Intelligent Agents for Data Mining and Information Retrieval

Masoud Mohammadian
University of Canberra, Australia

IDEA GROUP PUBLISHING
Hershey • London • Melbourne • Singapore

Acquisitions Editor: Mehdi Khosrow-Pour
Senior Managing Editor: Jan Travers
Managing Editor: Amanda Appicello
Development Editor: Michele Rossi
Copy Editor: Jennifer Wade
Typesetter: Jennifer Wetzel
Cover Design: Lisa Tosheff
Printed at: Yurchak Printing Inc.

Published in the United States of America by
        Idea Group Publishing (an imprint of Idea Group Inc.)
        701 E. Chocolate Avenue, Suite 200
        Hershey PA 17033
        Tel: 717-533-8845
        Fax: 717-533-8661
        E-mail: cust@idea-group.com
        Web site: http://www.idea-group.com

and in the United Kingdom by
        Idea Group Publishing (an imprint of Idea Group Inc.)
        3 Henrietta Street
        Covent Garden
        London WC2E 8LU
        Tel: 44 20 7240 0856
        Fax: 44 20 7379 3313
        Web site: http://www.eurospan.co.uk

Library of Congress Cataloging-in-Publication Data

Intelligent agents for data mining and information retrieval / Masoud Mohammadian, editor.
     p. cm.
   ISBN 1-59140-194-1 (hardcover) -- ISBN 1-59140-277-8 (pbk.) -- ISBN 1-59140-195-X (ebook)
   1. Database management. 2. Data mining. 3. Intelligent agents (Computer software). I. Mohammadian, Masoud.
   QA76.9.D3I5482 2004
   006.3'12--dc22
                              2003022613

British Cataloguing in Publication Data
A Cataloguing in Publication record for this book is available from the British Library.

Intelligent Agents for Data Mining and Information Retrieval

Table of Contents

Preface

There has been a large increase in the amount of information that is stored in and available from online databases and the World Wide Web. This information abundance has made the task of locating relevant information more complex. Such complexity drives the need for intelligent systems for searching and for information retrieval.

The information needed by a user is usually scattered in a large number of databases. Intelligent agents are currently used to improve the search for and retrieval of information from online databases and the World Wide Web. Research and development work in the area of intelligent agents and web technologies is growing rapidly. This is due to the many successful applications of these new techniques in very diverse problems. The increased number of patents and the diverse range of products developed using intelligent agents is evidence of this fact.

Most papers on the application of intelligent agents for web data mining and information retrieval are scattered around the world in different journals and conference proceedings. As such, journals and conference publications tend to focus on a very special and narrow topic. This book includes critical reviews of the state-of-the-art for the theory and application of intelligent agents for web data mining and information retrieval. This volume aims to fill the gap in the current literature.

The book consists of openly-solicited and invited chapters, written by international researchers in the field of intelligent agents and its applications for data mining and information retrieval. All chapters have been through a peer review process by at least two recognized reviewers and the editor. Our goal is to provide a book that covers the theoretical side, as well as the practical side, of intelligent agents. The book is organized in such a way that it can be used by researchers at the undergraduate and post-graduate levels. It can also be used as a reference of the state-of-the-art for cutting edge researchers.

The book consists of 18 chapters covering research areas such as: new methodologies for searching distributed text databases; computational intelligence techniques and intelligent agents for web data mining; multi-agent collaborative knowledge production; case-based reasoning and rule-based parsing and pattern matching for web data mining; multilingual concept-based web content mining; customization, personalization and user profiling; text processing and classification; textual document warehousing; web data repository; knowledge extraction and classification; multi-agent social coordination; agent-mediated user profiling; multi-agent systems for electronic catalog retrieval; concept matching and web searching; taxonomy-based fuzzy information filtering; web navigation using sub-graph and visualization; and networking e-learning hosts using mobile agents. In particular, the chapters cover the following:

In Chapter I, "Necessary Constraints for Database Selection in a Distributed Text Database Environment," *Yang* and *Zhang* discuss that, in order to understand the various aspects of a database, is essential to choose appropriate text databases to search with respect to a given user query. The analysis of different selection cases and different types of DTDs can help develop an effective and efficient database selection method. In this chapter, the authors have identified various potential selection cases in DTDs and have classified the types of DTDs. Based on these results, they analyze the relationships between selection cases and types of DTDs, and give the necessary constraints of database selection methods in different selection cases.

Chapter II, "Computational Intelligence Techniques Driven Intelligent Agents for Web Data Mining and Information Retrieval" by *Mohammadian* and *Jentzsch*, looks at how the World Wide Web has added an abundance of data and information to the complexity of information disseminators and users alike. With this complexity has come the problem of locating useful and relevant information. Such complexity drives the need for improved and intelligent search and retrieval engines. To improve the results returned by the searches, intelligent agents and other technology have the potential, when used with existing search and retrieval engines, to provide a more comprehensive search with an improved performance. This research provides the building blocks for integrating intelligent agents with current search engines. It shows how an intelligent system can be constructed to assist in better information filtering, gathering and retrieval.

Chapter III, "A Multi-Agent Approach to Collaborative Knowledge Production" by *Dodero*, *Díaz* and *Aedo*, discusses how knowledge creation or production in a distributed knowledge management system is a collaborative task that needs to be coordinated. The authors introduce a multi-agent architecture for collaborative knowledge production tasks, where knowledge-producing agents are arranged into knowledge domains or marts, and where a distributed interaction protocol is used to consolidate knowledge that is produced in a mart. Knowledge consolidated in a given mart can, in turn, be negotiated in higher-level foreign marts. As an evaluation scenario, the proposed architecture and protocol are applied to coordinate the creation of learning objects by a distributed group of instructional designers.

Chapter IV, "Customized Recommendation Mechanism Based on Web Data Mining and Case-Based Reasoning" by *Kim*, researches the blending of Artificial Intelligence (AI) techniques with the business process. In this research, the author suggests a web-based, customized hybrid recommendation mechanism using Case-based Reasoning (CBR) and web data mining. In this case, the author uses CBR as a supplementary AI tool, and the results show that the CBR and web data mining-based hybrid recommendation mechanism could reflect both association knowledge and purchase information about our former customers.

Chapter V, "Rule-Based Parsing for Web Data Extraction" by *Camacho*, *Aler* and *Cuadrado*, discusses that, in order to build robust and adaptable web systems, it is necessary to provide a standard representation for the information (i.e., using languages like XML and ontologies to represent the semantics of the stored knowledge). However, this is actually a research field and, usually, most of the web sources do not provide their information in a structured way. This chapter analyzes a new approach that allows for the building of robust and adaptable web systems through a multi-agent approach. Several problems, such as how to retrieve, extract and manage the stored information from web sources, are analyzed from an agent perspective.

Chapter VI, "Multilingual Web Content Mining: A User-Oriented Approach" by *Chau* and *Yeh*, presents a novel user-oriented, concept-based approach to multilingual web content mining using self-organizing maps. The multilingual linguistic knowledge required for multilingual web content mining is made available by encoding all multilingual concept-term relationships using a multilingual concept space. With this linguistic knowledge base, a concept-based multilingual text classifier is developed to reveal the conceptual content of multilingual web documents and to form concept categories of multilingual web documents on a concept-based browsing interface. To personalize multilingual web content mining, a concept-based user profile is generated from a user's bookmark file to highlight the user's topics of information interests on the browsing interface. As such, both explorative browsing and user-oriented, concept-focused information filtering in a multilingual web are facilitated.

Chapter VII, "A Textual Warehouse Approach: A Web Data Repository" by *Khrouf* and *Soulé-Dupuy*, establishes that an enterprise memory must be able to be used as a basis for the processes of scientific or technical developments. It has been proven that information useful to these processes is not solely in the operational bases of companies, but is also in textual information and exchanged documents. For that reason, the authors propose the design and implementation of a documentary memory through business document warehouses, whose main characteristic is to allow the storage, retrieval, interrogation and analysis of information extracted from disseminated sources and, in particular, from the Web.

Chapter VIII, "Text Processing by Binary Neural Networks" by *Beran* and *Macek*, describes the rather less traditional technique of text processing. The technique is based on the binary neural network Correlation Matrix Memory. The authors propose the use of a neural network for text searching tasks. Two methods of coding input words are described and tested; problems using this approach for text processing are then discussed.

In the world of artificial intelligence, the extraction of knowledge has been a very useful tool for many different purposes, and it has been tried with many different techniques. In Chapter IX, "Extracting Knowledge from Databases and ANNs with Genetic Programming: Iris Flower Classification Problem" by *Rivero*, *Rabuñal*, *Dorado*, *Pazos* and *Pedreira*, the authors show how Genetic Programming (GP) can be used to solve a classification problem from a database. They also show how to adapt this tool in two different ways: to improve its performance and to make possible the detection of errors. Results show that the technique developed in this chapter opens a new area for research in the field, extracting knowledge from more complicated structures, such as neural networks.

Chapter X, "Social Coordination with Architecture for Ubiquitous Agents — CONSORTS" by *Kurumatani*, proposes a social coordination mechanism that is realized with CONSORTS, a new kind of multi-agent architecture for ubiquitous agents. The author defines social coordination as mass users' decision making in their daily lives, such as the mutual concession of spatial-temporal resources achieved by the automatic negotiation of software agents, rather than by the verbal and explicit communication directly done by human users. The functionality of social coordination is realized in the agent architecture where three kinds of agents work cooperatively, i.e., a personal agent that serves as a proxy for the user, a social coordinator as the service agent, and a spatio-temporal reasoner. The author also summarizes some basic mechanisms of social coordination functionality, including stochastic distribution and market mechanism.

In Chapter XI, "Agent-Mediated Knowledge Acquisition for User Profiling" by *Andreevskaia*, *Abi-Aad* and *Radhakrishnan*, the authors discuss how, in the past few years, Internet shopping has been growing rapidly. Most companies now offer web service for online purchases and delivery in addition to their traditional sales and services. For consumers, this means that they face more complexity in using these online services. This complexity, which arises due to factors such as information overloading or a lack of relevant information, reduces the usability of e-commerce sites. In this study, the authors address reasons why consumers abandon a web site during personal shopping.

As Internet technologies develop rapidly, companies are shifting their business activities to e-business on the Internet. Worldwide competition among corporations accelerates the reorganization of corporate sections and partner groups, resulting in a break from the conventional steady business relationships. Chapter XII, "Development of Agent-Based Electronic Catalog Retrieval System" by *Nagano*, *Tahara*, *Hasegawa* and *Ohsuga*, represents the development of an electronic catalog retrieval system using a multi-agent framework, Bee-gent™, in order to exchange catalog data between existing catalog servers. The proposed system agentifies electronic catalog servers implemented by distinct software vendors, and a mediation mobile agent migrates among the servers to retrieve electronic catalog data and bring them back to the departure server.

Chapter XIII, "Using Dynamically Acquired Background Knowledge for Information Extraction and Intelligent Search" by *El-Beltagy*, *Rafea* and *Abdelhamid*, presents a simple framework for extracting information found in publications or documents that are issued in large volumes and which cover similar concepts or issues within a given domain. The general aim of the work described is to present a model for automatically augmenting segments of these documents with metadata, using dynamically acquired background domain knowledge in order to help users easily locate information within these documents through a structured front end. To realize this goal, both document structure and dynamically acquired background knowledge are utilized

Web search engines are one of the most popular services to facilitate users in locating useful information on the Web. Although many studies have been carried out to estimate the size and overlap of the general web search engines, it may not benefit the ordinary web searching users; they care more about the overlap of the search results on concrete queries, but not the overlap of the total index database. In Chapter XIV, "A Study on Web Searching: Overlap and Distance of the Search Engine Results" by *Zhu, Deng, Fang* and *Zheng*, the authors present experimental results on the comparison of the overlap of top search results from AlltheWeb, Google, AltaVista and Wisenut on the 58 most popular queries, as well as on the distance of the overlapped results.

Chapter XV, "Taxonomy Based Fuzzy Filtering of Search Results" by *Vrettos* and *Stafylopatis*, proposes that the use of topic taxonomies is part of a filtering language. Given any taxonomy, the authors train classifiers for every topic of it so the user is able to formulate logical rules combining the available topics, (e.g., Topic1 AND Topic2 OR Topic3), in order to filter related documents in a stream of documents. The authors present a framework that is concerned with the operators that provide the best filtering performance as regards the user.

In Chapter XVI, "Generating and Adjusting Web Sub-Graph Displays for Web Navigation" by *Lai, Huang* and *Zhang*, the authors relate that a graph can be used for web navigation, considering that the whole of cyberspace can be regarded as one huge graph. To explore this huge graph, it is critical to find an effective method of tracking a sequence of subsets (web sub-graphs) of the huge graph, based on the user's focus. This chapter introduces a method for generating and adjusting web sub-graph displays in the process of web navigation.

Chapter XVII, "An Algorithm of Pattern Match Being Fit for Mining Association Rules" by *Shi* and *Zhang*, discusses the frequent amounts of pattern match that exist in the process of evaluating the support count of candidates, which is one of the main factors influencing the efficiency of mining for association rules. In this chapter, an efficient algorithm for pattern match being fit for mining association rules is presented by analyzing its characters.

Chapter XVIII, "Networking E-Learning Hosts Using Mobile Agent" by *Quah, Chen* and *Leow*, discusses how, with the rapid evolution of the Internet, information overload is becoming a common phenomenon, and why it is necessary to have a tool to help users extract useful information from the Internet. A similar problem is being faced by e-learning applications. At present, commercialized e-learning systems lack information search tools to help users search for the course information, and few of them have explored the power of mobile agent. Mobile agent is a suitable tool, particularly for Internet information retrieval. This chapter presents a mobile agent-based e-learning tool which can help the e-learning user search for course materials on the Web. A prototype system of cluster-nodes has been implemented, and experiment results are presented.

It is hoped that the case studies, tools and techniques described in the book will assist in expanding the horizons of intelligent agents and will help disseminate knowledge to the research and the practice communities.

Acknowledgments

Many people have assisted in the success of this book. I would like to acknowledge the assistance of all involved in the collation and the review process of the book. Without their assistance and support, this book could not have been completed successfully. I would also like to express my gratitude to all of the authors for contributing their research papers to this book.

I would like to thank Mehdi Khosrow-Pour, Jan Travers and Jennifer Sundstrom from Idea Group Inc. for their assistance in the production of the book.

Finally, I would like to thank my family for their love and support throughout this project.

Masoud Mohammadian
University of Canberra, Australia
October 2003

Chapter I

Potential Cases, Database Types, and Selection Methodologies for Searching Distributed Text Databases

Hui Yang, University of Wollongong, Australia

Minjie Zhang, University of Wollongong, Australia

ABSTRACT

The rapid proliferation of online textual databases on the Internet has made it difficult to effectively and efficiently search desired information for the users. Often, the task of locating the most relevant databases with respect to a given user query is hindered by the heterogeneities among the underlying local textual databases. In this chapter, we first identify various potential selection cases in distributed textual databases (DTDs) and classify the types of DTDs. Based on these results, the relationships between selection cases and types of DTDs are recognized and necessary constraints of database selection methods in different cases are given which can be used to develop a more effective and suitable selection algorithm.

INTRODUCTION

As online databases on the Internet have rapidly proliferated in recent years, the problem of helping ordinary users find desired information in such an environment also continues to escalate. In particular, it is likely that the information needed by a user is scattered in a vast number of databases. Considering search effectiveness and the cost of searching, a convenient and efficient approach is to optimally select a subset of databases which are most likely to provide the useful results with respect to the user query.

A substantial body of research work has looked at database selection by using mainly quantitative statistics information (e.g., the number of documents containing the query term) to compute a ranking score which reflects the relative usefulness of each database (see Callan, Lu, & Croft, 1995; Gravano & Garcia-Molina, 1995; Yuwono & Lee, 1997), or by using detail qualitative statistics information, which attempts to characterize the usefulness of the databases (see Lam & Yu, 1982; Yu, Luk & Siu, 1978).

Obviously, database selection algorithms do not interact directly with the databases that they rank. Instead, the algorithms interact with a representative which indicates approximately the content of the database. In order for appropriate databases to be identified, each database maintains its own representative. The representative supports the efficient evaluation of user queries against large-scale text databases.

Since different databases have different ways of representing their documents, computing their term weights and frequency, and implementing their keyword indexes, the database representatives that can be provided by them could be very different. The diversity of the database representatives is often the primary source of difficulty in developing an effective database selection algorithm.

Because database representation is perhaps the most essential element of database selection, understanding various aspects of databases is necessary to developing a reasonable selection algorithm. In this chapter, we identify the potential cases of database selection in a distributed text database environment; we also classify the types of distributed text databases (DTDs). Necessary constraints of selection algorithms in different database selection cases are also given in the chapter, based on the analysis of database content, which can be used as the useful criteria for constructing an effective selection algorithm (Zhang & Zhang, 1999).

The rest of the chapter is organized as follows: The database selection problem is formally described. Then, we identify major potential selection cases in DTDs. The types of text databases are then given. The relationships between database selection cases and DTD types are analyzed in the following section. Next, we discuss the necessary constraints for database selection in different database selection cases to help develop better selection algorithms. At the end of the chapter, we provide a conclusion and look toward future research work.

PROBLEM DESCRIPTION

Firstly, several reasonable assumptions will be given to facilitate the database selection problem. Since 84 percent of the searchable web databases provide access to text documents, in this chapter, we concentrate on the web databases with text documents. A discussion of those databases with other types of information (e.g., image, video or audio databases) is out of the scope of this chapter.

Assumption 1. The databases are text databases which only contain text documents, and these documents can be searchable on the Internet.

In this chapter, we mainly focus on the analysis of database representatives. To objectively and fairly determine the usefulness of databases with respect to the user queries, we will take a simple view of the search cost for each database.

Assumption 2. Assume all the databases have an equivalent search cost, such as elapsed search time, network traffic charges, and possible pre-search monetary charges.

Most searchable large-scale text databases usually contain documents from multiple domains (topics) rather than from a single domain. So, a category scheme can help to better understand the content of the databases.

Assumption 3. Assume complete knowledge of the contents of these known databases. The databases can then be categorized in a classification scheme.

Now, the database selection problem is formally described as follows:

Suppose there are n databases in a distributed text database environment to be ranked with respect to a given query.

Definition 1:   A database S_i is a six-tuple, $S_i = <Q_i, I_i, W_i, C_i, D_i, T_i>$, where Q is a set of user queries; I_i is the indexing method that determines what terms should be used to index or represent a given document; W_i is the term weight scheme that determines the weight of distinct terms occurring in database S_i; C_i is the set of subject domain (topic) categories that the documents in database S_i come from; D_i is the set of documents that database S_i contains; and T_i is the set of distinct terms that occur in database S_i.

Definition 2:   Suppose database S_i has m distinct terms, namely, $T_i = \{t_1, t_2, ..., t_m\}$. Each term in the database can be represented as a two-dimension vector $\{t_i, w_i\}$ $(1 \le i \le m)$, where t_i is the term (word) occurring in database S_i, and w_i is the weight (importance) of the term t_i.

The weight of a term usually depends on the number of occurrences of the term in database S_i (relative to the total number of occurrences of all terms in the database). It may also depend on the number of documents having the term relative to the total number of documents in the database. Different methods exist for determining the weight. One popular term weight scheme uses the term frequency of a term as the weight of this term (Salto & McGill, 1983). Another popular scheme uses both the term frequency and the document frequency of a term to determine the weight of the term (Salto, 1989).

Definition 3:   For a given user query q, it can be defined as a set of query terms without Boolean operators, which can be denoted by $q = \{q_j, u_j\}$ $(1 \le j \le m)$, where q_j is the term (word) occurring in the query q, and u_j is the weight (importance) of the term q_j.

Suppose we know the category of each of the documents inside database S_i. Then we could use this information to classify database S_i (a full discussion of text database classification techniques is beyond this scope of this chapter).

Definition 4: Consider that there exist a number of topic categories in database S_i which can be described as $C_i = (c_1, c_2, ..., c_p)$. Similarly, the set of documents in database S_i can be defined as a vector $D_i = \{D_{i1}, D_{i2}, ..., D_{ip}\}$, where D_{ij} $(1 \leq j \leq p)$ is the subset of documents corresponding to the topic category c_j.

In practice, the similarity of database Si with respect to the user query q is the sum of the similarities of all the subsets of documents of topic categories.

For a given user query, different databases always adopt different document indexing methods to determine potential useful documents in them. These indexing methods may differ in a variety of ways. For example, one database may perform *full-text indexing*, which considers all the terms in the documents, while the other database employs *partial-text indexing*, which may only use a subset of terms.

Definition 5: A set of databases $S = \{S_1, S_2, ..., S_n\}$ is optimally ranked in the order of global similarity with respect to a given query q. That is, $Simi_G(S_1, q) \geq Simi_G(S_2, q) \geq ... \geq Simi_G(S_n, q)$, where $Simi_G(S_i, q)$ $(1 \leq i \leq n)$ is the global similarity function for the ith database with respect to the query q, the value of which is a real number.

For example, consider the databases S_1, S_2 and S_3. Suppose the global similarities of S_1, S_2, S_3 to a given user query q are 0.7, 0.9 and 0.3, respectively. Then, the databases should be ranked in the order $\{S_2, S_1, S_3\}$.

Due to possibly different indexing methods or different term weight schemes used by local databases, a local database may use a different local similarity function, namely $Simi_{Li}(S_i, q)$ $(1 \leq i \leq n)$. Therefore, for the same data source D, different databases may possibly have different local similarity scores to a given query q. To accurately rank various local textual databases, it is necessary for all the local textual databases to employ the same similarity function, namely $Simi_G(S_i, q)$, to evaluate the global similarity with respect to the user query (a discussion on local similarity function and global similarity function is out of the scope of this chapter).

The need for database selection is largely due to the fact that there are heterogeneous document databases. If the databases have different subject domain documents, or if the numbers of subject domain documents are various, or if they apply different indexing methods to index the documents, the database selection problem should become rather complicated. Identifying the heterogeneities among the databases will be helpful in estimating the usefulness of each database for the queries.

POTENTIAL SELECTION CASES IN DTDS

In the real world, a web user usually tries to find the information relevant to a given topic. The categorization of web databases into subject (topic) domains can help to alleviate the time-consuming problem of searching a large number of databases. Once the user submits a query, he/she is directly guided to the appropriate web databases with relevant topic documents. As a result, the database selection task will be simplified and become effective.

In this section, we will analyze potential database selection cases in DTDs, based on the relationships between the subject domains that the content of the databases may cover. If all the databases have the same subject domain as that which the user query involves, relevant documents are likely to be found from these databases. Clearly, under such a DTD environment, the above database selection task will be drastically simplified. Unfortunately, the databases distributed on the Internet, especially those large-scale commercial web sites, usually contain the documents of various topic categories. Informally, we know that there exist four basic relationships with respect to topic categories of the databases: (a) identical; (b) inclusion; (c) overlap; and (d) disjoint.

The formal definitions of different potential selection cases are shown as follows:

Definition 6: For a given user query q, if the contents of the documents of all the databases come from the same subject domain(s), we will say that an *identical selection case* occurs in DTDs corresponding to the query q.

Definition 7: For a given user query q, if the set of subject domains that one database contains is a subset of the set of subject domains of another database, we will say that an *inclusion selection case* occurs in DTDs corresponding to the query q.

For example, for database S_i, the contents of all its documents are only related to the subject domains, c_1 and c_2. For database S_j, the contents of all its documents are related to the subject domains, c_1, c_2 and c_3. So, $C_i \subset C_j$.

Definition 8: For a given user query q, if the intersection of the set of subject domains for any two databases is empty, we will say that a *disjoint selection case* occurs in DTDs corresponding to the query q. That is, $\forall\ S_i,\ S_j \in S\ (1 \leq i, j \leq n,\ i \neq j),\ C_i \cap C_j = \varnothing$.

For example, suppose database S_i contains the documents of subject domains c_1 and c_2, but database S_j contains the documents of subject domains c_4, c_5 and c_6. So, $C_i \cap C_j = \varnothing$.

Definition 9: For a given user query q, if the set of subject domains for database S_i satisfies the following conditions: $\forall\, S_j \in S\,(1{\le}j{\le}n,\, i{\ne}j)$, (1) $C_i \cap C_j \ne \varnothing$, (2) $C_i \ne C_j$, and (3) $C_i \not\subset C_j$ or $C_j \not\subset C_i$, we will say that an *overlap selection case* occurs in DTDs corresponding to the query q.

For example, suppose database S_i contains the documents of subject domains c_1 and c_2, but database S_j contains the documents of subject domains c_2, c_5 and c_6. So, $C_i \cap C_j = c_2$.

Definition 10: For a given user query q, $\forall\, S_i, S_j \in S\,(1{\le}i, j{\le}n,\, i{\ne}j)$, $c_k \in C_i \cap C_j\,(1{\le}k{\le}p)$ and the subsets of documents corresponding to topic category c_k in these two databases, D_{ik} and D_{jk}, respectively. If they satisfy the following conditions:

(1) the numbers of documents in both D_{ik} and D_{jk} are equal, and
(2) all these documents are the same,

then we define $D_{ik} = D_{jk}$. Otherwise, $D_{ik} \ne D_{jk}$.

Definition 11: For a given user query q, $\forall\, S_i, S_j \in S\,(1{\le}i, j{\le}n,\, i{\ne}j)$, if the proposition $c_k \in C_i \cap C_j\,(1{\le}k{\le}p)$, $D_{ik} = D_{jk} \to Simi_{Li}\,(D_{ik},\, q) = Simi_{Lj}$ $(D_{jk},\, q)$ is true, we will say that a *non-conflict selection case* occurs in DTDs corresponding to the query q. Otherwise, the selection is a *conflict selection case*. $Simi_{Li}\,(S_i,\, q)\,(1{\le}i{\le}n)$ is the local similarity function for the ith database with respect to the query q.

Theorem 1: A disjoint selection case is neither a non-conflict selection case nor a conflict selection case.

Proof: For a disjoint selection case, $\forall\, S_i, S_j \in S\,(1{\le}i, j{\le}n,\, i{\ne}j)$, $C_i \cap C_j = \varnothing$, and $D_i \ne D_j$. Hence, databases S_i and S_j are incomparable with respect to the user query q. So, this is neither a non-conflict selection case nor a conflict selection case.

By using a similar analysis to those on the previously page, we can prove that there are seven kinds of potential selection cases in DTDs as follows:

(1)   Non-conflict identical selection cases
(2)   Conflict identical selection cases
(3)   Non-conflict inclusion selection cases
(4)   Conflict inclusion selection cases
(5)   Non-conflict overlap selection cases
(6)   Conflict overlap selection cases
(7)   Disjoint selection cases

In summary, given a number of databases S, we can first identify which kind of selection case exists in a DTD based on the relationships of subject domains among them.

THE CLASSIFICATION OF TYPES OF DTDS

Before we choose a database selection method to locate the most appropriate databases to search for a given user query, it is necessary to know how many types of DTDs exist and which kinds of selection cases may appear in each type of DTD. In this section, we will discuss the classification of types of DTDs based on the relationships of the indexing methods and on the term weight schemes of DTDs. The definition of four different types of DTDs are shown as follows:

Definition 12: If all of the databases in a DTD have the same indexing method and the same term weight scheme, the DTD is called a *homogeneous* DTD. This type of DTD can be defined as:

$$\forall \ S_i, S_j \in S \ (1 \leq i, j \leq n, \ i \neq j), I_i = I_j$$
$$\forall \ S_i, S_j \in S \ (1 \leq i, j \leq n, \ i \neq j), W_i = W_j$$

Definition 13: If all of the databases in a DTD have the same indexing method, but at least one database has a different term weight scheme, the DTD is called a *partially homogeneous* DTD. This type of DTD can be defined as:

$$\forall \ S_i, S_j \in S \ (1 \leq i, j \leq n, \ i \neq j), I_i = I_j$$
$$\exists \ S_i, S_j \in S \ (1 \leq i, j \leq n, \ i \neq j), W_i \neq W_j$$

Definition 14: If at least one database in a DTD has a different indexing method from other databases, but all of the databases have the same term weight scheme, the DTD is called a *partially heterogeneous* DTD. This type of DTD can be defined as:

$$\exists\ S_i, S_j \in S\ (1 \le i, j \le n,\ i \ne j),\ I_i \ne I_j$$
$$\forall\ S_i, S_j \in S\ (1 \le i, j \le n,\ i \ne j),\ W_i = W_j$$

Definition 15: If at least one database in a DTD has a different indexing method from other databases, and at least one database has a different term weight scheme from the other databases, the DTD is called a *heterogeneous* DTD. This type of DTD can be defined as:

$$\exists\ S_i, S_j \in S\ (1 \le i, j \le n,\ i\ , j),\ I_i \ne I_j$$
$$\exists\ S_i, S_j \in S\ (1 \le i, j \le n,\ i \ne j),\ W_i \ne W_j$$

RELATIONSHIPS BETWEEN POTENTIAL SELECTION CASES AND DTD TYPES

We have identified selection cases and classified DTD types in the above sections. Now, we can briefly summarize the relationships between selection cases and DTD types as follows:

Theorem 2: For a given user query q, the database selection in a homogeneous DTD may be either a non-conflict selection case or a disjoint selection case.

Proof: In a homogeneous DTD, $\forall\ S_i, S_j \in S\ (1 \le i, j \le n,\ i \ne j),\ I_i = I_j,\ W_i = W_j$. If:

(1) Suppose $C_i \cap C_j \ne \varnothing, c_k \in C_i \cap C_j\ (1 \le k \le p), D_{ik} = D_{jk}$, is valid since they use the same indexing method and the same term weight scheme to evaluate the usefulness of the databases. Then, $Simi_{Li}(D_{ik}, q) = Simi_{Lj}(D_{jk}, q)$ is true. So, the database selection in this homogeneous DTD is a non-conflict selection case (recall Definition 11).

(2) Suppose $C_i \cap C_j = \varnothing$ is valid. Then, the database selection in this homogeneous DTD is a disjoint selection case (recall Definition 8).

Theorem 3: Given a user query q, for a partially homogeneous DTD, or a partially heterogeneous DTD, or a heterogeneous DTD, any potential selection case may exist.

Proof: In a partially homogeneous DTD, or a partially heterogeneous DTD, or a heterogeneous DTD, $\forall\ S_i, S_j \in S\ (1 \le i, j \le n,\ i \ne j),\ \exists\ 1 \le i, j \le n,\ i \ne j,\ I_i \ne I_j$ or $\exists\ 1 \le i, j \le n,\ i \ne j,\ W_i \ne W_j$ is true. If:

(1) Suppose $C_i \cap C_j \ne \varnothing,\ c_k \in C_i \cap C_j\ (1 \le k \le p),\ D_{ik} = D_{jk}$, is valid, but since the databases employ different index methods or different term weight schemes, $Simi_{Li}(D_{ik}, q) = Simi_{Lj}(D_{jk}, q)$ is not always true. So, the selection case in these three DTDs is either a conflict selection case or a non-conflict selection case.
(2) Suppose $C_i \cap C_j = \varnothing$ is valid. Then, the database selection in these three DTDs is a disjoint selection case.

By combining the above two cases, we conclude that any potential selection case may exist in all the DTD types except the homogeneous DTD.

NECESSARY CONSTRAINTS OF SELECTION METHODS IN DTDS

We believe that the work of identifying necessary constraints of selection methods, which is absent in others' research in this area, is important in accurately determining which databases to search because it can help choose appropriate selection methods for different selection cases.

General Necessary Constraints for All Selection Methods in DTDs

As described in the previous section, when a query q is submitted, the databases are ranked in order $S_1, S_2, ..., S_n$, such as S_i is searched before S_{i+1}, $1 \le i \le n-1$, based on the comparisons between the query q and the representatives of the databases in DTDs, and not based on the order of selection priority. So, the following properties are general necessary constraints that a reasonable selection method in DTDs must satisfy:

(1)   The selection methods must satisfy the *associative* law. That is, $\forall S_i, S_j,$ $S_k \in S$ $(1 \leq i, j, k \leq n, i \neq j \neq k)$, $Rank$ $(Rank$ $(S_i, S_j), S_k) = Rank$ $(S_i, Rank$ $(S_j, S_k))$, where $Rank$ ( ) is the ranking function for the set of databases S;

(2)   The selection methods must satisfy the *commutative* law. That is, $Rank$ $(S_i, S_j) = Rank$ (S_j, S_i).

Special Necessary Constraints of Selection Methods for Each Selection Case

Before we start to discuss the special necessary constraints of selection methods for each selection case, we first give some basic concepts and functions in order to simplify the explanation. In the following section, we will mainly focus on the selection of three databases. It is easy to extend the selection process to any number of databases in DTDs. Suppose that there exist three databases in a DTD, S_i, S_j and S_k, respectively. $S_i = <Q_i, I_i, W_i, C_i,$ $D_i, T_i>, S_j = <Q_j, I_j, W_j, C_j, D_j, T_j>$ and $S_k = <Q_k, I_k, W_k, C_k, D_k, T_k>$. q is a given user query, and c_t is the topic domain of interest for the user query. $Simi_G(S_t, q)$ is the global similarity score function for the lth database with respect to the query q, and $Rank$ ( ) is the ranking function for the databases. All these notations will be used through the following discussions.

The objective of database selection is to find the potential "good" databases which contain the most relevant information that a user needs. In order to improve search effectiveness, a database with a high rank will be searched before a database with a lower rank. Therefore, the correct order relationship among the databases is the critical factor which judges whether a selection method is "ideal" or not.

A database is made up of numerous documents. Therefore, the work of estimating the usefulness of a text database, in practice, is the work of finding the number of documents in the database that are sufficiently similar to a given query. A document d is defined as the most likely similar document to the query q if $Simi_G (d, q) \geq t_d$, where t_d is a global document threshold. Here, three important reference parameters about textual databases are given as follows, which should be considered when ranking the order of a set of databases based on the usefulness to the query.

(1)   *Database size*. That is, the total number of the documents that the database contains.

For example, if databases S_i and S_j have the same number of the most likely similar documents, but database S_i contains more documents than database S_j, then S_j is ranked ahead of S_i. That is, $Rank\ (S_i, S_j)=\{S_j, S_i\}$.

(2) *Useful document quality in the database*. That is, the number of the most likely similar documents in the database.

For example, if database S_i has more of the most likely documents than database S_j, then S_i is ranked ahead of S_j. That is, $Rank\ (S_i, S_j)=\{S_i, S_j\}$.

(3) *Useful document quantity in the database*. That is, the similarity degree of the most likely similar documents in the database.

For example, if databases S_i and S_j have the same number of the most likely similar documents, but database S_i contains the document with the largest similarity among these documents, then S_i is ranked ahead of S_j. That is, $Rank\ (S_i, S_j)=\{S_i, S_j\}$.

Now, some other special necessary constraints for each potential selection case are given in following discussion:

(a) In *an identical selection case*, all the databases have the same topic categories. That is, they have an equal chance to contain the relevant information of interest. If $Simi_G\ (S_i, q)=Simi_G\ (S_j, q)$ and $D_{it} > D_{jt}$, then $Rank\ (S_i, S_j)=\{S_j, S_i\}$. The reason for this is that, for the same useful databases, more search effort will be spent in database S_i than in database S_j because database S_i has more documents needed to search for finding the most likely similar documents.

(b) In *an inclusion selection case*, if $C_i \subset C_j$, it means that database S_j has other topic documents which database S_i does not. Therefore, in order to reduce the number of non-similar documents to search in the database, the special constraint condition of selection method for the inclusion selection case can be described as follows:

If $Simi_G\ (S_i, q) = Simi_G\ (S_j, q)$ and $C_i \subset C_j$, $c_t \in C_i \cap C_j$, then $Rank\ (S_i, S_j) = \{S_i, S_j\}$.

(c) In *an overlap selection case*, any two databases not only have some same subject-domain documents, but also have different subject-domain documents, respectively. So, there exist two possible cases: (1) $c_t \in C_i \cap C_j$; and (2) $c_t \notin C_i \cap C_j$. Then, under these two cases, the constraint conditions that a suitable selection method must satisfy can be described as:

(1) If $c_t \in C_i \cap C_j$ and $c_t \notin C_k$, then $Simi_G (S_i, q)$, $Simi_G (S_j, q) > Simi_G (S_k, q)$; and $Rank (S_i, S_j, S_k)=\{S_i, S_j, S_k\}$ or $\{S_j, S_i, S_k\}$.

(2) If $c_t \notin C_i \cup C_j$ and $c_t \in C_k$, then $Simi_G (S_i, q)$, $Simi_G (S_j, q) < Simi_G (S_k, q)$; and $Rank (S_i, S_j, S_k)=\{S_k, S_i, S_j\}$ or $\{S_k, S_j, S_i\}$.

(d)   In *a disjoint selection case*, since any two databases do not have the same subject-domain documents, it is obvious that only one database most likely contains the relevant documents of interest to the user. So, the selection method must satisfy the following necessary constraint:

If $c_t \in C_i$, then $Simi_G (S_i, q) > Simi_G (S_j, q), Simi_G (S_k, q)$; and $Rank (S_i, S_j, S_k)= \{S_i, S_j, S_k\}$ or $\{S_i, S_k, S_j\}$.

CONCLUSION AND FUTURE WORK

In this chapter, we identified various potential selection cases in DTDs and classified the types of DTDs. Based on these results, we analyzed the relationships between selection cases and types of DTDs, and gave the necessary constraints of database selection methods in different selection cases.

Understanding the various aspects of each local database is essential for choosing appropriate text databases to search with respect to a given user query. The analysis of different selection cases and different types of DTDs can help develop an effective and efficient database selection method. Very little research in this area has been reported so far. Further work is needed to find more effective and suitable selection algorithms based on different kinds of selection problems and available information.

ACKNOWLEDGMENTS

This research was supported by a large grant from the Australian Research Council under contract DP0211282.

REFERENCES

Callan, J., Lu, Z., & Croft, W. B. (1995). Searching distributed collections with inference networks. *The 19th Annual International ACM SIGIR Conference on Research and Development in Information Retrieval,* Seattle, Washington (pp. 21-28).

Gravano, L. & Garcia-Molina, H. (1995). *Generalizing GlOSS to vector-space databases and broker hierarchies.* Stanford, CA: Stanford University, Computer Science Department. (Technical Report)

Lam, K. & Yu, C. (1982). A clustered search algorithm incorporating arbitrary term dependencies. *ACM Transactions on Database Systems,* 500-508.

Salto, G. (1989). *Automatic Text Processing: The Transformation, Analysis, and Retrieval of Information by Computer.* New York: Addison-Wesley.

Salto, G. & McGill, M. (1983). *Introduction to Modern Information Retrieval.* New York: McGraw-Hill.

Yu, C., Luk, W., & Siu, M. (1978). On the estimation of the number of desired records with respect to a given query. *ACM Transactions on Database Systems, 3*(4), 41-56.

Yuwono, B. & Lee, D. (1997). Server ranking for distributed text resource system on the Internet. *The 5th International Conference on Database Systems for Advanced Application,* Melbourne, Australia (pp. 391-400).

Zhang, M. & Zhang, C. (1999). Potential cases, methodologies, and strategies of synthesis of solutions in distributed expert system. *IEEE Transactions on Knowledge and Database Engineering, 11*(3), 498-503.

Chapter II

Computational Intelligence Techniques Driven Intelligent Agents for Web Data Mining and Information Retrieval

Masoud Mohammadian, University of Canberra, Australia

Ric Jentzsch, University of Canberra, Australia

ABSTRACT

The World Wide Web has added an abundance of data and information to the complexity of information for disseminators and users alike. With this complexity has come the problem of finding useful and relevant information. There is a need for improved and intelligent search and retrieval engines. Current search engines are primarily passive tools. To improve the results returned by searches, intelligent agents and other technology have the potential, when used with existing search and retrieval engines, to provide a more comprehensive search with an improved performance. This research provides the building blocks for integrating intelligent agents with current search engines. It shows how an intelligent system can be constructed to assist in better information filtering, gathering and retrieval. The research is unique in the way the intelligent agents are directed and in how computational intelligence techniques (such as evolutionary computing and fuzzy logic) and intelligent agents are combined to improve information filtering and retrieval. Fuzzy logic is used to access the performance of the system and provide evolutionary computing with the necessary information to carry out its search.

INTRODUCTION

The amount of information that is potentially available from the World Wide Web (WWW), including such areas as web pages, page links, accessible documents, and databases, continues to increase. Research has focused on investigating traditional business concerns that are now being applied to the WWW and the world of electronic business (e-business). Beyond the traditional concerns, research has moved to include those concerns that are particular to the WWW and its use. Two of the concerns are: (1) the ability to accurately extract and filter user (business and individuals) information requests from what is available; and (2) finding ways that businesses and individuals can more efficiently utilize their limited resources in this dynamic e-business world.

The first concern is, and continues to be, discussed by researchers and practitioners. Users are always looking for better and more efficient ways of finding and filtering information to satisfy their particular needs. Existing search and retrieval engines provide more capabilities today then ever before, but the information that is potentially available continues to grow exponentially. Web page designers have become familiar with ways to ensure that existing search engines find their material first, or at least in the top 10 to 20 hits. This information may or may not be what the users really want. Thus, the search engines, even though they have now become sophisticated, cannot and do not provide sufficient assistance to the users in locating and filtering out the relevant information that they need (see Jensen, 2002; Lawrence & Giles, 1999). The second area, efficient use of resources, especially labor, continues to be researched by both practitioners and researchers (Jentzsch & Gobbin, 2002).

Current statistics indicate that, by the end of 2002, there will be 320 million web users (http://www.why-not.com/company/stats.htm). The Web is said to contain more than 800 million pages. Statistics on how many databases and how much data they have are, at best, sparse. How many page links and how many documents (such as pdf) and other files can be searched via the WWW for their data is, at best, an educated guess. Currently, existing search engines only partially meet the increased need for an efficient, effective means of finding, extracting and filtering all this WWW-accessible data (see Sullivan, 2002; Lucas & Nissenbaum, 2000; Cabri, 2000; Lawrence, 1999; Maes, 1994; Nwana, 1996; Cho & Chung et al., 1997).

Part of the problem is the contention between information disseminators (of various categories) and user needs. Businesses, for example, want to build web sites that promote their products and services and that will be easily found and moved to the top of the search engine result listing. Business web designers are particularly aware of how the most popular search engines work and of how to get their business data and information to the top of the search engine result listing. For many non-business information disseminators, it is either not as important or they do not have the resources to get the information their web sites need to get to the top of a search engine result listing.

Users, on the other hand, want to be able to see only what is relevant to their requests. Users expect and trust the search engines they use to filter the data and information before it comes to them. This, as stated above, is often in contention with what information disseminators (business and non-business) provide. Research needs to look at ways to better help and promote the user needs through information filtering methods. To do this will require a concentration of technological efficiencies with user requirements and needs analysis. One area that can be employed is the use of intelligent agents to search, extract and filter the data and information available on the WWW while meeting the requirements of the users.

SEARCH ENGINES

Search engines, such as AltaVista, Excite, Google, HotBot, Infoseek, Northernlight, Yahoo, and numerous others, offer a wide range of web searching facilities. These search engines are sophisticated, but not as much as one might expect. Their results can easily fall victim to intelligent and often deceptive web page designers. Depending on the particular search engine, a web site can be indexed, scored and ranked using many different methods (Searchengine.com, 2002). Search engines' ranking algorithms are often based on the use of the position and frequency of keywords for their search. The web pages with the most instances of a keyword, and the position of the keywords in the web page, can determine the higher document ranking (see Jensen, 2002; Searchengine.com, 2002; Eyeballz, 2002). Search engines usually provide the users with the top 10 to 20 relevant hits.

There is limited information on the specific details of the algorithms that search engines employ to achieve their particular results. This is logical as it can make or break a search engine's popularity as well as its competitive edge. There is generalized information on many of the items that are employed in search engines such as keywords, the reading of tags, and indexes. For example, AltaVista ranks documents, highest to lowest, based on criteria such as the number of times the search appears, proximity of the terms to each other, proximity of the terms to the beginning of the document, and the existence of all the search terms in the document. AltaVista scores the retrieved information and returns the results. The way that search engines score web pages may cause very unexpected results (Jensen, 2002).

It is interesting to note that search results obtained from search engines may be biased toward certain sites, and may rank low a site that may offer just as much value as do those who appear on the top-ranked web site (Lucas & Nissenbaum, 2000). There have often been questions asked without substantial responses in this area.

Like search engines on the Web, online databases on the WWW have problems with information extraction and filtering. This situation will continue to grow as the size of the databases continues to grow (Hines, 2002). Between database designer and web page designers, they can devise ways to either promote their stored information or to at least make something that sounds like the information the user might want come to the top of the search engine result listing. This only adds to the increased difficulties in locating and filtering relevant information from online databases via the WWW.

INTELLIGENT AGENTS

There are many online information retrieval and data extraction tools available today. Although these tools are powerful in locating matching terms and phrases, they are considered passive systems. Intelligent Agents (see Watson, 1997; Bigus & Bigus, 1998) may prove to be the needed instrument in transforming these passive search and retrieval systems into active, personal user assistants. The combination of effective information retrieval techniques and intelligent agents continues to show promising results in improving the performance of the information that is being extracted from the WWW for users.

Agents are computer programs that can assist the user with computer applications. Intelligent Agents (i-agents or IAs) are computer programs that assist the user with their tasks. I-agents may be on the Internet, or they can be on mobile wireless architectures. In the context of this research, however, the tasks that we are primarily concerned with include reading, filtering and sorting, and maintaining information.

Agents can employ several techniques. Agents are created to act on behalf of its user(s) in carrying out difficult and often time-consuming tasks (see Jensen, 2002; Watson, 1997; Bigus & Bigus, 1998). Most agents today employ some type of artificial intelligence technique to assist the users with their computer-related tasks, such as reading e-mail (see Watson, 1997; Bigus & Bigus, 1998), maintaining a calendar, and filtering information. Some agents can be trained to learn through examples in order to improve the performance of the tasks they are given (see Watson, 1997; Bigus & Bigus, 1998).

There are also several ways that agents can be trained to better understand user preferences by using computational intelligence techniques, such as using evolutionary computing systems, neural networks, adaptive fuzzy logic and expert systems, etc. The combination of search and retrieval engines, the agent, the user preference, and the information retrieval algorithm can provide the users with the confidence and trust they require in agents. A modified version of this approach is used throughout this research for intelligent information retrieval from the WWW.

The user who is seeking information from the WWW is an agent. The user agent may teach the i-agent by example or by employing a set of criteria for the i-agent to follow. Some i-agents have certain knowledge (expressed as rules) embedded in them to improve their filtering and sorting performance. For an agent to be considered intelligent, it should be able to sense and act autonomously in its environment. To some degree, i-agents are designed to be adaptive to their environments and to the changes in their environments (see Jensen, 2002; Watson, 1997; Bigus & Bigus, 1998).

This research considers i-agents for transforming the passive search and retrieval engines into more active, personal user assistants. By playing this role, i-agents can be considered to be collaborative with existing search engines as a more effective information retrieval and filtering technique in support of user needs.

INTELLIGENT AGENTS FOR INFORMATION FILTERING AND DATA MINING

Since the late '90s, intranets, extranets and the Internet have provided platforms for an explosion in the amount of data and information available to WWW users. The number of web-based sites continues to grow exponentially. The cost and availability of hardware, software and telecommunications currently continues to be at a level that user worldwide can afford. The ease of use and the availability of user-oriented web browsers, such as Netscape and Internet Explorer, have attracted many new computer users to the online world. These factors, among others, continue to create opportunities for the design and implementation of i-agents to assist users in doing complex computing tasks associated with the WWW.

There are three major approaches for building agents for the WWW. The first approach is to integrate i-agents into existing search engine programs. The agent follows predefined rules that it employs in its filtering decisions. Using this approach has several advantages.

The second approach is a rule-based approach. With this approach, an agent is given information about the application. A knowledge engineers is required to collect the required rules and knowledge for the agent.

The third approach is a training approach. In this approach the agent is trained to learn the preferences and actions of its user (Jensen, 2002).

This research aims to describe an intelligent agent that is able to perceive the world around it. That is, to recognize and evaluate events as they occur, determine the meaning of those events, and then take actions on behalf of the user(s). An event is a change of state within that agent's environment, such as when an email arrives and the agent is to filter the email (see Watson, 1997; Bigus & Bigus, 1998), or when new data or information becomes available in one of the many forms described earlier.

An i-agent must be able to process data. I-agents may have several processing strategies. They may be designed to use simple strategies (algorithms), or they could use complex reasoning and learning strategies to achieve their tasks. The success of i-agents depends on how much value they provide to their users (see Jensen, 2002; Lucas & Nissenbaum, 2000; Watson, 1997; Bigus & Bigus, 1998) and how easily they can be employed by their user(s).

I-agents in this research are used to retrieve data and information from the WWW. Technical issues of the implementation of the system using HTTP protocol are described. The Java programming language was used in this research to create an i-agent. The i-agent developed actively searches out desired data and information on the Web, and filters out unwanted data and information in delivering its results.

EVOLUTIONARY COMPUTING, FUZZY LOGIC AND I-AGENTS FOR INFORMATION FILTERING

Evolutionary computing are powerful search optimization and learning algorithms based on the mechanism of natural selection and, among other operations, use operations of reproduction, crossover and mutation on a population of solutions. An initial set (population) of candidate solutions is created. In this research, each individual in the population is a candidate-relevant homepage that is represented as a URL-string. A new population of such URL-strings is produced at every generation by the repetition of a two-step cycle. Firstly, each individual URL-string's ability is assessed. Each URL-string is assigned a fitness value, depending on how well it performed (how relevant the page is). In the second stage, the fittest URL-strings are preferentially chosen to form the next generation. A modified-mutation is used to add diversity within a small population of URL-strings. It is used to prevent premature convergence to a non-optimal solution. The modified-mutation operator adds new URL-strings to the evolutionary computing population when it is called.

Evolutionary computing is used to assist in improving i-agent performance. This research is based on the successful simulations of employing an i-agent.

The simulation assumes that, first, a connection to the WWW via a protocol, such as HTTP (HyperText Transport Protocol), is done. Next, it assumes that a URL (Universal Resource Locator) object class can be easily created. The URL class represents a pointer to a "resource" on the WWW. A resource can be something as simple as a file or a directory, or it can be a reference to a more complicated object, such as a query result via a database or a search engine.

The resulting information obtained by the i-agent resides on a host machine. The information on the host machine is given by a name that has an html extension. The exact meaning of this name on the host machine is both protocol-dependent and host-dependent. The information normally resides in an existing file, but it could be generated "on the fly." This component of the URL is called the *file component*, even though the information is not necessarily in a file. The i-agent facilitates the search for and retrieval of information from WWW searches according to keywords provided by the user. Filtering and retrieval of information from the WWW using the i-agent, with the use of evolutionary computing and fuzzy logic according to keywords provided by the user, is described:

Phase 1:

(1)   Select the required search engine(s), such as AltaVista, Excite, Google, HotBot, Infoseek, Northernlight, etc.;

(2)   Combine the keywords $(k_1, k_2, ..., k_n)$ given by the user in a form understandable to the search engine(s) and submit the keywords to the i-agent;

(3)   Obtain the results of the search from the selected search engine(s). The host machine (of the search engine) returns the requested information and data with no specific format or acknowledgment.

Phase 2:

(1)   The i-agent program then calls its routines to identify all related URLs obtained from search engine(s) and inserts them into a temporary list (only the first 600 URLs returned are chosen) referred to as "TempList";

(2)   For each URL in the TempList, the following tasks are performed:
(2.1) Once all URLs are retrieved, initialize the generation zero (of the evolutionary computing population) using the supplied URL by the i-agent (Given an URL address from TempList, connect to that web page);
(2.2) Once the connection is established, read the web page and rank it as described:

More weight is assigned to the query term shown applied to the web page with a frequency of occurrence higher than the other terms $(k_1, k_2, ..., k_n)$. Both position and frequency of keywords are used to assign a position and frequency score to a page. If the instances of the keywords on the web page are more frequent, and the position earlier on the web page than those with the other occurrence instances, the higher the web page's ranking. The following fuzzy rules are used to evaluate and assign a score to a web page:

If *Frequency_of_keywords* = **High**, then *Frequency_Score* = **High**;
If *Frequency_of_keywords* = **Medium**, then *Frequency_Score* = **Medium**;
If *Frequency_of_keywords* = **Low**, then *Frequency_Score* = **Low**;

The score obtained from applying these fuzzy rules is called the *Frequency_Score*. The position of a keyword on a web page is used to assign a position score for the web page. The following fuzzy rules are used to evaluate and assign a position score to a web page:

If *Position_of_keywords* = **Close_To_Top**, then *Position_Score* = **High**;
If *Position_of_keywords* = **More_&_Less_Close_To_Top**, then *Position_Score* = **Medium**;
If *Position_of_keywords* = **Far_From_Top**, then *Position_Score* = **Low**;

The score obtained from the above fuzzy rules is called *Position_Score*.

The number of links on a web page is used to assign a link score for the web page. The following fuzzy rules are used to evaluate and assign a link score to a web page:

If *Number_of_Links* = **Large**, then *Link_Score* = **High**;
If *Number_of_Links* = **Medium**, then *Link_Score* = **Medium**;
If *Number_of_Links* = **Small**, then *Link_Score* = **Low**;

The score obtained from the previous fuzzy rules is called *Link_Score*.

A final calculation, based on the scores for each page by aggregating all scores obtained from the fuzzy rules above, is created. That is, for each web page, a score according to the following is derived:

Score = (2*Frequency_Score) + *Position_Score* + *Links_Score*

(2.2.1) For web pages with high scores, identify any URL link in this web page (we call these links **child URLs**) and create a list of these URLs;
(2.2.2) For each child URL found on the web page, connect to that web page, evaluate, and assign a score as described in 2.2. Store the URLs with their scores in a list called FitURLs.
(2.3.3) Process the information, read, and save it locally.

(3) The next (modified crossover) step involves the selection of the two **child URLs** (see 2.2.1) that have the highest score (the score for a page will be referred to as "fitness" from here on).

(4) Modified-mutation is used to provide diversity in the pool of URLs in a generation. For modified-mutation, we choose a URL from the list of already created FitURLs, URLs with high fitness (see 2.2.2). The process of selection, modified-crossover, and modified-mutation is repeated for a number of generations until a satisfactory set of URLs is found or until a predefined number of generations (200 was the limit for our simulation) is reached. In some cases, the simulation found that the evolutionary computing system converged fairly quickly and had to be stopped before 200 generations.

(5) Finally, display the URLs with their fitness.

SIMULATION RESULTS

Several keyword(s) were submitted to test the i-agent. The keywords covered a broad range of topics. Keywords submitted were single keywords, such as "Conference" and "Tennis," and multiple keywords, such as "Conference Australia," "Intelligent Agents" and "Information Retrieval." Volunteers tested the results of searching, first, by using the keyword(s) and their chosen search engine (AltaVista, Excite, Google, HotBot, Infoseek, Northernlight, etc.). The volunteers then used the i-agent program for search and retrieval from the WWW by giving the same keyword(s). The results from the two searches were then compared. For example, in one experiment, a volunteer used the keywords "Conference Australia" and performed a search using the AltaVista, Excite, Lycos and Yahoo search engines. These search engines, shown below, returned a large number of results.

Table 1. Search Results as of June 2002

Search query: Conference Australia

Search Engines	Number of pages returned
AltaVista	Conference: 26,194,461 and Australia: 34,334,654
Excite	2,811,220
Lycos	673,912
Yahoo	40 categories and 257 sites

Table 2. Search Results as of July 2002

Search Engines	Number of pages returned
AltaVista	766,674
Google	1,300,000
HotBot	807,500
Lycos	3,688,456
Northernlight	103,748
Yahoo	251 pages with 20 hits per page

It is very unlikely that a user will search the 26,194,461 results shown in the AltaVista query in Table 1. This could be due to users' past experience in not finding what they want, or it could be due to the time constraint that users have when looking for information. A business would consider the cost of obtaining the information and just what value exists after the first 600 pages found. It is very unlikely that a user will search more than 600 pages in a single query, and most users likely will not search more than the first 50.

In a more recent experiment, a volunteer used the search query of "Conference Australia." This volunteer extended the search to include several other search engines that are considered more popular in their use. The results illustrate that search engines and the results are changing dynamically. However, it is still very unlikely that a user will, for example, search the 1,300,000 results as shown in Google or the 3,688,456 shown in Lycos. The following table illustrates their results.

Table 3. Search Results and Evaluation as of June 2002

Search query: Conference Australia

Search Engines	Number of pages returned	Number of relevant pages	I-agent relevant pages	Number of relevant pages from i-agent and evolutionary algorithms
AltaVista	Conference: 26,194,461 and Australia: 34,334,654	2,050	180	179 from 200 pages returned
Excite	2,811,220	1,889		
Lycos	673,912	2,210		
Yahoo	40 categories and 257 sites	84 sites were relevant		

The dynamics of web data and information means that the simulation could be done any day and different results will be obtained. The essence of this research takes that into account by providing a way to continuously provide the user with their desired information while taking into account the dynamics of information on the Web. To evaluate the performance of the information filtering and retrieval of the above system, several simulations were performed. Simulation results for some of the keywords that are used to check the performance of the systems were: Conference, Conference Australia, Intelligent Agents, Information Retrieval, and Tennis. The results obtained were then passed to the evolutionary computing system, and final results were passed to volunteers for testing. The evolutionary computing, as described above, was then used to find the most relevant pages to this search query. The evolutionary computing was run for 200 generations. The top 200 URLs returned from the evolutionary computing were then presented to the volunteers to assess the results. The volunteers then compared the results obtained from i-agents to their own opinion from the web sites they visited and evaluated. It is interesting to see that the results obtained by combined i-agent and evolutionary computing are very good.

The number of URLs returned is feasible, and the users are provided with relevant web pages. Out of another 62 experiments performed, the combined i-agent and evolutionary computing system performance was good. The volunteers have reported that in more than 70 percent of the experiments (out of 62 experiments), the results of the combined i-agent and evolutionary computing system were very satisfactory. Table 4 shows that relevancy of the

Table 4. Search Results by i-Agent and Combined i-Agent and Evolutionary Computing as of July 2002

Search query	Number of pages returned i-agent	Number of relevant pages returned by i-agent and evolutionary computing and fuzzy logic
Conference	180 from 215 pages returned	169 from 200 pages returned
Conference and Australia	127 from 223 pages returned	127 from 200 pages returned
Intelligent Agents, and Tennis.	189 from 348 pages returned	132 from 200 pages returned
Information Retrieval	117 from 216 pages returned	111 from 200 pages returned
Information Retrieval	127 from 223 pages returned	108 from 200 pages returned

URLs, based on some of the queries given to i-agent and evolutionary computing.

CONCLUSION

The amount of information potentially available from the World Wide Web (WWW), including such areas as web pages, page links, accessible documents, and databases, continues to increase. This information abundance increases the complexity of searching and locating relevant information for users. This chapter suggests intelligent agents as a way to improve the performance of search and retrieval engines. The use of search engines, the i-agent, evolutionary computing, and fuzzy logic has been shown to be an effective way of filtering data and information retrieval from the World Wide Web.

In this research, an intelligent agent was first constructed to assist in better information filtering, information gathering, and ranking from the World Wide Web than simply using existing search engines. Simulation results show that the performance of the system using the intelligent agent provides better results than conventional search engines. It is not very surprising since agents use the results of search engines and then filter the irrelevant web pages. In most of the simulated cases, the combination of evolutionary computing, fuzzy logic, and i-agents in filtering data and information provided improved results over traditional search engines. This research is unique in the way the agents are constructed and in the way evolutionary computing and fuzzy logic are incorporated to help users. The method described in this chapter demonstrates that using i-agents, evolutionary computing, and fuzzy logic together has a great deal of promise. In particular, the method employed shows that it can:

- collect and rank relevant web pages;
- reduce the size of the result set and recommend the more relevant web pages according to a given query;
- increase the precision of the results by displaying the URLs of relevant web pages.

The methods employed and described here require further study. The first study that is being looked at is directed at individuals. This includes having more volunteers to test and compare the methods. Given the information that these volunteers obtain, evaluate the value of the resulting information. Then, compare the results among the individuals. The second study that is being looked at is for business competitiveness. This study employs the methods described in this chapter and evaluates the information that a business needs in its industry to maintain a watch on its current and new competitors.

ACKNOWLEDGMENT

The authors would like to acknowledge the assistance of *Mr. Long Tan* and *Mr. Thien Huynh* in programming efforts on several parts of this research project.

REFERENCES

Bigus, J. P. & Bigus, J. (1998). *Constructing Intelligent Agents with Java — A Programmer's Guide to Smarter Applications*. Hoboken, NJ: Wiley InterScience.

Cabri, G., Leonardi, L., & Zambonelli, F. (2000, February). Mobile-agent coordination models for Internet applications. *IEEE Spectrum*.

Chen, H., Chung, Y., Ramsey, M., & Yang, C. (1997). Intelligent spider for Internet searching. In *Proceedings of the 30th Hawaii International Conference on System Sciences* (vol. IV, pp. 178-188).

Cho, H. J., Garcia-Molina, H., & Page, L. (1998). Efficient crawling through URL ordering. *Proceedings of the 7th International Web Conference*, Brisbane, Australia (April 14-18).

Chong, C. W., Ramachandran, V., & Eswaran, C. (1999). *Equivalence class approach for web link classification*. Malaysia: University Telekom, Faculty of Engineering and Information Technology (Conference Paper).

Eyeballz. (2002). *Search engine marketing in New Zealand*. Last accessed May 24, 2002, from: http://www.eyeballz.co.nz/search_engine_statistics.htm

Hines, M. (2002). The problem with petrabytes. *The Information Architect*. Last accessed June 5, 2002, from: http://www.techtarget.com.au

Jensen, J. (2002). *Using an intelligent agent to enhance search engine performance*. Retrieved January 2002, from: http://www.firstmonday.dk/issues/issue2_3/jansen/index.htm

Jentzsch, R. & Gobbin, R. (2002). An e-commerce communicative multi-agent agent model. *Proceedings of the IRMA 2002 Conference*, Seattle, Washington (May 19-22).

Lawrence, S. & Giles, C. L. (1999). Accessibility of information on the Web. *Nature*, *400*, 107-109.

Lucas, I. & Nissenbaum, H. (2000, June). The politics of search engine. *IEEE Spectrum*.

Maes, P. (1994). Agents that reduce work and information overload. *Communications of the ACM*, *19*(1), 31-40.

Nwana, H. S. (1996). Software agents: An overview. *Knowledge Engineering Review*, *11*(3), 205-244.

Searchengines.com. (2002). Last accessed June 10, 2002, from: http://www.searchengines.com/searchEnginesRankings.html

Searchengines.com. (2002). Last accessed June 10, 2002, from: http://www.searchengines.com/search_engine_statistics.html

Sullivan, D. (ed.). Nielsen//NetRatings search engine ratings. *Current Audience Reach*. Last accessed May 9, 2002, from: http://www.searchenginewatch.com/reports/netratings.html

Watson, M. (1997). *Intelligent Java Applications for the Internet and Intranet*. San Francisco, CA: Morgan Kaufmann.

ELECTRONIC REFERENCES

AltaVista: http://www.altavista.com/

America On Line: http://www.aol.com

Excite: http://www.excite.com/

Google: http://www.Google.com/

InfoSeek: http://www.infoseek.com/

Lycos: http://www.Lycos.com/

MSN: http://www.msn.com (aka: http://dellnet.msn.com)

Northernlight: http://www.Northernlight.com/

Yahoo: http://www.yahoo.com/

Chapter III

A Multi-Agent Approach to Collaborative Knowledge Production

Juan Manuel Dodero, Universidad Carlos III de Madrid, Spain

Paloma Díaz, Universidad Carlos III de Madrid, Spain

Ignacio Aedo, Universidad Carlos III de Madrid, Spain

ABSTRACT

Knowledge creation or production in a distributed knowledge management system is a collaborative task that needs to be coordinated. A multi-agent architecture for collaborative knowledge production tasks is introduced, where knowledge-producing agents are arranged into knowledge domains or marts, and where a distributed interaction protocol is used to consolidate knowledge that is produced in a mart. Knowledge consolidated in a given mart can, in turn, be negotiated in higher-level foreign marts. As an evaluation scenario, the proposed architecture and protocol are applied to coordinate the creation of learning objects by a distributed group of instructional designers.

INTRODUCTION

Knowledge management (KM) authors quote many verbs to describe the processes that transform the intellectual capital of an organization or group of people into value (Stewart, 1997) — creation, acquisition, distribution, application, sharing and reposition, among others — but they can be summarized in three categories, depending on the direction of the information flow, i.e., production, acquisition and transfer.

Knowledge is not frequently well-structured enough to be appropriately used and exploited, so acquisition and transfer techniques are needed to facilitate the sharing and re-use of the group-wide available knowledge. On the other hand, knowledge emerges from the social interaction between actors, with production being the creative process of formulating information, which has to be validated as useful to the group before it becomes fully-fledged knowledge. According to empiric (Goldman, 1991) and organizational learning (Argyris, 1993) approaches, we consider knowledge as the subset of information that is applied in order to cause an impact in the influenced environment and which is subject to necessary validation tests that corroborate its applicability.

Recent works (Clases et al., 2002) advocate collaboration in support of knowledge production in socially distributed systems. Collaborative production stands out as a tool to mediate, but not eliminate, the differences between views of the design of a system. This chapter outlines a new approach for collaborative knowledge production based upon a multi-agent architecture. This approach organizes knowledge production in a distributed interaction environment to complete the distributed KM scenario. As a case study, our approach is applied to the collaborative development of learning objects by a distributed group of instructional designers.

In the rest of this section, we introduce the subject of collaborative knowledge production and our working thesis. The following section presents a structured and coordinated model of interaction between knowledge-producing agents. Next, the architecture is tested in an instructional design scenario devoted to the collaborative creation of learning objects. Finally, we present some conclusions and future work drawn from the application of the architecture.

Collaborative Knowledge Production

Several authors on the topic of KM cite production or generation of knowledge referring to the creation of new knowledge. When Davenport and Prusak (1998) tell about *knowledge generation*, they are referring both to externally acquired knowledge and knowledge developed within the bosom of an organization without distinguishing between acquisition and generation. In our study, we consider *generation* as distinct from *acquisition*. From our point of view, knowledge generation or production is the creation of new knowledge as the result of the social interaction between actors in a workgroup or organization, according to their interests and the regulations that apply. On the other side, knowledge is acquired when it comes from outside of an organization or workgroup — i.e., it is generated outside and thereafter adopted by the organization.

Coordination is a key pattern of interaction that is needed to obtain good-quality knowledge that has been validated by means of contrast and/or consensus in the group. Although KM research in distributed knowledge acquisition and sharing efforts are worth considering, knowledge production still lacks the interaction models and methods of coordinating a group of autonomous users in the collaborative generation of knowledge.

A Multi-Agent Approach

Multi-agent systems have been successful in the distributed implementation of KM processes. Knowledge acquisition agents have been one of the most successful applications of software agents, specifically in the Internet (Etzioni, 1995), where knowledge-collector agents operate within available information resources and validate them in accordance with the users' interests. On the other hand, knowledge transfer lies in an end-to-end routing of knowledge that is generated by some actor, and it is another typical task that has been realized by software agents (Genesereth & Tenenbaum, 1991). Therefore, it is reasonable to approach the multi-agent paradigm for knowledge production. Knowledge-producing agents need to do formulations in keeping with a validation scheme that supports the knowledge construction. Multi-agent systems can support the coordinated interaction needed to achieve an agreement on the knowledge that is eventually generated. They can also support the validation scheme.

Advances in multi-agent systems as an alternative way to build distributed systems have made agents a facilitator of human-computer interaction. Agents have been proven as helpful tools for the coordination of people who are performing a given task (Maes, 1994). Agent interaction protocols govern the exchange of a series of messages among agents, in accordance with the interaction style among actors. The interaction styles of individual agents can be competitive, cooperative or negotiating. But, both the group behavior and the authoring of knowledge objects are social, group-level issues, more than individual subjects, and it is there where multi-agent systems can give their contribution.

The architecture presented in this work is a bottom-up, multi-agent approach for knowledge production. Our working hypothesis is that a group of agents can help in the collaborative production of knowledge by coordinating their creation activities. Therefore, different agents can act as representatives of knowledge-producing actors, according to the following principles:

- Agents can be structured into separable knowledge domains of interaction. This structuring reflects the knowledge differences between developers.
- A dynamic rethinking of the structure of interactions in different domains can help to reduce conflicts during the process.

A KNOWLEDGE PRODUCTION ARCHITECTURE

A system can be described from the following perspectives: (1) the function and structure of the system; (2) the relation and interaction of the system with its environment; and (3) the dynamics of the system. This section deals with the first two perspectives of a reference architecture used to build knowledge production systems:

- The function of our knowledge production architecture is to consolidate knowledge created in an agent-coordinated interaction environment. The structure is hierarchical and is based upon interaction domains that we call *knowledge marts*, as described in this chapter.
- Agent interaction in a mart fulfills the rules of the protocol described in this section, while the interaction between different marts is guided by the multilevel architecture of subsection "Multi-Level Architecture."

Knowledge Marts

Knowledge-producing agents usually operate within the boundaries of a knowledge domain that we call a *knowledge mart*. Such a mart consists of a distributed group of agents, whose purpose is to generate knowledge objects in a knowledge domain. The basic elements of a mart are:

- A set of collaborative agents which can communicate in order to consolidate the knowledge that is being produced.
- A multicasting transport support that guarantees the reliable delivery of messages to every member in the mart.
- An interaction protocol that governs coordination between agents.
- An interaction policy that defines the kind of relationship established between agents, which may be mainly competitive or cooperative.
- An ontology to represent domain-level knowledge that is produced by agents affiliated with the mart.

Knowledge Consolidation

Agents in a mart should coordinate their interactions with the aim of consolidating the knowledge that is being generated. *Consolidation* is the establishment of knowledge as accepted by every agent in the mart in such a way that every agent in the group eventually knows about it. The knowledge body is built through the progressive consolidation of proposals, which then become knowledge.

Interaction between agents is carried out by exchanging proposals in a FIPA-like common language (FIPA, 1999) that is driven by the participants' goals and needs, therefore shaping a social interaction-level knowledge (Jennings & Campos, 1997). By *proposal*, we mean each formulation act of an agent that intends to consolidate a given knowledge in its group. Since a proposal exhibits an intentional nature, we will not refer to it as fully-fledged knowledge until it becomes consolidated. An agent may be involved in several simultaneous interaction processes. The protocol described below is used to advance each interaction process by executing it in a separate thread.

Multi-Level Architecture

In our architecture, knowledge-producing agents can operate within the boundaries of a specific domain or knowledge mart, as shown in Figure 1. Nevertheless, interaction among different domains is also supported through a number of proxy agents. In order to facilitate interaction between domains, marts can be structured in a hierarchical way. In this architecture, domains are modeled as knowledge marts, and these are arranged into *knowledge warehouses*, in a similar way to data warehousing systems. A knowledge warehouse is the place where knowledge consolidated in foreign marts is merged in a structured fashion.

Figure 1. Multilevel Architecture of Marts for Knowledge Production

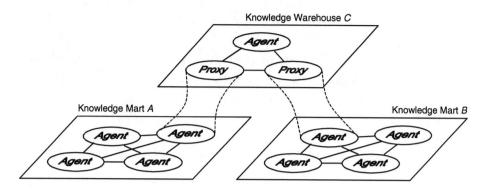

Two or more marts can interact using representatives in a common warehouse. When knowledge produced in a mart can affect performance in some other domain, a special proxy agent can act as a representative in the foreign mart so that interaction between marts is not tightly coupled.

In this hierarchical structure, when a mart sets up a proxy agent in another higher-level mart, a *participative* relationship is defined between both marts, since agents in the lower-level mart can have influence in production tasks carried out in the upper one.

Agent Interaction in a Knowledge Mart

The minimum requirement to interact is that agents can build and deliver proposals, which can be accepted or rejected. An example is the contract net protocol (Smith & Davis, 1981). The protocol is more sophisticated when recipients have a chance to build counterproposals that alter certain issues that were not satisfactory in the original proposal. A more elaborate form of interaction allows parties to send justifications or arguments along with the proposals. Such arguments indicate why proposals should be accepted (Sycara, 1990).

Interaction between agents is carried out by exchanging proposals in a common language, or ACL (Agent Communication Language) (Mayfield et al., 1995). Proposal interchange is directed by the goals and needs of participating agents. Although the formalization of agents' language and goals is not our concern, we need to assume a set of conventions:

(1) Agent rationality is modeled in terms of *preference relationships*, or *relevance functions*, in order to allow agents to evaluate and compare proposals. Nevertheless, other preference structures can be easily integrated, e.g., linguistic-expressed preferences (Delgado et al., 1998).

(2) Relevant aspects of the interaction can be modeled as *issues* and *values* that change as the interaction progresses. This is not despite of more powerful, ontology-based possibilities to represent the same aspects (Gruber, 1991).

(3) Concerning our protocol, the following types of messages can be exchanged between agents:

- *propose(k, n)*: Given an interaction process n, an agent sends a *propose* message to inform the rest of agents about its desire for a piece of knowledge k to be consolidated.
- *consolidate(k, n)*: Agents send a *consolidate* message when they want a previously submitted proposal k to be consolidated in an interaction process n.

Both types of messages can be respectively identified with *propose* and *inform* declaratives from FIPA ACL specification (FIPA, 1997). Nevertheless, since FIPA ACL provides them with a well-defined semantics — especially different in the case of *consolidate* — we prefer to use the types of messages recently described.

A proposal reflects the intention of an agent to generate a given knowledge that was previously formulated. The *attributes* of a proposal are elementary criteria that should be considered when comparing it to another in a mart. Some examples of proposal attributes are:

- The submitter's hierarchical level, useful when agents present different decision privileges in the mart about the acceptance of proposals (e.g., lecturer vs. assistant in a faculty staff).
- The degree of fulfillment of a set of goals. For instance, before the development of a learning content, a set of educational objectives should be defined. In the case of corporate learning, these goals will be determined by the training needs of the organization.
- A time-stamp of the moment when a proposal was first submitted in the mart (this is normally considered in the last case, when the rest of attributes cannot decide).

We define the *relevance* of a proposal as the set of proposal attributes that are considered in fact during a message interaction. In order to measure the relevance of a proposal, a *relevance function* can be defined.

The relevance function $u(k)$ of a proposal k in a mart returns a numeric value, dependent on attributes of k, in such a way that, if $k_i \neq k_j$, then $u(k_i) \neq u(k_j)$. A way to express the relevance is by means of *preference relationships*, where a proposal k_1 is preferred to another k_2 in a mart, denoted as $k_1 > k_2$, if $u(k_1) > u(k_2)$.

Interaction Protocol

An agent A_i may participate in several interaction processes. Each interaction process is handled separately by initiating a new execution thread of the protocol, as depicted in the following algorithm:

Algorithm: Let $\mathcal{A}_M = \{A_1, \ldots, A_n\}$ be a discrete set of agents participating in a knowledge mart $\mathcal{M}$.

Start: When A_i wants a knowledge piece k to be consolidated in $\mathcal{M}$, it sends a *propose*(k_i,*n*) to every agent in $\mathcal{M}$, initiating a new interaction process n. Then, A_i sets a timeout t_0 before confirming its proposal. During t_0, messages can arrive from any other agent A_j, with $j \neq i$, consisting of new proposals — maybe the original, though modified — referring to the same interaction process n.

Rule 1:   If A_i does not receive any message referred to n during t_0, it considers that there is no agent against its proposal. It tries to ratify it by sending a *consolidate*(k_i,*n*) to every agent in $\mathcal{M}$. At the same time, A_i starts a new timeout t_1.

Rule 2:   When A_i receives a *propose*(k_j,*n*) message from other agent A_j, referring to the same interaction process n, A_i evaluates the new proposal k_j. If $k_i < k_j$, then A_i sets a new timeout t_1, waiting for proposal k_j to be ratified. Then, A_i proceeds as follows:

(2.1) If A_i does not receive any proposal referred to interaction process n before t_1 expires, then A_i initiates the protocol again with the same proposal k_i.

(2.2) If A_i receives a *consolidate*(k_j,n), with $k_j > k_i$, for $j \neq i$, before t_1 expires, and referring to the same interaction process n, then A_i gives up the initial proposal and the protocol finishes unsuccessfully.

(2.3) If A_i receives a new *propose*(k_j,n), with $k_i < k_j$, it extends the timeout t_1.

The interaction protocol described above uses two message types (i.e., *propose* and *consolidate*), but some variants using additional message types to express different semantics can also be formulated — e.g., *retract*, *substitute* or *reject*. These types of messages can speed up the development of the protocol, but they are not completely necessary for the success of the consolidation process.

EVALUATION IN AN INSTRUCTIONAL DESIGN SCENARIO

An important contribution to the e-learning arena is happening in the way of designing, locating and delivering educational contents in the Internet. *Learning objects* lead the set of theories devoted to the design and development of learning contents, also known as *instructional design* (Merrill, 1994). A concrete case of a system for the shared creation of knowledge is one dedicated to the development of learning objects. During the process, a number of instructional designers may wish to contribute. They could, for example, make some modification to the structure of a course or add some learning resource to the course contents. Interaction between authors should be coordinated to extend or modify the educational material. Authors try to meet a protocol that reflects their different interaction styles.

Under a constructivist instructional design approach (Koper, 1997), in the creation of educational content, not only must teachers take part, but also the receivers of the training (i.e., students). Therefore, consumers and designers of learning objects have a participative relationship, where the subordinated agents can also participate in the instructional design process, although the final decision lies with the higher-level agents.

Evaluation Scenario

The evaluation scenario consists of a knowledge mart where three agents are producing knowledge in the representation of a docent coordinator (C_1) and two instructors $(I_1$ and $I_2)$. The goal of agents in the mart is the development of a IMS/SCORM (IMS, 2001) learning object — a course named 'XML Programming' — that fulfills a set of educational objectives. Although there is room in IMS standards for describing each part of the learning object — e.g., organizations, resources, metadata, etc. — we will restrict the discussion to the ToC structure, devoting the interaction process n to it.

When authors submit proposals, they will include the differences between both ToCs and will refer to the same interaction. The interaction protocol is executed by every receiving author until the proposal is eventually accepted or replaced with a further elaborated proposal. This process continues until some proposal wins all evaluations, an agreement is reached, or until some degree of consensus is achieved (depending on the kind of interaction, i.e., competitive, negotiating or cooperative). Although the authors' behavior is an asynchronous process, the agents' interaction protocol helps to synchronize their operations.

Objectives

These are the educational objectives that define the preference relation used to evaluate proposals about the ToC of the course:

1. Ability to program XHTML (i.e., XML-generated HTML) web applications
2. Ability to program server-side web applications
3. Ability to program XML data exchange applications

The degree of fulfillment of educational objectives is modeled as a three-component vector $\mathbf{x} = (x_1, x_2, x_3)$, with $x_k \in I = [0,1]$ for $k=1,2,3$. Let $f: I^3 \to I$ be a numerical measure of how well a proposal meets the objectives.

Evaluation Criteria

The relevance of a proposal is graded by the fulfillment of the educational objectives described above. All objectives being equally satisfied, the rank of the agent will decide (coordinator is higher that instructor). If ranks are the same, the time when the proposal was issued will decide. To determine the instant of generation, every proposal will include a time-stamp.

Each proposal $\mathbf{p}$ is described by a three-component vector (p_1, p_2, p_3), where:

- $p_1 = f(\mathbf{x})$ measures the degree of fulfillment of educational objectives.
- p_2 is the numerical rank held by the submitter agent.
- p_3 is a time-stamp.

Notation for Proposals

To simplify the notation, proposals are represented by x_{ij}, where x_i is an identification of the author, and j is a sequence number ordered by the instant of generation of the proposal. Using this notation, the following proposals will be elaborated by agents in the mart:

- i_{11}: Create a unique chapter for "XML script programming."
- i_{12}: Divide "XML script programming" into two new chapters: "Client-side XML script programming" and "Server-side XML script programming."
- i_{21}: Add a chapter about "Document Type Definitions (DTD)."
- i_{22}: Add a chapter about "DTD and XML schemas."
- c_{11}: Add a chapter about "Using XML as data."

Preference Relationship

A preference relationship $>$ is defined between any two proposals $\mathbf{p} = (p_1, p_2, p_3)$ and $\mathbf{q} = (q_1, q_2, q_3)$:

$$\mathbf{p} > \mathbf{q} \Leftrightarrow (p_1 > q_2) \vee [(p_1{=}q_1) \wedge (p_2 > q_2)] \vee [(p_1{=}q_1) \wedge (p_2{=}q_2) \wedge (p_3 > q_3)] \quad (1)$$

The preference relation given in (1) defines a partial order, where $i_{11} < i_{12} < i_{21} < i_{22} < c_{11}$, in accordance with the evaluation criteria.

Sequence of Events

The sequence of events generated by agents in the mart is made up of three *acts*, which are depicted in Figure 2 and traced as follows:

(1) I_1 starts by sending a proposal i_{11}. When i_{11} is about to be consolidated, I_2 agent will issue a better evaluated proposal i_{21}. C_1 does nothing and silently accepts every proposal that comes to it.

(2) I_1 and I_2 elaborate two respective proposals i_{12} and i_{22}, approximately at the same time during the distribution phase. The proposal from I_2 has a better evaluation than I_1's, and both are better than those in the first act.

(3) C_1 builds and sends the best-evaluated proposal of this scene, which will eventually win the evaluation.

The series of messages exchanged during act (2) is depicted in more detail in Figure 3 and is described as follows:

(a)   Both I_1 and I_2 receive each other's proposal and begin the distribution phase, therefore starting timeout t_0. Proposals $\mathbf{i}_{12}$ and $\mathbf{i}_{22}$ also arrive at C_1, which is not participating in the process and silently receives them.

(b) I_1 compares $\mathbf{i}_{22}$ to $\mathbf{i}_{12}$, turning out that its proposal has a worse evaluation. It is reasonable that an evaluation of proposal $\mathbf{i}_{12}$ obtains a higher value than $\mathbf{i}_{22}$, as for the second objective described above. Concerning the first and third objectives, any relevance function should result in similar values for both proposals, so they would not be decisive. Then, I_1 starts timeout t_1, giving $\mathbf{i}_{22}$ a chance to be consolidated. On the other hand, I_2 also compares both proposals and reminds I_1 of the results by again sending $\mathbf{i}_{22}$, then extending timeout t_0 in order to give a chance for other agents' proposals to come.

(c)   When timeout t_0 expires, I_2 sends a consolidation message for $\mathbf{i}_{22}$ that arrives to every agent in the mart. At the reception, I_1 finishes the protocol because it is expecting the consolidation for $\mathbf{i}_{22}$. C_1 simply accepts the notification.

(d)   Finally, at the expiration of t_1, I_2 is notified about the end of the consolidation phase for $\mathbf{i}_{22}$, and its execution of the protocol finishes successfully. Therefore, every agent in the mart will eventually know about the consolidation of the proposal.

These tests have been carried out to examine how far the multi-agent architecture facilitates the coordination of a group of actors that are producing learning objects. In this educational scenario, quantitative measurements of performance and throughput were taken concerning observable actions and behaviors about a number of aspects, such as conflict-solving facility, effectiveness in coordinating the production process, fair participation of members from other groups, overall quality of the final results, and speed and quality of the generated knowledge.

In this context, the agent-mediated solution has been found to facilitate the following aspects of the distributed creation of learning objects during the instructional design process:

- Bring together instructional designers' different paces of creation.
- Take advantage of designers' different skills in the overall domain and tools that are managed.
- Reduce the number of conflicts provoked by interdependencies between different parts of the learning objects.
- In a general sense, avoid duplication of effort.

Figure 2.   Sequence of Events for the Learning Object Evaluation Scenario

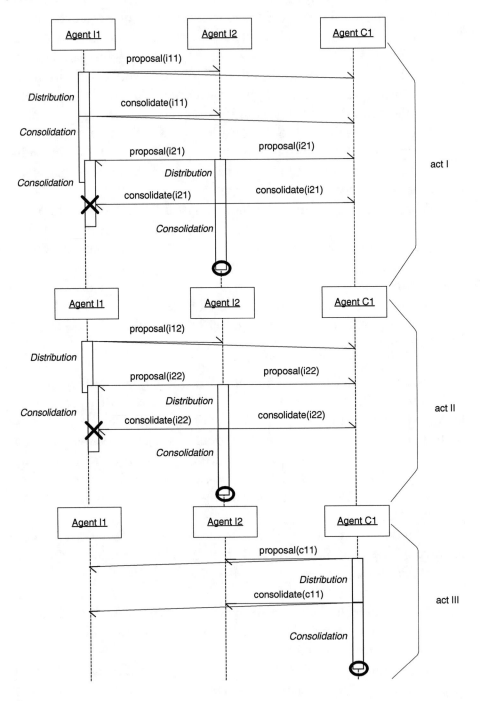

Figure 3. Execution Example of the Interaction Protocol

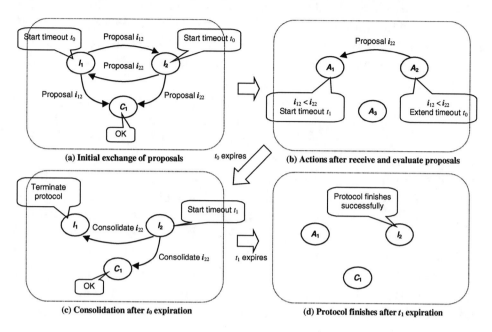

(a) Initial exchange of proposals

(b) Actions after receive and evaluate proposals

t_0 expires

(c) Consolidation after t_0 expiration

(d) Protocol finishes after t_1 expiration

CONCLUSION

This work presents a participative multi-agent architecture to develop knowledge production systems. Multi-agent interaction approaches and protocols are designed according to top-down or bottom-up approaches. The architecture presented in this chapter is a bottom-up approach to the design of collaborative multi-agent systems, where every mart holds responsibilities on some domain-level knowledge, while coordination-level knowledge interfaces to other domains are well-defined. This structuring of knowledge marts can help to reduce inconsistencies between agent territories.

The participative approach presented in this work has been successfully applied to the development of learning objects, but is also applicable to other knowledge production tasks (Dodero et al., 2002). Results obtained from single-mart and two-mart evaluation scenarios have been contrasted, with the result that the coordination protocol improves conflict-solving and coordination during the shared development process. Moreover, the absence of participation of some agent does not delay the overall process. Nevertheless, in order to test the multilevel architecture, these results need to be confirmed in more complex scenarios, consisting of two or more groups of participative agents working in different knowledge marts. We are also conducting tests of the impact of the number of agents on the overall effectiveness of the model. Further validation is also needed to assess the usefulness of the approach in different application scenarios, such as software development, especially in the analysis and design stages.

The structuring of heterogeneous knowledge domains into marts presents a number of issues: What would happen if an agent changes the kind of knowledge that it is producing, and is this better classified in another mart? As time progresses, will knowledge that is being produced in a mart be biased towards a different category? As a future work, it seems reasonable to dynamically establish the membership of agents into the marts, such that an agent can change its membership to some other mart if the knowledge produced by the agent affects interaction processes carried out in that mart. Then, division and/or fusion of marts may be needed to better reflect the knowledge-directed proposed structure. In that case, clustering techniques can be readily applied to solve those issues. As well, it will be helpful that mart generation and affiliation of agents to marts be dependent on agents' ontology-based interests.

REFERENCES

Argyris, C. (1993). *Knowledge for Action*. San Francisco, CA: Jossey-Bass.

Clases, C. & Wehner, T. (2002). Steps across the border - Cooperation, knowledge production and systems design. *Computer Supported Cooperative Work, 11*, 39-54.

Davenport, T. H. & Prusak, L. (1998). *Working Knowledge: How Organizations Manage What They Know*. Boston, MA: Harvard Business School Press.

Delgado, M., Herrera, F., Herrera-Viedma, E., & Martínez, L. (1998). Combining numerical and linguistic information in group decision making. *Information Sciences, 7*, 177-194.

Dodero, J. M., Aedo, I., & Díaz, P. (2002). Participative knowledge production of learning objects for e-books. *The Electronic Library, 20*, 296-305.

Etzioni, O. & Weld, D. S. (1995). Intelligent agents on the Internet: Fact, fiction, and forecast. *IEEE Expert, 10*, 44-49.

Foundation for Intelligent Physical Agents (FIPA). (1997). *Specification Part 2 - Agent Communication Language*. Geneva, Switzerland: FIPA. (Technical Report)

Genesereth, M. & Tenenbaum, J. (1991). *An agent-based approach to software*. Stanford, CA: Stanford University Logic Group. (Technical Report)

Goldman, A. H. (1991). *Empirical Knowledge*. Berkeley, CA: University of California.

Gruber, T. R. (1991). The role of common ontology in achieving sharable, reusable knowledge bases. In J. Allen, R. Fikes & E. Sandewall (Eds.), *Proceedings of the 2nd International Conference on Principles of Knowledge Representation and Reasoning,* San Mateo, California (pp. 601-602). San Francisco, CA: Morgan Kaufmann.

IMS Global Learning Consortium. (2001). *IMS content packaging information model, version 1.1.2.* Burlington, MA: IMS Global Learning Consortium. (Technical Report)

Jennings, N. R. & Campos, J. R. (1997). Towards a social level characterisation of socially responsible agents. *IEEE Proceedings on Software Engineering, 144,* 11-25.

Koper, E. J. R. (1997). A method and tool for the design of educational material. *Journal of Computer Assisted Learning, 14,* 19-30.

Maes, P. (1994). Agents that reduce work and information overload. *Communications of the ACM, 37,* 31-40.

Mayfield, J., Labrou, Y. & Finin, T. (1995). Desiderata for agent communication languages. In *AAAI Spring Symposium on Information Gathering* (pp. 123-130).

Merrill, M. D. (1994). *Instructional Design Theory*. Englewood Cliffs, NJ: Educational Technology Publications.

Smith, R. G. & Davis, R. (1981). Frameworks for cooperation in distributed problem solving. *IEEE Transactions on Systems, Man, and Cybernetics, 11,* 61-70.

Stewart, T. A. (1997). *Intellectual Capital: The New Wealth of Organizations*. New York: Doubleday.

Sycara, K. (1990). Persuasive argumentation in negotiation. *Theory and Decision, 28,* 203-242.

Chapter IV

Customized Recommendation Mechanism Based on Web Data Mining and Case-Based Reasoning

Jin Sung Kim, Jeonju University, Korea

ABSTRACT

One of the attractive topics in the field of Internet business is blending Artificial Intelligence (AI) techniques with the business process. In this research, we suggest a web-based, customized hybrid recommendation mechanism using Case-Based Reasoning (CBR) and web data mining. CBR mechanisms are normally used in problems for which it is difficult to define rules. In web databases, features called attributes are often selected first for mining the association knowledge between related products. Therefore, data mining is used as an efficient mechanism for predicting the relationship between goods, customers' preference, and future behavior. If there are some goods, however, which are not retrieved by data mining, we can't recommend additional information or a product. In this case, we can use CBR as a supplementary AI tool to recommend the similar purchase case.

Web log data gathered in a real-world Internet shopping mall was given to illustrate the quality of the proposed mechanism. The results showed that the CBR and web data mining-based hybrid recommendation mechanism could reflect both association knowledge and purchase information about our former customers.

INTRODUCTION

This study examines whether the quality of a web recommendation system is associated with an AI-based reasoning mechanism for the Internet consumer focused on Business to Consumer Internet Business. The 1990s have seen an explosive growth of global networks and Internet Business systems that cross-organizational boundaries. Forrester Research, an Internet research firm, estimates that revenues in the Business to Consumer segment will grow from $614 billion in 2002 to $6.3 trillion by 2004 (Forrester Research, 2002).

In the field of Internet Business, recommendation systems can serve as intermediaries between the buyers and the sellers, creating a "cyber market-place" that lowers the buyer's cost and time for acquiring information about seller prices and product offerings (see Changchien & Lu, 2001; Cho et al., 2002; Hui & Jha, 2000). As a result, Internet Business customers could reduce the inefficiencies caused by information search costs.

Customer purchase support or recommendation is becoming an integral part of most Internet Business companies. For this purpose, many companies have a customer service department or marketing department called a Customer Relationship Management (CRM) center which provides direct one-to-one marketing, advertising, promotion, and other relationship management services (see Cho et al., 2002; Choy et al., 2002; Hui & Jha, 2000; Kannan & Rao, 2001; Kim et al., 2002; Kohli et al., 2001; Lee et al., 2002; Song et al., 2001).

Marketing managers, especially, should know and predict the customer's intentions for purchase and future behaviors to select information that corresponds to the special good. Insufficient understanding of a customer's behavior can lead to problems such as low profit. Web data mining is a new technology, which emerged as one of the attractive topics in the filed of Internet-based marketing. With the advent of CRM issues in Internet Business, most of the modern companies operating web sites for several purposes are now adopting web data mining as a strategic way of capturing knowledge about the potential needs of target customers and future trends in the market (see Cho et al., 2002; Hui & Jha, 2000; Lee et al., 2002).

To find effective solutions for CRM, many researchers use a lot of machine learning technologies, data mining, and other statistical methodologies (see Cho et al., 2002; Choy et al., 2002; Hui & Jha, 2000; Kannan & Rao, 2001; Kim et al., 2002; Kohli et al., 2001; Lee et al., 2002). As a result, most companies use knowledge bases established by web data mining tools for recommendation in an Internet marketplace.

However, the most critical problems with web data mining are poor reasoning information and a lack of adaptability. If the knowledgebase for a recommendation system has no inference rule, it may provide no additional purchase information to Internet customers (see Aha, 1991; Chiu, 2002; Choy et al., 2002; Finnie & Sun, 2002; Fyfe & Corchado, 2001; Hui & Jha, 2000; Jung et al., 1999; Kolodner et al., 1993; Lee et al., 2002; Schirmer, 2000; Yamaoka & Nishida, 1997). Therefore, we may say that the older data mining techniques are limited in their quality of reasoning and environmental adaptability. In this sense, we propose web data mining and CBR as a supplementary mechanism, which can improve the recommendation system's reasoning ability and environmental adaptability.

BACKGROUND

Data Mining

Data mining, also known as Knowledge Discovery in Databases (KDD) (Chen et al., 1996; Lee et al., 2002), has been recognized as a rapidly emerging research area. This research area can be defined as efficiently discovering human knowledge and interesting rules from large databases. This technology is motivated by the need for new techniques to help analyze, understand and visualize the huge amount of stored data gathered from scientific and business applications, where business applications include attached mailing, add-on sales, customer satisfaction, etc. Data mining involves the semiautomatic discovery of interesting knowledge, such as patterns, associations, changes, anomalies and significant structures, from large amounts of data stored in databases and other information repositories.

Data mining differs from traditional statistics in several ways. First, statistical inference is assumption-driven, in the sense that a hypothesis is formed and validated against the data. By contrast, data mining is discovery-driven; patterns and hypotheses are automatically extracted from large databases. Second, the goal of data mining is to extract qualitative models which can easily be translated into business patterns, associations or logical rules. The major data mining functions that have been developed for the commercial and research communities include summarization, classification, association, prediction and clustering. Therefore, it can be used to help decision makers make better decisions in order to stay competitive in the marketplace.

Data mining functions can be implemented using a variety of technologies, such as database-oriented techniques, machine learning, statistical techniques, and other AI methods (Hui & Jha, 2000). In general, determining which data mining technique and function to apply depends very much on the application domain and on the nature of the data available. Recently, a number of data mining applications and prototypes have been developed for a variety of domains, including online marketing, banking, finance, manufacturing, CRM, and health care. In the Internet Business space, data mining techniques have the potential to provide companies with competitive advantages (Dhond et al., 2000).

Web Data Mining

One of the key steps in KDD is to create a suitable target data set for the data mining tasks. In web data mining, data can be collected at several sites, such as proxy servers, web servers, or an organization's operational databases, which contain business data or consolidated web log data. Web data mining has the same objective as data mining in that both attempt to search for valuable and meaningful knowledge from databases or data warehouses. However, web data mining differ from data mining in that the former is a more unstructured task than the latter. The difference is based on the characteristics of web documents or web log files which represent unstructured relationships with little machine-readable semantics, while data mining is aimed at dealing with a more structured database.

In recent years, several web search engines were suggested as the advent of web technology. Since 1960, those search engines have been credited with many achievements in the field of information retrieval, such as index modeling, document representation and similarity measure. Recently, some researchers applied database concept to the web database and presented some new methods of modeling and querying web content at a finger granularity level instead of a page level. Nevertheless, web data mining is concerned with discovering patterns or knowledge from web documents or web log files.

As shown in Figure 1, web data mining is classified into roughly three domains: web content mining, web structure mining, and web usage mining.

Pyle (1999) and Srivastava et al. (2000) presented a detailed taxonomy for web usage mining methods and systems. Web content mining is the process of extracting knowledge from the content of a number of web documents. Web content mining is related to using web search engines, the main role of which is to discover web contents according to the user's requirements and constraints. In recent years, the web content mining approach of using the traditional search engine has migrated into intelligent agent-based mining and database-driven mining, where intelligent software agents for specific tasks support the search for more relevant web contents by taking domain characteristics and user profiles into consideration more intelligently. They also help users interpret the discovered web contents.

Many agents for web content mining appeared in literature such as Harvest (Brown et al., 1994), FAQ-Finder (Hammond et al., 1995), Information Manifold (Kirk et al., 1995), OCCAM (Kwok & Weld, 1996), and ParaSite (Spertus, 1997). The techniques used to develop agents include various information retrieval techniques (see Frakes & Baeza-Yates, 1992; Liang & Huang, 2000), filtering and categorizing techniques (see Broder et al., 1997; Chang & Hsu, 1997; Maarek & Shaul, 1996; Bonchi et al., 2001), and individual preferences learning techniques (see Balabanovic et al., 1995; Park et al., 2001). Database approaches for web content mining have focused on techniques for organizing structured collections of resources and for using standard database querying mechanisms.

Figure 1. Taxonomy of Web Data Mining (Adapted from Pyle, 1999, and Srivastava et al., 2000)

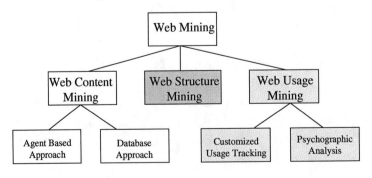

As to the query language, Konopnicki and Shmueli (1995) combined structure queries based on the organization of hypertext documents, and combined content queries based on information retrieval techniques. Lakshmanan et al. (1996) suggest a logic-based query language for restructuring to extract information from web information sources. On the basis of semantic knowledge, efficient ways of mining intra-transaction association rules have been proposed by Ananthanarayana et al. (2001) and Jain et al. (1999). A frame metadata model was developed by Fong et al. (2000) to build a database and extract association rules from online transactions stored in the database. Web log data warehousing was built by Bonchi et al. (2001) to perform mining for intelligent web caching.

Web structure mining is the process of inferring knowledge from the organization and links on the Web, while web usage mining is the automatic discovery of user access patterns from web servers. Our approach is belonging to web usage mining because we are aimed at proposing the way of amplifying the inference value from the web log files, which potential users left through surfing the target web site. Web structure includes external structure, internal structure, and URL itself. External structure mining is therefore related with investigating hyperlinked relationships between web pages under consideration, while internal structure mining analyzes the relationships of information within the web page. URL mining is to extract URLs that are relevant to decision maker's purpose. Spertus (1997) and Chakrabarti et al. (1999) proposed some heuristic rules by investigating the internal structure and the URL of web pages. Craven et al. (1998) used first-order learning technique in categorizing hyperlinks to estimate the relationship between web pages. Brin and Page (1998) considered citation counting of referee pages to find pages that are relevant on particular topics. To mine the community structure on the Web, Kumar et al. (1999) proposed a new hyperlink analysis method. Zaiane (2001) presented building virtual web views by warehousing the web structure that would allow efficient information retrieval and knowledge discovery.

Web usage mining applies the concept of data mining to the web log file data, and automatically discovers user access patterns for a specific web page. Web usage mining can also use *referrer logs* as a source. Referrer logs contain information about the referring pages for each page reference, and user registration or survey data gathered via CGI scripts (Jicheng et al., 1999). The results of web usage mining give decision makers crucial information about the life-time value of customers, cross-marketing strategies across products, and the effectiveness of promotional campaigns. Among other things, web usage mining helps organizations analyze user access patterns to targeted ads or web pages, categorize user preferences, and restructure a web site to create a more effective management of workgroup communication and organizational infrastructure.

Web usage mining provides the core basis for our system by supporting customized web usage tracking analysis and psychographics analysis. This customized web usage tracking analysis focuses on optimizing the structure of web sites based on the co-occurrence patterns of web pages (Perkowitz & Etzioni, 1999), predicting future HTTP request to adjust network and proxy caching (Schechter et al., 1998), deriving marketing intelligence (see Buchner & Mulvenna, 1999; Cooley et al., 1997, 1999; Spiliopoulou & Faulstich, 1999; Hui & Jha, 2000; Song et al., 2001), and predicting future user behavior on a specific web site by clustering user sessions (see Shahabi et al., 1997; Yan et al., 1996; Changchien & Lu, 2001; Lee et al., 2001). Psychographics analysis, which gives insights about the behavioral patterns of specific web site visitors, requires data about routes taken by visitors through a web site, the time spent on each page, route differences based on differing entry points to the web site, the aggregated route behavior, and general click stream behavior, etc. (Cooley et al., 1997, 1999). Based on these data, the psychographics analysis tries to answer marketing intelligence-related questions about which menu shoppers are using to buy a product, how long shoppers stay in the product description menu before making a decision to buy, and how shoppers feel about specific ads on the Web, etc.

METHODOLOGY

Our proposed hybrid recommendation mechanism is composed of four phases, as shown in Figure 2. The first phase is to extract association rules from the web log database. Among the data mining techniques, association rules mining algorithm has been popular in marketing intelligence fields (Lee et al., 2002). Therefore, we applied association rules mining to the web data mining tasks. The web log database, which has been used in data mining, includes the web surfing log files (time, frequency, duration, products, etc.) users made on a target shopping mall or web site. From a data preprocessing viewpoint, the web log data poses the following challenges: (1) large errors, (2) unequal sampling, and (3) missing values. To remove these noises included in data, we applied preprocessing techniques to web log data. Through web data mining, we can usually find the hidden informative relationships between those products and the interrelated hyperlinks users visited while web surfing. Association

Table 1. Pseudo Code of the Association Rules Mining Algorithm

---
C_k : Candidate transaction set of size k
L_k : Frequency transaction set of size k
L_j = {frequent items};
For (k=1; L_k !=∅; k++) **Do Begin**
C_{k+1} = Candidates generated from L_k;
For Each transaction t in database **Do**
   Increment the count of all candidates in C_{k+1}
   that are contained in tL_{k+1} = candidates in C_{k+1} with min_support
End Return L_k;

---

rules are similar to IF-THEN rules, in which a condition clause (IF) triggers a conclusion clause (THEN). In addition, association rules include the support and confidence (Agrawal et al., 1993a, 1993b). The association rules mining algorithm is shown in Table 1.

In the second phase, after the extraction of the association rules, we adapt CBR to extend the quality of reasoning and recover the limitation of rule-based reasoning. CBR is both a paradigm for computer-based problem-solvers and a model of human cognition. Therefore, cases extracted from the customer database may imply the customer's knowledge of products and predict his future behavior. Through this phase, CBR shows significant promise for improving the effectiveness of complex and unstructured decision-making.

The third phase is to build a hybrid knowledge base. In this phase, we combine rule base with case base. The key features to combining these two different knowledge bases are the customer's profile and the products.

The final phase of the proposed hybrid recommendation mechanism is to apply inference procedures to the hybrid knowledge base and extract the inference results. Figure 2 shows our proposed mechanism.

IMPLEMENTATION

To prove the quality of the hybrid recommendation mechanism, we implemented the prototype system using the Excel and VBA languages in a Windows XP environment. We call this prototype system CAR (CBR & Association rule-based Recommendation systems). CAR is composed of five components (Figure 3). The five components are: (1) rule generator, (2) knowledge base, (3) inference engine, (4) justifier, and (5) user interface.

Figure 2. Research Methodology of Hybrid Recommendation

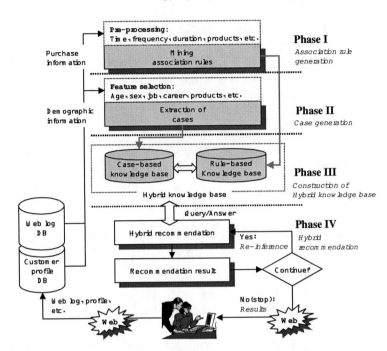

Phase I: Association Rule Generation

Web log data, which was used in web data mining, was collected from an Internet-based RC (remote-controlled plastic model) shopping mall. This shopping mall focused on selling remote-controlled products, such as cars, tanks, helicopters, gliders, yachts and ships. The original web log data was contaminated by several types of irrelevant and redundant information including

Figure 3. The Structure of CAR

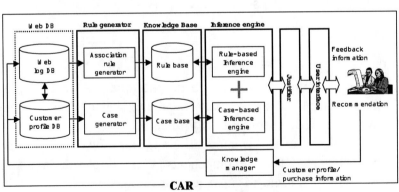

Figure 4. Preprocessed Web Log Database

	A	B	C	D	E	F	G	H	I	J	K
1	Name	Sec-No.	Address	Position	Registration	Sex	Phone	E-Mail	Products	Order date	rder complete
2	K. Kang	223-18501	1210-3, Na	Undergradute student	07 22 2002 12:40AM	Male	2-223-408	@hanma	X SPEED Stock	16-Aug-02	16-Aug-02
3	K. Kang	223-18501	1210-3, Na	Undergradute student	07 22 2002 12:40AM	Male	2-223-408	@hanma	GRT-T11	16-Aug-02	16-Aug-02
4	K. Kang	223-18501	1210-3, Na	Undergradute student	07 22 2002 12:40AM	Male	2-223-408	@hanma	RT-12	16-Aug-02	16-Aug-02
5	T. Kang	212-1247	ing, 209-7, P	Manufacture	12 20 2001 11:29PM	Male	1-237-50	@samsun	[kit] Castrol Mugen NSX(58233)	21-Dec-01	21-Dec-01
6	W. Goo	006-1648	yscom, Ami-	etc.	Jul 30 2001 8:43PM	Male	1-639-8	@hysyscor	GLINT 25L	19-Apr-02	19-Apr-02
7	W. Goo	006-1648	yscom, Ami-	etc.	Jul 30 2001 8:43PM	Male	1-639-8	@hysyscor	Power Supplier	19-Apr-02	19-Apr-02
8	M. Kwon	619-1405	406, Mannyu	Independent enterprise	11 28 2001 3:47PM	Male	kmk@ltech.cc		RC Car GuideBook	28-Nov-01	28-Nov-01
9	S. Kwon	305-1802	nggok-Dong	Independent enterprise	10 28 2001 9:42PM	Male	4-456-5	mi66@dau	MASTER 30%(1G)(Airplane, He	28-Oct-01	28-Oct-01
10	S. Kwon	305-1802	nggok-Dong	Independent enterprise	10 28 2001 9:42PM	Male	4-456-5	mi66@dau	12V Battery(7A)	28-Oct-01	28-Oct-01
11	S. Kwon	305-1802	nggok-Dong	Independent enterprise	10 28 2001 9:42PM	Male	4-456-5	mi66@dau	FRP 550D Roter(symmetry)	28-Oct-01	28-Oct-01
12	ae H. Kwo	702-1775	uhan-Myun	Undergradute student	26-Jun-01	Male	3) 544-2	1c@hanm	RC Car GuideBook	02-Aug-01	02-Aug-01
13	Jung H. Ke	405-1379	un-Dong 19	Undergradute student	Aug 27 2001 2:19AM	Male	-9616-7	mh@korea	MSX3	16-Oct-01	16-Oct-01
14	Jung H. Ke	405-1379	un-Dong 19	Undergradute student	Aug 27 2001 2:19AM	Male	-9616-7	mh@korea	TOYOTA CELICA(58248)	02-May-02	02-May-02
15	K. Kim	412-1623	ngwon Kyung	Businessman	02 20 2002 5:15PM	Male	5-278-41	isi@empa	Booster Charger	20-Feb-02	20-Feb-02

slashes (/, \), file name suffixes (htm, html, gif, jpg, jsp, etc.), and other information for query communications (&, =, <=, ?, etc.).

To mine a meaningful set of association rules from the web log database, the first step is to cleanse the original web log data so that the preprocessed web log data may become more traceable (Lee et al., 2002). Figure 4 shows a preprocessed web log database.

The web data mining algorithm we adopted here is an APRIORI algorithm (Agrawal et al., 1993a, 1993b), which is known to yield a set of association rules. Based on the preprocessed web log database in Figure 4, the corresponding association rules were extracted with a threshold of 20 percent confidence. Table 2 shows an excerpt of the derived association rules. The association rules shown in Table 2 are straightforward and easy to understand and interpret.

Phase II & III: Case Generation & Construction of Hybrid Knowledge Base

In this phase, we briefly outline the CBR mechanism, which may help the decision maker in classifying cases which occur in the web log database. The concepts of similarity and similarity relations used in CBR play a fundamental role in many fields of pure and applied science.

The simplest CBR or CBL (Case-Based Learning) algorithm is CBL1. Its preprocess linearly normalizes all numeric feature values (Aha, 1991). CBL1 defines the similarity of cases C_1 and C_2 as:

$$\text{Similarity}(C_1, C_2, P) = 1 \frac{1}{\sqrt{\sum_{i \in P} Feature\_dissimilarity(C_1, C_2)}}$$

Table 2. Example of Association Rules from Web Log Database

Pocket Booster (Checker)	<=	RC car guidebook (5:4.673%, 0.2)
ACE 2000	<=	7.2V low speed charger (5:4.673%, 0.4)
7.2V low speed charger	<=	ACE 2000 (4:3.738%, 0.5)
15% SM15 (1G)	<=	7.2V low speed charger (5:4.673%, 0.2)
Booster	<=	Plus wrench (S) (3:2.804%, 0.667)
GP 20(1Q)	<=	Booster charger (3:2.804%, 0.667)

where P is the set of predictor features and

$$Feature\_dissimilarity\ (C_1, C_2) \begin{cases} (C_{1i} - C_{2i})^2 & \text{if feature } i\text{'s values are numeric} \\ 0 & \text{if } C_{1i} = C_{2i} \\ 1 & \text{otherwise} \end{cases}$$

The CBL algorithm used in this study is summarized in Table 3.

The prototype system CAR supports a CBL algorithm shown in Table 3, and transforms the case extraction results into a case-based knowledge base. Figure 5 summarizes seven cases extracted from the web log database and the customer profile database.

After the extracting association rules and related cases, the rule-based knowledge base and the case-based knowledge base are combined using the customer's profile and web log information. At this time, the most important key points are the customer's ID and his web surfing information.

Phase IV: Hybrid Recommendation

The prototype system CAR uses the rule-based knowledge base and the case-based knowledge base concurrently. After the hybrid knowledge base is

Table 3. CBL Algorithm

Similarity = Customer's characteristics + probability of success

$$\text{Probability of success} = \frac{\text{former frequency of the purchase}}{\text{possible maximum frequency of the purchase}} \times constant$$

$$\text{Customer's characteristics} = \sum_{i=1}^{n} CS_i$$

$$CS_i = weight \times \left(1 - \frac{|\text{customer's } characteristic - \text{selected customer's } characteristic|}{\text{maximum degree of } characteristic} \right)$$

Figure 5. Case-Based Knowledge Base

	A	B	C	D	E	F	G
1	Age	Age class	Sex	Position code	Experience	Interest	Products
2	17	1	1	1	19	1	Crytal (for Hutaba-40) set
3	41	4	1	4	5	2	Seawind
4	17	1	1	1	19	1	Red wind (forward, backward)
5	41	4	1	3	8	1	Super nova 3000S
6	37	3	1	3	2	3	SENSATION
7	35	3	1	5	5	3	GLINT 25L
8	23	2	1	4	19	1	SP3-II chassis kit

(*Experience: months experienced, Interest: 1=car/tank, 2=yacht/ship, 3=airplane/ helicopter)

built, CAR can execute inference. In this phase, CAR may suggest the results of hybrid recommendation to the customer and then wait for the customer's feedback and response. Before the inference, Table 4 shows the web customer's brief profile and preferences to validate our hybrid recommendation mechanism.

First, the customer will search and select the guidebook for a remote-controlled car. If this web site is a common shopping mall, however, he can't get additional information about the ability to control the remote-controlled car. Therefore, the web site may lose this potentially loyal customer. In this case, CAR can present more intelligent and additional information to customers. Figure 6 shows the hybrid recommendation results of CAR.

In Figure 6, the customer finds additional information describing other products suggested by CAR. Finally, the recommended products (information) are 'SuperNova 3000S (re-charger for a worn out battery),' 'Switching Power 15A (high capacity power supplier),' and '3-Mode Charger (re-charger for remote controller, receiver and battery).' These products are the most important and basic goods for controlling the remote-controlled plastic models. As a result, the customer may purchase the product he wants and, at the same time, find additional products.

Table 4. Customer's Profile and Preference

Customer's profile *Birth: February 1963 / Sex: Male / Position: Businessman /* *Experience (career): 7 months /* *Interest: Car (remote controlled car)* **Customer's preference**: *Purchasing the **Guidebook** for remote-controlled car*

Figure 6. Hybrid Recommendation Results of CAR

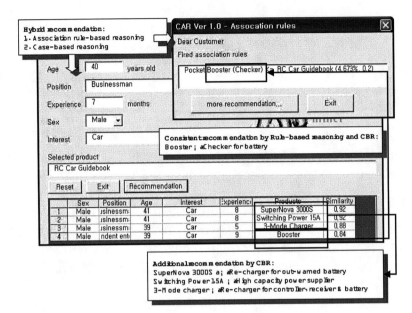

CONCLUSION

This chapter suggests a hybrid recommendation mechanism and a prototype system called CAR. The hybrid recommendation mechanism is based on association rule mining and on CBR, which is aimed at enriching the recommended information.

The proposed mechanism consists of a four phase-association rule generation, case generation, construction of a hybrid knowledge base, and hybrid recommendation. The result of our experiment with an illustrative web log database proved to be valid and robust.

In conclusion, this study shows how the tacit knowledge within a web site can be brought together to create valuable decision support tools for an Internet Business focused on B2C (Business to Consumer). It is expected that the proposed recommendation mechanism will have a significant impact on the research domain related to B2C Internet Business and CRM. Further research topics still remaining are as follows:

(1) The basic technology of data mining used for this study needs to be improved so that more complicated customer knowledge can be analyzed.

(2)   CBR needs to be integrated with other artificial intelligence-based reasoning algorithms, such as fuzzy cognitive map (FCM), so that more complicated web-based decision problems can be analyzed effectively.

(3)   CAR, our prototype system, needs to be updated with other commercial functions so that more practical recommendation problems can be solved easily.

ACKNOWLEDGMENTS

This work was supported by a Korea Research Foundation Grant (KRF-2002-003-B00099).

REFERENCES

Agrawal, R., Imielinski, T., & Swami, A. (1993a). Mining association rules between sets of items in large databases. *Proceedings of the ACM SIGMOD Conference on Management of Data*, Washington, DC (pp. 207-216).

Agrawal, R., Imielinski, T., & Swami, A. (1993b). Database mining: A performance perspective. *IEEE Transactions on Knowledge and Data Engineering, 5*(6), 914-925.

Aha, D.W. (1991, May). Case-based learning algorithm. *Proceedings of the Case-Based Reasoning Workshop* (pp. 157-158).

Ananthanarayana, V.S., Murty, N.M., & Subramanian, D.K. (2001). Multi-dimensional semantic clustering of large databases for association rule mining. *Pattern Recognition, 34*, 939-941.

Balabanovic, M., Shoham, Y., & Yun, Y. (1995). An adaptive agent for automated web browsing. *Journal of Visual Communication and Image Representation, 6*(4), 165-173.

Bonchi, F. et al. (2001). Web log data warehousing and mining for intelligent web caching. *Data & Knowledge Engineering, 39*, 165-189.

Brin, S. & Page, L. (1998). The anatomy of a large-scale hypertextual web search engine. *Proceedings of the 7th International World Wide Web Conference.*

Broder, A.Z., Glassman, C., Manasse, M.S., & Zweig, G. (1997). Syntactic clustering of the Web. *Proceedings of the 6th International World Wide Web Conference.*

Brown, C.M., Danzig, B.B., Hardy, D., Manber, U., & Schwartz, M.F. (1994). The harvest information discovery and access system. *Proceedings of the 2nd International World Wide Web Conference.*

Buchner, A. & Mulvenna, M.D. (1999). Discovering Internet marketing intelligence through online analytical web usage mining. *SIGMOD Record, 4,* 27-35.

Chakrabarti, S. et al. (1999). Mining the Web's link structure. *Computer, 32,* 60-67.

Chang, C. & Hsu, C. (1997). Customizable multiengine search tool with clustering. *Proceedings of the 6th International World Wide Web Conference.*

Changchien, S.W. & Lu, T.C. (2001). Mining association rule procedure to support online recommendation by customers and products fragmentation. *Expert Systems with Applications, 20,* 325-335.

Chen, M.S., Han, J., & Yu, P.S. (1996). Data mining: An overview from a database perspective. *IEEE Transactions on Knowledge and Data Engineering, 8(6),* 866-883.

Chiu, C. (2002). A case-based customer classification approach for direct marketing. *Expert Systems with Applications, 22(2),* 163-168.

Cho, Y.H., Kim, J.K., & Kim, S.H. (2002). A personalized recommender system based on web usage mining and decision tree induction. *Expert Systems with Applications, 23(3),* 329-342.

Choy, K.L., Lee, W.B., & Lo, V. (2002). Development of a case-based intelligent customer-supplier relationship management system. *Expert Systems with Applications, 23(3),* 281-297.

Cooley, R., Mobasher, B., & Srivastava, J. (1997). Web mining: Information and pattern discovery on the World Wide Web. *Proceedings of the Tools with Artificial Intelligence 9th IEEE International Conference* (pp. 558-567).

Cooley, R., Mobasher, B., & Srivastava, J. (1999). Data preparation for mining World Wide Web browsing patterns. *Knowledge and Information Systems, 1(1),* 1-27.

Craven, M., Slattery, S., & Nigam, K. (1998). First-order learning for web mining. *Proceedings of the 10th European Conference on Machine Learning,* Chemnitz, Germany.

Dhond, A., Gupta, A., & Vadhavkar, S. (2000). Data mining techniques for optimizing inventories for electronic commerce. *Proceedings of the 6th ACM SIGKDD International Conference on Knowledge Discovery and Data Mining*, Boston, Massachusetts (August 20-24, 2000, pp. 480-486).

Diffenbach, J. (1982). Influence diagrams for complex strategic issues. *Strategic Management Journal, 3*, 133-146.

Downes, L., Mui, C., & Negroponte, N. (2000). *Unleashing the Killer App: Digital Strategies for Market Dominance.* Cambridge, MA: Harvard Business School Press.

Finnie, G. & Sun, Z. (2002). Similarity and metrics in case-based reasoning. *International Journal of Intelligent Systems, 17*, 273-287.

Fong, J., Hughes, J.G.. & Zhu, J. (2000). Online web mining transactions association rules using frame metadata model. *Proceedings of the 1st International Conference on Web Information Systems Engineering* (Vol. 2, pp. 121-129).

Forrester Research (2002). http://www.forrester.com/

Frakes, W.B. & Baeza-Yates, R. (1992). *Information Retrieval Data Structures and Algorithms.* Englewood Cliffs, NJ: Prentice Hall.

Fyfe, C. & Corchado, J.M. (2001). Automating the construction of CBR systems using kernel methods. *International Journal of Intelligent Systems, 16*, 571-586.

Hammond, K., Bruke, R., Martin, C., & Lytinen, S. (1995). FAQ-finder: A case-based approach to knowledge navigation. In *Working Notes of the AAAI Spring Symposium: Information Gathering from Heterogeneous Distributed Environments.* Menlo Park, CA: AAAI Press.

Hui, S.C. & Jha, G. (2000). Data mining for customer service support. *Information & Management, 38*, 1-13.

Jain, A.K., Murty, N.M., & Flynn, P.J. (1999). Data clustering: A review. *ACM Computer Surveys, 31*(3), 264-323.

Jicheng, W., Yuan, H., Gangshan, W., & Fuyan, Z. (1999). Web mining: Knowledge discovery on the Web. *Systems, Man, and Cybernetics, IEEE SMC '99 Conference Proceedings* (Vol. 2, pp. 137-141).

Jung, C., Han, I., & Suh, B. (1999). Risk analysis for electronic commerce using case-based reasoning. *International Journal of Intelligent Systems in Accounting, Finance & Management, 8*, 61-73.

Kannan, P.K. & Rao, H.R. (2001). Introduction to the special issue: Decision support issues in customer relationship management and interactive marketing for e-commerce. *Decision Support Systems, 32*(2), 83-84.

Kim, E., Kim, W., & Lee, Y. (2002). Combination of multiple classifiers for the customer's purchase behavior prediction. *Decision Support Systems, 34*(2), 167-175.

Kirk, T., Levy, A. Y., Sagiv, Y., & Srivastava, D. (1995). The information manifold. *Working Notes of the AAAI spring symposium: Information gathering from heterogeneous distributed environments.* Menlo Park, CA: AAAI Press.

Kohli, R., Piontek, F., Ellington, T., VanOsdol, T., Shepard, M., & Brazel, G. (2001). Managing customer relationships through e-business decision support applications: A case of hospital-physician collaboration. *Decision Support Systems, 32*(2), 171-187.

Kolodner, J. (1993). *Case-Based Reasoning.* San Francisco, CA: Morgan Kaufmann.

Konopnicki, D. & Shmueli, O. (1995). W3QS: A query system for the World Wide Web. *Proceedings of the 21st VLDB Conference* (pp. 54-65).

Kumar, R., Raghavan, P., Rajagopalan, S., & Tomkins, A. (1999). Trawling the Web for emerging cyber-communities. *Computer Networks, 31,* 1481-1493.

Kwok, C. & Weld, D. (1996). Planning to gather information. *Proceedings of the 14th National Conference on AI* (pp. 54-65).

Lakshmanan, L., Sadri, F., & Subramanian, I.N. (1996). A declarative language for querying and restructuring the Web. *Proceedings of the 6th International Workshop on Research Issues in Data Engineering: Interoperability of Non-traditional Database Systems.*

Lee, C.H., Kim, Y.H., & Rhee, P.K. (2001). Web personalization expert with combining collaborative filtering and association rule mining technique. *Expert Systems with Applications, 21,* 131-137.

Lee, K.C., Kim, J.S., Chung, N.H., & Kwon, S.J. (2002). Fuzzy cognitive map approach to web-mining inference amplification. *Expert Systems with Applications, 22,* 197-211.

Liang, T.P. & Huang, J.S. (2000). A framework for applying intelligent agents to support electronic trading. *Decision Support Systems, 28*(4), 305-317.

Maarek, Y.S. & Shaul, I.Z.B. (1996). Automatically organizing bookmarks per contents. *Proceedings of the 5th International World Wide Web Conference,* Paris, France.

Noh, J.B., Lee, K.C., Kim, J.K., Lee, J.K., & Kim, S.H. (2000). A case-based reasoning approach to cognitive map-driven tacit knowledge management. *Expert Systems with Applications, 19,* 249-259.

Park, S.C., Piramuthu, S., & Shaw, M.J. (2001). Dynamic rule refinement in knowledge-based data mining systems. *Decision Support Systems, 31*(2), 205-222.

Perkowitz, M. & Etzioni, O. (1999). Adaptive web sites: Automatically synthesizing web pages. *Proceedings of the 15th National Conference on Artificial Intelligence,* Madison, Wisconsin.

Pyle, D. (1999). *Data Preparation for Data Mining.* San Francisco, CA: Morgan Kaufmann Publishers.

Schechter, S., Krishnan, M., & Smith, M.D. (1998). Using path profiles to predict HTTP requests. *Proceedings of the 7th International World Wide Web Conference,* Brisbane, Australia.

Schirmer, A. (2000). Case-based reasoning and improved adaptive search for project scheduling. *Naval Research Logistics, 47,* 201-.

Shahabi, C., Zarkest, A.M., Adibi, J., & Shah, V. (1997). Knowledge discovery from users' web-page navigation. *Proceedings of the Workshop on Research Issues in Data Engineering,* Birmingham, UK.

Smith, J.R. (2001). Quantitative assessment of image retrieval effectiveness. *Journal of the American Society for Information Science and Technology, 52*(11), 969-979.

Song, H.S., Kim, J.K., & Kim, S.H. (2001). Mining the change of customer behavior in an Internet shopping mall. *Expert Systems with Applications, 21,* 157-168.

Spertus, E. (1997). ParaSite: Mining structural information on the Web. *Proceedings of the 6th International World Wide Web Conference.*

Spiliopoulou, M. & Faulstich, L. C. (1999). WUM: A web utilization miner. In *Proceedings of the EDBT Workshop WebDB98,* Valencia, Spain, (LNCS 1590). Berlin: Springer-Verlag.

Srivastava, J., Cooley, R., Deshpende, M. & Tan, P.N. (2000). Web usage mining: Discovery and applications usage patterns from web data. *SIGKDD Explorations, 1*(2), 12-23.

Yamaoka, T. & Nishida, S. (1997). A case-based decision support method incorporating recognition of the designer's intentions. *Electronics and Communications in Japan,* Part 3, *80*(2), 46-62.

Yan, T., Jacobsen, M., Garcia-Molina, H., & Dayal, U. (1996). From user access patterns to dynamic hypertext linking. *Proceedings of the Fifth International World Wide Web Conference,* Paris.

Zaiane, O.R. (2001). Building virtual web views. *Data & Knowledge Engineering, 39,* 143-163.

Chapter V

Rule-Based Parsing for Web Data Extraction

David Camacho, Universidad Carlos III de Madrid, Spain

Ricardo Aler, Universidad Carlos III de Madrid, Spain

Juan Cuadrado, Universidad Carlos III de Madrid, Spain

ABSTRACT

How to build intelligent robust applications that work with the information stored in the Web is a difficult problem for several reasons which arise from the essential nature of the Web: the information is highly distributed, it is dynamic (both in content and format), it is not usually correctly structured, and the web sources will be unreachable at some times. To build robust and adaptable web systems, it is necessary to provide a standard representation for the information (i.e., using languages such as XML and ontologies to represent the semantics of the stored knowledge). However, this is actually a research field and usually most web sources do not provide their information in a structured way.

This chapter analyzes a new approach that allows us to build robust and adaptable web systems by using a multi-agent approach. Several problems, including how to retrieve, extract, and manage the stored information from web sources, are analyzed from an agent perspective. Two difficult problems will be addressed in this chapter: designing a general architecture to deal with the problem of managing web information sources; and how these agents could work semiautomatically, adapting their behaviors to the dynamic conditions of the electronic sources.

To achieve the first goal, a generic web-based multi-agent system (MAS) will be proposed, and will be applied in a specific problem to retrieve and manage information from electronic newspapers. To partially solve the problem of retrieving and extracting web information, a semiautomatic web parser will be designed and deployed like a reusable software component. This parser uses two sets of rules to adapt the behavior of the web agent to possible changes in the web sources. The first one is used to define the knowledge to be extracted from the HTML pages; the second one represents the final structure to store the retrieved knowledge. Using this parser, a specific web-based multi-agent system will be implemented.

INTRODUCTION

The World Wide Web (Web) is an interesting and growing environment for different research fields, e.g., Agents and multi-agent systems (see Balabanovic et al., 1995; Knoblock et al., 2000), Information Retrieval (Baeza-Yates & Ribeiro-Neto, 1999; Jones & Willett, 1997), Software Engineering (Petrie, 1996), etc. Over the past two decades, the evolution of the Web, and especially the stored information that can be obtained from the connected electronic sources, have led to an explosion of system development and research efforts.

However, the success of the Web could be its main pitfall: the enormous growth of the information stored creates so many problems that building and maintaining a web application is difficult. Actually, there is increasing interest in building systems which could reuse the information stored in the Web (Fan & Gauch, 1999). To build these systems, several problems need to be analyzed and solved, i.e. how to retrieve, extract and reuse the stored information.

Information extraction (see Freitag, 1998; Kushmerick et al., 1997) is a complex problem because many of the electronic sources connected in the

Web do not provide their information in a standardized way. So, it will be necessary to use several types of specialized agents (or any other type of applications) to retrieve and extract the stored knowledge from the HTML pages. Once this knowledge is extracted, it could be used by the other agents.

Several solutions for information extraction have been proposed. Some of the most popular solutions, which have actually been implemented, are related to the Semantic Web (Berners-Lee et al., 2001). Others use XML-based specifications (Bremer & Gertz, 2002) and ontologies (Gruber, 1993) to represent, in a coherent way, the information stored in the Web. In the near future, this approach will provide the possibility of building robust distributed web applications. However, the Semantic Web is still evolving. So, if we wish to build an application that could reuse the information, we need to use other approaches that allow the system to extract the information.

The *Wrapper* approach (Sahuguet & Azavant, 1999) is one of the most widely used. It uses *wrappers* (see Sahuguet & Azavant, 2001; Serafini & Ghidini, 2000) which allow access to the Web as a relational database (see Ashish & Knoblock, 1997; Camacho et al., 2002c; Fan & Gauch, 1999). Building those wrappers may be a complex task because, when the information source changes, it is necessary to reprogram the wrappers as well. Several toolkits, including W4F (Sahuguet & Azavant, 2001) and WrapperBuilder (Ashish & Knoblock, 1997), have been deployed to help engineers build and maintain wrappers.

The main goal of this work is to search for mechanisms that allow for the design and implementation of robust and adaptable multi-agent web systems. These mechanisms should also integrate, like a particular skill of some specialized agents (web agents), the ability to automatically filter and extract the available web knowledge. Toward this end, our approach will use a semiautomatic web parser, or simply *WebParser*, that is deployed as a reusable software component.

The WebParser is used by different web agents, and they can change its behavior by modifying two sets of rules. The first rules are used by the agents to define the knowledge to be extracted from the HTML pages (i.e., different agents can access different sources), and the second set of rules is used to represent the final structure for store the knowledge that has been retrieved (so that any agent can adapt the extracted knowledge). Finally, this parser will be used as a specific skill in several agents to build a specific multi-agent web system (such as SimpleNews).

GENERIC MULTI-AGENT
WEB ARCHITECTURE

Several authors have proposed multi-agent approaches in different domains to deal with web information (see Camacho et al., 2002b; Decker et al., 1997; Knoblock et al., 2000), some general conclusions could be summarized from those works to describe a possible generic multi-agent architecture, which could be used to implement adaptable and robust web systems. Figure 1 shows a schematic representation of this architecture. The architecture is built using a three-layer model. The functionality of those layers can be summarized in:

- **User → System Interaction.** This layer usually provides a set of agents that is able to deal with the users. These agents (UserAgents, IntefaceAgents, etc.) could use different techniques, such as learning (see Howe & Dreilinger, 1997; Lieberman, 1995), to facilitate the communication between the users and the whole system. In the past few years, this interaction has sparked interest in Human-Computer Interaction (Lewerenz, 2000).

Figure 1. Generic Web Multi-Agent Based Architecture

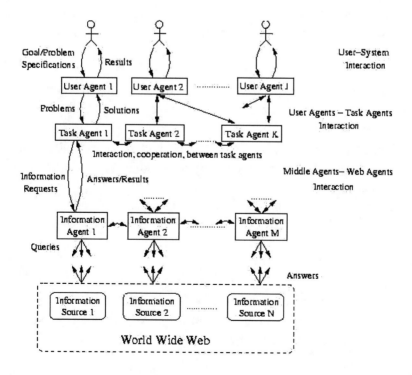

- **User Agents → Task Agents.** This layer is usually built by a set of specialized agents which achieve a specific goal. We call these specialized agents Task Agents, although different architectures refer to them as Middle Agents, Execution Agents, Planning or Learning Agents, etc. Several models of MAS require that the control agents necessary for the system to work correctly be in this layer (usually named as ANS agents, AMR, Control Agents, etc.). Characteristics of this layer, i.e., coordination, organization, cooperation, negotiation, etc., are widely studied (see Nwana, 1996; Rosenschein, 1985; Sycara, 1989).

- **Middle Agents → Web Agents.** This layer involves agents, such as Information Agents, Web Agents, SoftBots, Crawlers (Selberg & Etzioni, 1997), and Spiders (Chen et al., 2001), which specialize in accessing, retrieving and filtering information from the Web. These types of agents retrieve entire pages or specific parts of those pages (usually the information belongs to <meta> tags). These agents could be characterized because they are able to access different web servers, extract some information, filter that information, and finally store the retrieved document. These agents usually use one or more wrappers (see Kushmerick, 2000; Sahuguet & Azavant, 2001; Serafini & Ghidini, 2000) to wrap the web source and retrieve the available information.

The multi-agent approaches that deal with web information have several advantages and disadvantages. They are summarized as follows:

Advantages of a Multi-Agent Approach:
- These systems have *better adaptability* when unexpected problems in web servers occur. It is easy to add new agents specialized in new web sources.
- The *software maintenance* is usually simpler than the traditional monolitic applications because the whole system can be split into several simple elements.
- These systems are more *robust* (have a better fault tolerance) because, if some of the agents are down, the whole system could still work.

Disadvantages of a Multi-Agent Approach:
- It is more complex to design the system than a single-agent approach because it is necessary to design the different relations between the agents; new problems, such as coordination, control, or organization, need to be performed to obtain a complete operative system.

- These systems could cause new problems, e.g., the coordination or cooperation among the agents that the engineer could need to solve. These new problems arise from the utilization of multi-agent techniques that could be avoided in a monolitic approach.
- The increasing number of elements (agents) involved in achieving the goal set by the user increases the number of communication messages between the agents. The communication process could be a serious obstacle to a good performance by the whole system.

However, if the main goal is to obtain robust, adaptable, and fault-tolerant web-based systems, we believe that the multi-agent based approach is a suitable one, which provides many important advantages in obtaining the desired systems.

Characteristics to Implement Robust MAS-Web Systems

From the previous generic MAS architecture, three important aspects for characteristics (related to the layers shown in Figure 1) need to be performed to achieve the desired goal:

(1) It is necessary to provide a flexible and user-friendly user agent to adapt the behavior of the system to the needs of the user.
(2) The agent and multi-agent model used to implement the final system is a critical aspect. To build the system, it is possible to use several frameworks and toolkits, such as Jade (Bellifemine et al., 1999), JATLite (Petrie, 1996), ZEUS (Collis et al., 1998), etc. These frameworks allow to the engineers to reuse libraries and agent templates to facilitate the design and implementation phases. The selection of the agent and multi-agent architecture will be an important aspect in the implementation of the system.
(3) For any system that uses web sources, the problems of accessing, retrieving, filtering, representing and, finally, reusing this information need to be overcome.

This chapter addresses the latter characteristic. The first two characteristics will not be analyzed. The process of knowledge extraction is difficult, but it is an essential characteristic for any system that needs to solve problems using web knowledge.

WEBPARSER: SEMI-AUTOMATIC WEB KNOWLEDGE EXTRACTION

This section describes our approach to designing flexible and simple methods for information extraction from web sources. We have designed and implemented a parser, named WebParser, which, through the definition of several rules, can extract knowledge from HTML pages. If any changes are produced in the web page, it will only be necessary to redefine the rules to allow the parser to work correctly again. The utilization of rules creates flexibility and adaptability for the web agents that may use this parser.

However, it is necessary to define what kind of knowledge can be extracted and filtered from the available web pages. We will consider that all web pages can be roughly classified into two knowledge categories:

(1) *Non-structured knowledge*. The stored information in the page is represented using *natural language*, so it will be necessary to apply NLP (Natural Language Processing) techniques to allow the information extraction.

(2) *Semi-structured knowledge*. It is possible to find, inside the page, a structure (e.g., a table or list) which stores the information by using some kind of marks to delimit the data (e.g., <table>, </table>, <ul>, </ul>, <ol>, </ol>... tags in HMTL).

The WebParser proposed is a simple software module, which is specialized in the extraction of knowledge stored in the second kind of pages. Therefore, the knowledge extracted by the parser will be stored in a specific structure inside the web page.

The WebParser Architecture

A parser can be defined as: *A module, library or program that is able to translate an input (usually a text file) into an output with an internal representation.* The main goal of the WebParser is to accept web pages and generate a data-output structure that contains the filtered information. The WebParser uses as input the HTML page to be filtered along with several sets of rules that must be defined by the engineer to obtain the information.

Figure 2 shows the rule-based architecture for the semiautomatic web knowledge parser. The definition of several rules allows the engineer to modify the behavior of the parser and adapt it in a simple way. These rules will be used

Figure 2. Semi-Automatic Web Parser Architecture

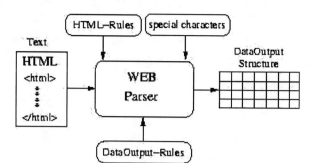

by the parser to represent the knowledge to extract, and the output structure
to store the knowledge respectively. Two main types of rules must to be
defined:

- *HTML-Rules*. These rules define the *type of knowledge* to extract
  (tables, lists, etc.), and the *position* where this knowledge is inside the
  page.
- *DataOutput-Rules*. This set of rules defines the final data (output)
  structure that will be generated by the parser when the extraction process
  ends.

We have used the term *"semiautomatic"* because, once the engineer
defines the two sets of rules to describe the knowledge to be extracted, the rest
of the processes are automatic. If the page changes, or if we want to extract
other knowledge inside the same page, it will only be necessary to modify those
rules. Several limitations and conditions have been considered in the process
of designing the parser. These can be summarized as:

(1) The WebParser uses a set of predefined rules (*special characters*) which
      are used by the parser to preprocess the HMTL page. These special
      characters (e.g.: á, é....., ñ, etc.) that have their HTML representations
      (as: á é ..... ñ etc.) are first translated into standard
      characters (e.g.: a, e, n, etc.) to avoid possible problems in the extraction
      process.
(2) These sets of rules are written by the engineer, and those rules will be
      stored into text files to facilitate the modification.

(3) Only the following types of web pages are actually parsed:
• Web pages which contain one or more *tables* (<table>...</table>) can be parsed.
• Web pages which contain one or more *lists*. It is possible to extract information from unordered (<ul>...</ul>), ordered (<ol>...</ol>), and definition (<dt>...</dt>) lists.
• Web pages that contain nested structures built using tables and/or lists.

(4) The code and final implementation of the WebParser will be written in the Java language to obtain a portable and reusable software. This implementation decision was made after taking into account that our main goal is to integrate this software into web agents. Actually, Java is a suitable and very popular language used by a large number of researchers and companies to implement their agent-based and web applications.

Definition of the Sets Rules in the WebParser

From the architecture designed for the WebParser (shown in Figure 2), it is necessary to provide two different rules to extract the information from a given page.

HTML-Rules. Although it is possible to define different rules, the WebParser uses a specific HTML-Rule for filtering each page. This rule is used to select what structures will be filtered from the page. These filtering rules have two attributes:

- *Type*. This attribute tells the parser what type of structure will be filtered. Only *list* and *table* attributes are allowed.

- *Position*. If the web page stores several structures (tables, lists, etc.), this attribute is used to locate which of those structures are the target of the extraction process. If there are nested structures, we can use the dot (".") to locate the exact position of the structure, i.e., *struc1.struc2.strucj* represents that information stored in the *j-th* structure, that is nested with two level depth, will be extracted.

DataOutput-Rules. These rules define the output data structure and what knowledge will be extracted from the page. Only one of those rules (as in the HTML-Rules) is used for every page. These rules are built using the following attributes:

- *Data Level*. This attribute shows where the data is located within the structure.

- *Begin-mark/End-mark*. Once the cells that store the data are fixed (using the previous attribute), it is necessary to set the begin and end patterns which are used to enclose the data. For instance, when the data is stored in a table (it will be stored between the tags <td> and </td>), it is possible to use as begin-mark the symbol <td>...data...</td> to show the string that represents the data begins from this symbol (it is possible to use any string to indicate the beginning and ending of the pattern).

- *Attribute-name*. Once the information is selected, it is necessary to provide the name of the attributes that will be associated with the retrieved information.

- *Attribute distribution*. This attribute shows the attributes-name when the structure to be filtered is a **table**. In this situation, we have a *horizontal* (Table 2 inside the third structure in Figure 3) or a *vertical* (Table 3 inside the third structure in the example) distribution in the tables. This attribute could have a *null* value if the structure does not have any attribute name (e.g., a table with only numerical information). If the structure to filter is a *list*, the value will be *null* because no distribution is necessary for the parser (the different items retrieved will be stored in a Java vector).

- *Data types*. The predefined value of any attribute or data extracted is *String*. However, the parser can extract other types of data such as: integer (int), float (flo), doubles (doub), etc. The WebParser will cast the extracted string into the desired type of data.

- *Data structure*. Finally, it is necessary to provide the final data output structure that the parser will generate. It can be either a vector or a table. It is possible to select a horizontal table (*tableh*: the attributes will be put in the first row and the data in the next rows) or a vertical table (*tablev*: the attributes will be put in the first column and the data in the next columns). If the extracted information is a list, it will be stored in a vector.

Figure 3 shows an example of a simple web page (and its related HMTL code) that stores three different structures: a simple unordered list, a table, and a nested structure which combines lists and tables recursively. For instance, if we wish to extract only the second simple table and the ordered list stored in the third structure (that is nested inside into a table, and inside into a list) from the web page, it will only be necessary to define the rules (HTML and DataOutput) shown in Figure 4. The attributes shown in these rules are used by the parser to:

- **HTML-Rule (a)** describes that the structure to extract is a *table*, and that it is the second (*position = 2*) structure stored in the page. **DataOutput-Rule (a)** shows that the data is in the second cell of the table, and that the *<td>* tag is used as begin-end pattern. The names of the attributes are

Figure 3.   Web Page Example and HTML Code with Several Types of Structures

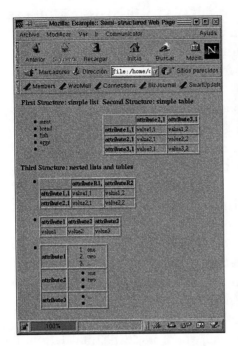
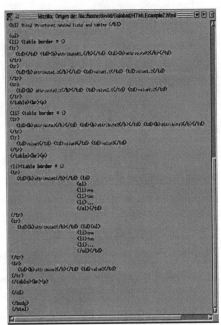

provided in that order to the parser. So, if the distribution of the attributes in the table is *horizontal/vertical* (*distrib=hv*), we will first indicate the name of the attributes in the rows ({att1,1+att1,2+att1,3}) and then name the attributes in the columns ({att2,1+att3,1}). The *data type* to retrieve will be *String* values and, finally, the WebParser will generate a table (*data struc= tablehv*) to store the retrieved data.

- **HTML-Rule (b)** describes that the structure to extract is a *list* which is stored inside the third structure (*position=3*). **DataOutput-Rule (b)** shows that the data is stored in the *second* cell of the table, which is stored in third position in the list (*data Level=3.3.2*), and that it possibly uses the *<li>* tag as the begin-end pattern. There are no names associated with the data to retrieve (*attrib={null}*), and no distribution of them is necessary. The *data type* to retrieve will be *integer* values and, finally, the WebParser will generate a vector (*data struc=sortlist*) to store the retrieved data.

Actually, the output of the WebParser is a Java object (vector or tables), so this output will be modified by the agent as needed.

Figure 4. HTML and DataOutput-Rules to Extract the Information Stored in the Selected Structures

Rule (a): table	**Rule (b): list**
- HTML rule:	- HTML rule:
type= table	type= list
position= 2	position= 3
- DataOutput rule:	- DataOutput rule:
data Level= 2	data Level= 3.3.2
begin-mark= <td>	begin-mark= <li>
end-mark= </td>	end-mark= </li>
attrib= {att1,1+att2,1+att2,1}	attib = {null}
{att2,1+att3,1}	
distrib= hv	distrib = (null)
data type= (str)	data type = (int)
data struc= tablehv	data struc = sortlist

DEPLOYING A WEB-MAS USING THE WEBPARSER

The WebParser has been implemented as a Java reusable software component. This allows us to:

- Modify, in a flexible way, the behavior of the parser by changing only the rules.
- Integrate this component, like a new skill, in a specialized web agent.

We have deployed a Java application from this WebParser to test different rules retrieved from the selected web pages. This allows the engineer to test the behavior of the parser before it will be integrated as a new skill in the web agent.

We used a simple model to design our web agents. This model allows to us to migrate the designed agent to any predefined architecture that will ultimately be used to deploy the multi-agent web system. Figure 5 shows the model that defines a basic web agent using the next modules:

- *Communication module.* This module defines the protocols and languages used by the agents to communicate with other agents in the system [i.e., KQML (Finin et al., 1994) or FIPA-ACL (FIPA.org, 1997)].

Figure 5. Architecture for a Web Agent

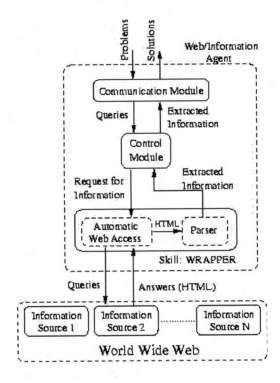

- *Skill: wrapper.* This basic skill must be implemented by every agent that wishes to retrieve information from the Web. This module needs to be able to do the following tasks: access the web source automatically; retrieve the HTML answer; filter the information; and, finally, extract the knowledge.
- *Control.* This module coordinates and manages all the tasks in the agents.

To correctly integrate the WebParser in the web agent, or to change the actual wrapper skill if the agent is deployed, it will be necessary to adapt this agent's functionality to the behavior of the software component. To achieve successful migration to the WebParser, it will be necessary to change or modify the following:

- The processes which are used by the agent to access to the information source and to extract the knowledge (*Automatic Web Access* and *Parser* modules respectively).

- The answers retrieved by the agent (HTML pages) will be provided as input to the parser (and the rules defined by the engineer).

Once the web agent is correctly designed, the integration of the WebParser only needs to define the two set of rules analyzed in the previous section, and then use the API provided with the WebParser to correctly execute this software module.

SimpleNews: A MetaSearch System for Electronic News

SimpleNews (Camacho et al., 2002a) is a meta-search engine that, by means of several specialized and cooperative agents, searches for news in a set of electronic newspapers. SimpleNews uses a very simple topology (as Figure 6 shows), where all of the web agents solve the queries sent by the UserAgent. The motivation for designing and implementing SimpleNews was to obtain a web system that could be used to evaluate and compare empirically different multi-agent frameworks in the same domain. Actually, SimpleNews has been implemented using the Jade, JATLite, SkeletonAgent (Camacho et al., 2002b), and ZEUS frameworks.

The SimpleNews engine uses a set of specialized agents to retrieve information from a particular electronic newspaper. SimpleNews can retrieve information from the selected electronic sources, filter the different answers from the specialized agents, and show them to the user. As Figure 6 shows, the architecture of SimpleNews can be structured in several interconnected layers:

- *UserAgent Interface.* This agent only provides a simple Graphical User Interface to allow users to make requests for news from the selected electronic papers. SimpleNews uses a UserAgent that provides a simple graphical user interface for making queries, the number of solutions requested, and the agents that will be consulted. The interface used by this agent allows to the user to know: the actual state of the agents (active, suspended, searching or finished) and the messages and contents sent between the agents. Finally, all requests retrieved by the agents are analyzed (only different requests are taken into account) and the UserAgent builds an HTML file, which is subsequently displayed to the user.
- *Control Access Layer.* Jade, JATLite, or any other multi-agent architecture needs to use specific agents to manage, run or control the whole system (*AMS, ACC, DF* in Jade, or *AMR* in JATLite). This level represents the set of necessary agents (for the architecture analyzed) that

Figure 6. SimpleNews Architecture

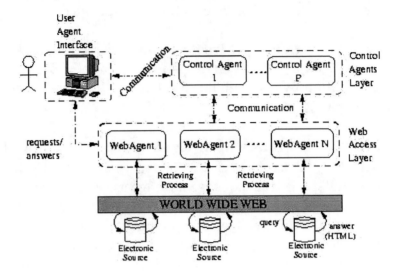

will be used by SimpleNews to work correctly. This layer resolves the differences from the two versions of SimpleNews that are implemented (from Jade framework and from JATLite).

- *Web Access Layer.* Finally, this layer represents the specialized web agents that retrieve information from the specific electronic sources in the Web.

The meta-search engine includes a UserAgent and six specialized web agents. The specialized web agents can be classified into the following categories:

(1) *Financial Information.* Two web agents have been implemented, and they will specialize in financial newspapers: *Expansion* (http://www.expansion.es), and *CincoDias* (http://www.cincodias.es).

(2) *Sports information.* Two other web agents specialize in sportive newspapers: *Marca* (http://www.marca.es) and *Futvol.com* (http://www.futvol.com).

(3) *General information.* Finally, two more web agents have been implemented to retrieve information from generic newspapers: *El Pais* (http://www.elpais.es) and *El Mundo* (http://www.elmundo.es).

Copyright © 2004, Idea Group Inc. Copying or distributing in print or electronic forms without written permission of Idea Group Inc. is prohibited.

The selected electronic sources are Spanish to allow a better evaluation of the retrieval process. It is difficult to evaluate the performance of a particular web agent when using a query in a different language. Another reason is that most of those sources are widely used in Spain, so the information stored in them should be enough to test an MAS built with those web agents.

From all the possible available versions of SimpleNews, we selected the Jade 2.4 version for several reasons:

- This framework provides an excellent API, and it is easy to change or modify some Java modules of the agents.
- The performance evaluation shows us that the system has a good fault tolerance.
- It is a multi-agent framework widely used in this research field. So, more researchers can analyze the possible advantages of integrating this module into their agent-based or web-based applications.

WebParser Integration into SimpleNews

This section provides a practical example which shows how the WebParser could be integrated into several web agents that belong to a deployed MAS (SimpleNews). The following steps must be taken by the engineer to replace the actual skill (wrapper) in the selected agent:

(1) Analyze the actual wrapper used by the web agent. Then, identify which modules (or classes) are responsible for the extraction of the information.
(2) Analyze the web source. It will be necessary to generate the set of rules to extract the information and generate the information in the appropriate format. The WebParser provides a simple Java object for storing the extracted information. If a more sophisticated structure is necessary, the engineer may need to program a method that translates these objects into the internal representation of the agent.
(3) Change the actual wrapper module used by the WebParser and use the tested rules as input to the parser.
(4) Test the web agent. If the integration is successful, the behavior does not change in any of the possible situations (information not found, server down, etc.) managed by the agent.

For instance, assume that we want to integrate the WebParser into the specialized web agent *www-ElPais* that belongs to SimpleNews. The method of achieving the previous steps is outlined below:

(1) The architecture of this agent is quite similar to the one shown in Figure 5. The wrapping process is achieved by several Java classes that belong to a specialized package (agent wrapper).

(2) The web source is shown in Figure 8. The figure on the left shows the answer (using the query: "*bush*") to the search engine used by this electronic newspaper. The figure on the right shows the HTML request. It is interesting to see how the information is stored in a nested table (our system only retrieves news headlines). Figure 7 shows the HTML and DataOutput rules necessary to extract the information.

(3) Once the previous rules have been tested (using several pages retrieved from the information sources) and the different situations have been considered, the classes or package identified in the first step are changed by the WebParser and the related rules.

(4) Finally, the web agent is tested with some test that has been used previously, and the results are compared.

These two rules will be stored in two different files, which will be used by the WebParser when the wrapping skill of the agent is used to extract the knowledge in the source request. The final integration of the WebParser will be achieved by the engineer through exchanging the actual Java classes in the agent for a simple method invocation with several parameters (like the name of the rules and the page to be filtered).

Figure 7. HTML and DataOutput-Rules to Extract the Headlines from the Web Page Request

```
- HTML rule:
  type= table
  position= 1
- DataOutput rule:
  data Level= 1.2
  begin-mark= <td><b>
  end-mark= </b></td>
  attrib= {null}
  distrib= (null)
  data type= (str)
  data struc= sortlist
```

Figure 8. Web Page Example and HTML Code Provided by www.elpais.es

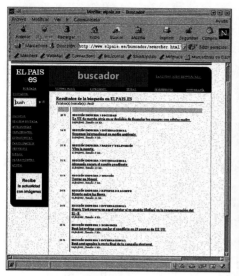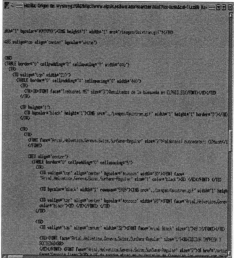

Verification and Test

This section shows how complex it is to integrate the WebParser into a deployed system. So, previous processes were repeated for every agent in the selected version of SimpleNews. This version uses six web agents, specialized in three type of news. Two groups of three different agents were made and were modified by different programmers. We have evaluated seven phases:

(1) *Architecture Analyses*. This stage is used by the engineer to study and analyze the architecture of the implemented MAS.

(2) *WebParser Analyses*. It is necessary to study the API (http://scalab.uc3m.es/~agente/Projects/WebParser/API) provided by the WebParser to correctly integrate the new software module.

(3) *Web Source Analyses*. The possible answers and requests from the web source are analyzed.

(4) *Generate/Test Rules*. The HTML and DataOutput Rules are generated by the engineer. Using the WebParser application, the engineer tests the rules, using as examples some of the possible HTML requests from the web source.

(5)   *Change Skill*. When the rules work correctly, the WebParser is changed for the actual Java classes.
(6)   *Test Agent*. The agent with the integrated parser is tested in several possible situations.
(7)   *Test Multi-Agent System*. Finally, all the web agents are tested. If the integration process is successful, then the new system should not present any differences.

Table 1 shows the average measures obtained by two students who used the deployed system to change the skill of all the web agents. Each programmer modified three agents (one of each type), and the table shows the average effort for each integration phase. It is important to note that the order of modifying the different agents is shown in the table; the General Information agents (www-Elpais, www-ElMundo) were modified first. From this table, it is possible to show when the multi-agent system is analyzed (and when the functionality and software modules of the agents are properly understood by the engineers). Changing and modifying the actual wrapping skill in the agents only required a few hours to adapt it in the first agent. When this process is successfully implemented, the next agents only need about one hour to build the rules, to change the skill and to test the new agents. This average time is measured over deployed agents (so it is necessary to change the implemented modules). If we are building new agents from scratch or using an MAS framework, it is not necessary to implement the *Change Skill* phase, so the implementation of a wrapper agent could take about 30 minutes (the wrapper skill). This means that the time and effort to program (and to reprogram these classes when the sources change) the agent is highly reduced.

Table 1. Average Time (Hours) for Each Integration Phase

Phase	General Information	Finantial Information	Sportive Information
Analyze SimpleNews	13.4	0	0
Analyaze WebParser	34.2	0	0
Analize Web Source	1.6	0.4	0.7
Generate/Test Rules	1	0.2	0.15
Change agent Skill	4.3	0.3	0.3
Test Web agent	0.9	0.5	0.3
Test MAS	2	0.6	0.3

CONCLUSIONS AND FUTURE WORK

The main contributions of this chapter can be summarized as follows:

- Our approach tries to obtain a reusable and portable software that could be used by different web agents to extract knowledge from specific web sources.
- The utilization of rules provides two advantages: the flexible modification of the parser behavior when the source changes; and easy reutilization of the well-tested rules for similar web sources.
- Once the API of the WebParser is analyzed by the programmer, it is easy to use it as a new skill module inside the web agent. This could improve the implementation of web-based multi-agent systems and gathering systems.

Currently, we have implemented an initial version of the WebParser, and have integrated it into several web agents that belong to a simple multi-agent web system.

However, there are several important points that will be addressed to obtain a fully portable and reusable software for extracting web knowledge. These points can be summarized as:

- To study the flexibility of the rules that can be defined in the WebParser. Is it possible to extract other types of stored knowledge with this simple representation?
- To study other agent-based and multi-agent technologies and frameworks that actually have been used by different researchers and companies, including ZEUS (Collis et al., 1998) and JATLite (Petrie, 1996), and to see if it is possible to implement web or wrapper agents which integrate the parser inside the agents implemented with those technologies.

REFERENCES

Ashish, N. & Knoblock, C. A. (1997). *Semi-automatic wrapper generation for Internet information sources*. Second IFCIS Conference on Cooperative Information Systems (CoopIS), Charleston, South Carolina.

Baeza-Yates, R. & Ribeiro-Neto, B. (1999). *Modern Information Retrieval*. Boston, MA: Addison-Wesley Longman.

Balabanovic, M., Shoham, Y., & Yun, T. (1995). *An adaptive agent for automated web browsing*.

Bellifemine, F., Poggi, A., & Rimassa, G. (1999). Jade - A FIPA-compliant agent framework. In *Proceedings of the Conference on Practical Applications of Agents and Multi-Agents (PAAM'99)*, London (pp. 97-108).

Berners-Lee, T., Hendler, J., & Lassila, O. (2001). The semantic web. *Scientific American*.

Bremer, J. M. & Gertz, M. (2002). *Xquery/ir: Integrating XML documents and data retrieval*.

Camacho, D., Aler, R., Castro, C., & Molina J. M. (2002). Performance evaluation of Zeus, Jade and skeleton agent frameworks. In *Proceedings of the IEEE Systems, Man, and Cybernectics Conference (SMC-2002)*, Hammamet, *Tunisia*. New York: IEEE Press.

Camacho, D., Molina J. M., Borrajo, D., & Aler, R. (2002). Mapweb: Cooperation between planning agents and web agents. *Information & Security: An International Journal, Special issue on Multi-agent Technologies*, 8.

Camacho, D., Molina J. M., Borrajo, D., & Aler, R. (2002). Solving travel problems by integrating web information with planning. In *Proceedings of the 13th International Symposium on Methodologies for Intelligent Systems (ISMIS 2002)*, Lyon, France. Berlin: Springer-Verlag.

Chen, H., Chung, Y., Ramsey, M., & Yang, C. (2001). A smart itsy bitsy spider for the Web. *Journal of the American Society for Information Science*.

Collis, J., Ndumu, D., Nwana, H. S., & Lee, L. (1998). The Zeus agent building tool-kit. *The British Telecom Technology Journal, 16*(3), 60-68.

Decker, K., Sycara, K. & Williamson, M. (1997). Middle-agents for the Internet. *Proceedings of the 15th International Joint Conference on Artificial Intelligence*, Nagoya, Japan.

Fan, Y. & Gauch, S. (1999). Adaptive agents for information gathering from multiple, distributed information sources. *Proceedings of the 1999 AAAI Symposium on Intelligent Agents in Cyberspace*, Stanford University, California.

Finin, T., Fritzson, R., Mackay, D. & McEntire, R. (1994). KQML as an agent communication language. In *Proceedings of the 3rd International Conference on Information and Knowledge Management (CIKM94)*, *Gaithersburg, Maryland* (pp. 456-463). New York: ACM Press.

FIPA.org. (1997) *Agent communication language*. Foundation for Intelligent Physical Agents. (Technical Report)

Freitag, D. (1998). Information extraction from HTML: Application of a general learning approach. In *Proceedings of the 15th National Conference on Artificial Intelligence (AAAI-98)*. Menlo Park, CA: AAAI Press.

Gruber, T. R. (1993). A translation approach to portable ontologies. *Knowledge Acquisition*, 5(2), 199-220.

Howe, A. E. & Dreilinger, D. (1997). Savvysearch: A metasearch engine that learns which search engines to query. *AI Magazine, 18*(2), 19-25.

Jones, K. S. & Willett, P. (1997). *Readings in Information Retrieval*. San Francisco, CA: Morgan Kaufmann.

Knoblock, C. A. et al. (2000). The Ariadne approach to web-based information integration. *International Journal on Cooperative Information Systems (IJCIS) Special Issue on Intelligent Information Agents: Theory and Applications.*

Kushmerick, N. (2000). Wrapper induction: Efficiency and expressiveness. *Artificial Intelligence, 118*(1-2), 15-68.

Kushmerick, N., Weld, D. S., & Doorenbos, R. B. (1997). Wrapper induction for information extraction. In *Proceedings of the International Joint Conference on Artificial Intelligence (IJCAI'97)* (pp. 729-737).

Lewerenz, J. (2000). *Automatic generation of human-computer interaction in heterogeneous and dynamic environments based on conceptual modelling.*

Lieberman, H. (1995). Letizia: An agent that assists web browsing. In *Proceedings of the International Joint Conference on Artificial Intelligence (IJCAI'95)* (pp. 924-929).

Nwana, H. S., Lee, L. C. & Jennings, N. R. (1996). Coordination in software agent systems. *The British Telecom Technical Journal, 14*(4), 79-88.

Petrie, C. (1996). Agent-based engineering, the Web, and intelligence. *IEEE Expert, 11*(6), 24-29.

Rosenschein, J. (1985). *Rational interaction: Cooperation among intelligent agents*. Stanford, CA: Standford University. (PhD Thesis).

Sahuguet, A. & Azavant, F. (1999). Building light-weight wrappers for legacy web data-sources using W4F. *Proceedings of the International Conference on Very Large Databases (VLDB).*

Sahuguet, A. & Azavant, F. (2001). Building intelligent web applications using lightweight wrappers. *Data & Knowledge Engineering, 36*(3), 283-316.

Selberg, E. & Etzioni, O. (1997, January/February). The metacrawler architecture for resource aggregation on the Web. *IEEE Expert*, 8-14.

Serafini, L. & Ghidini, C. (2000). Using wrapper agents to answer queries in distributed information systems. *Proceedings of the 4th International Conference on Multiagent Systems.*

Sycara, K. P. (1989). Multiagent compromise via negotiation. In *Distributed Artificial Intelligence* (vol. II, pp. 119-138). San Mateo, CA: Morgan Kaufmann.

Chapter VI

Multilingual Web Content Mining:
A User-Oriented Approach

Rowena Chau, Monash University, Australia

Chung-Hsing Yeh, Monash University, Australia

ABSTRACT

This chapter presents a novel user-oriented, concept-based approach to multilingual web content mining using self-organizing maps. The multilingual linguistic knowledge required for multilingual web content mining is made available by encoding all multilingual concept-term relationships using a multilingual concept space. With this linguistic knowledge base, a concept-based multilingual text classifier is developed. It reveals the conceptual content of multilingual web documents and forms concept categories of multilingual web documents on a concept-based browsing interface. To personalize multilingual web content mining, a concept-based user profile is generated from a user's bookmark file to highlight the user's topics of information interest on the browsing interface. As such, both explorative browsing and user-oriented, concept-focused information filtering in multilingual web are facilitated.

INTRODUCTION

The rapid expansion of the World Wide Web throughout the globe means electronically accessible information is now available in an ever-increasing number of languages. With the majority of this web data being unstructured text (Chakrabarti, 2000), web content mining technology capable of discovering useful knowledge from multilingual web documents, thus, holds the key to exploiting the vast human knowledge hidden beneath this largely untapped multilingual text. Moreover, users' information interests differ. Knowledge useful to one user may not be useful to another. Mining the multilingual web content and delivering the discovered knowledge without considering the user's information interest may not be effective.

To help each user discover knowledge specific to his domain of interest from the multilingual web, a user-oriented approach to multilingual web content mining is required. The user-oriented, concept-based, multilingual web content mining approach introduced in this chapter is such an approach. The objective of this approach is to facilitate personalized multilingual web content mining, which is important, especially when the user's motive for information seeking is personalized global knowledge discovery.

BACKGROUND

Web content mining has attracted much research attention in recent years (Kosala & Blockeel, 2000). It has emerged as an area of text mining specific to web documents, focusing on analyzing and deriving meaning from textual collections on the Internet (Chang et al., 2001). Currently, web content mining technology is still limited to processing monolingual web documents.

The challenge of discovering knowledge from textual data which are significantly linguistically diverse has been well recognized by text mining research (Tan, 1999). In a monolingual environment, the conceptual content of documents can be discovered by directly detecting patterns of frequent features (i.e., terms) without precedential knowledge of the concept-term relationship. Documents containing an identical known term pattern, thus, share the same concept. However, in a multilingual environment, *vocabulary mismatch* among diverse languages implies that documents exhibiting a similar concept will not contain identical term patterns. This *feature incompatibility* problem, thus, makes the inference of conceptual contents using term pattern matching inapplicable.

To enable multilingual web content mining, linguistic knowledge of concept-term relationships is essential to exploit any knowledge relevant to the domain of a multilingual document collection. Without such linguistic knowledge, no text or web mining algorithm can effectively infer the conceptual content of the multilingual documents.

In addition, in the multilingual WWW, a user's motive for information seeking is global knowledge exploration. As such, major multilingual web content mining activities include: (a) *explorative browsing* that aims to gain a general overview of a certain domain; and (b) *user-oriented concept-focused information filtering* that looks only for knowledge relevant to the user's personal topics of interest. To support global knowledge exploration, it is necessary to reveal the conceptual content of multilingual web documents by suggesting some scheme of document browsing to the user that suits his information seeking needs.

USER-ORIENTED, CONCEPT-BASED APPROACH

To address the various issues of personalized multilingual web content mining, a user-oriented, concept-based approach for multilingual web content mining is proposed. This is achieved by constructing a multilingual concept space as the linguistic knowledge base. The concept space encodes all multilingual concept-term relationships from parallel corpus using a self-organizing map. Given this concept space, concept-based multilingual web document classification is achieved with a multilingual text classifier using a second self-organizing map. By highlighting a user's personal topics of interests on the concept-based document categories, as defined by the multilingual text classifier, explorative browsing and user-oriented concept-focused information filtering are both facilitated on the same browsing space.

In subsequent sections, we first present an overview of the user-oriented, concept-based approach for multilingual web content mining and describe the technical details about the development of the concept space for encoding the multilingual linguistic knowledge. We then develop a concept-based multilingual text classifier for classifying multilingual web documents by concepts. Finally, we generate a user profile using the user's bookmark file to highlight the user's topics of information interest on a personal concept-based document browsing interface.

An Overview

The concept-based approach to multilingual web content mining is due to a notion that, while languages are culture-bound, concepts expressed by these languages are universal (Soergel, 1997). Moreover, the conceptual relationships among terms are inferable from the way that terms are set down in the text. Therefore, the domain-specific multilingual concept-term relationship can be discovered by analyzing relevant multilingual training documents. Using this multilingual concept-term relationship as the multilingual linguistic knowledge, the semantic content of all multilingual web documents can then be detected. Figure 1 shows the framework for this concept-based approach for user-oriented multilingual web content mining.

First, a parallel corpus, which is a collection of documents and their translations, is used as training documents for constructing a concept space using a self-organizing map (Kohonen, 1995). The concept space encodes all multilingual concept-term relationships as the linguistic knowledge base for multilingual text classification. With the concept space, a concept-based multilingual text classifier is developed by organizing the training documents on a second self-organizing map.

This text classifier is then used to classify multilingual web documents, using the concept space as the linguistic knowledge base. Multilingual documents describing similar concepts will then be mapped onto a browsing

Figure 1. User-Oriented, Concept-Based Approach for Multilingual Web Content Mining

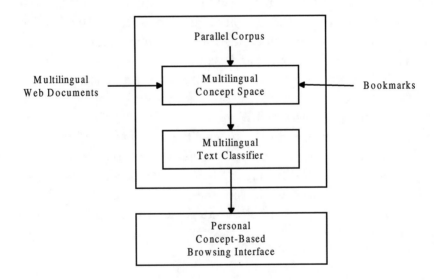

interface as document clusters. To personalize the browsing result, a concept-based user profile, using the user's bookmark file as the indicator of his information interests, is generated.

Finally, each user's personal topics of interest are highlighted on the browsing interface, mapping the user profile to relevant document clusters. As a result, explorative browsing aimed toward gaining an overview of a certain domain and toward user-oriented concept-focused information filtering is achieved.

Development of a Multilingual Concept Space

From the viewpoint of automatic text processing, the relationships among the meaning of terms are inferable from the way that the terms are set down in the text. Natural language is used to encode and transmit concepts. A sufficiently comprehensive sample of natural language text, such as a well-balanced corpus, may offer a fairly complete representation of the concepts and the conceptual relationship applicable within specific areas of discourse. Given corpus statistics of term occurrence, the associations among terms become measurable, and sets of semantically/conceptually-related terms are detected.

To construct multilingual, linguistic knowledge base encoding, lexical relationships among multilingual terms, parallel corpora containing sets of documents and their translations in multiple languages are ideal sources of multilingual lexical information. Parallel documents, basically, contain identical concepts expressed by different sets of terms. Therefore, multilingual terms used to describe the same concept tend to occur with very similar inter- and intra-document frequencies across a parallel corpus. An analysis of paired documents has been used to infer the most likely translation of terms between languages in the corpus (see Carbonell et al., 1997; Davis, 1996; Landauer & Littman, 1990). As such, co-occurrence statistics of multilingual terms across a parallel corpus can be used to determine clusters of conceptually-related multilingual terms.

Given a parallel corpus D, consisting of P pairs of parallel documents, meaningful terms from every language covered by the corpus are extracted. They form the set of multilingual terms for constructing the multilingual concept space. Each term is represented by an n-dimensional term vector. Each feature value of the term vector corresponds to the weight of the nth document, indicating the significance of that document in characterizing the meaning of the term. Parallel documents which are translated versions of one another within the corpus are considered as the same feature. To determine the significance of each document in characterizing the contextual content of a term based on the term's occurrences, the following weighting scheme is used. It calculates the feature value w_{kp} of a document d_p for $p = 1,...,P$ in the vector of term t_k.

$$
w_{kp} = \begin{cases} \dfrac{tf_{kp} \cdot log\left(\dfrac{|T|}{|d_p|}\right)}{\sqrt{\sum\limits_{q=1}^{P}\left(tf_{kq} \cdot log\left(\dfrac{|T|}{|d_q|}\right)\right)}} & \text{for } tf_{kp} > 0 \\[20pt] 0 & \text{for } tf_{kp} = 0 \end{cases} \tag{1}
$$

where

tf_{kp} is the occurrence of term t_k in document d_p;

$log\left(\dfrac{|T|}{|d_p|}\right)$ is the inverse term frequency of document d_p; $|T|$ is the number of terms in the whole collection, and $|d_p|$ is the number of terms in document d_p. The longer the document d_p, the smaller the inverse term frequency;

$1\bigg/\sqrt{\sum\limits_{q=1}^{P}\left(tf_{iq} \cdot log\left(\dfrac{|T|}{|d_q|}\right)\right)}$ is the normalization factor. With this normaliza-

tion factor, the feature value relating a document to a term t_k is reduced according to the total number of documents in which the term occurs.

When the contextual contents of every multilingual term are well represented, they are used as the input into the self-organizing algorithm for constructing the multilingual concept space.

Let $\mathbf{x}_i \in R^N (1 \leq i \leq M)$ be the term vector of the ith multilingual term, where N is the number of documents in the parallel corpus for a single language (i.e., the total number of documents in the parallel corpus divided by the number of languages supported by the corpus), and where M is the total number of multilingual terms. The self-organizing map algorithm is applied to form a multilingual concept space, using these term vectors as the training input to the map. The map consists of a regular grid of nodes. Each node is associated with an N-dimensional model vector. Let $\mathbf{m}_j = [m_{jn} \mid 1 \leq n \leq N]$ $(1 \leq j \leq G)$ be the model vector of the jth node on the map. The algorithm for forming the multilingual concept space is given below.

Step 1: Select a training multilingual term vector $\mathbf{x}_i$ at random.

Step 2: Find the winning node s on the map with the vector $\mathbf{m}_s$ which is closest to $\mathbf{x}_i$ such that:

$$\|\mathbf{x}_i - \mathbf{m}_s\| = \min_j \|\mathbf{x}_i - \mathbf{m}_j\| \tag{2}$$

Step 3: Update the weight of every node in the neighborhood of node s by:

$$\mathbf{m}_t^{new} = \mathbf{m}_t^{old} + \alpha(t)(\mathbf{x}_i - \mathbf{m}_t^{old}) \tag{3}$$

where $\alpha(t)$ the gain term at time t $(0 \leq \alpha(t) \leq 1)$ that decreases in time and converges to 0.

Step 4: Increase the time stamp t and repeat the training process until it converges.

After the training process is completed, each multilingual term is mapped to the grid node closest to it on the self-organizing map. A multilingual concept space is, thus, formed. This process corresponds to a projection of the multidimensional term vectors onto an orderly two-dimensional concept space, where the proximity of the multilingual terms is preserved as faithfully as possible. Consequently, conceptual similarities among multilingual terms are explicitly revealed by their locations and neighborhood relationships on the map.

To represent the relationship between every language-independent concept and its associated multilingual terms on the concept space, each term vector representing a multilingual term is input once again to find its corresponding winning node on the self-organizing map. All multilingual terms for which a node is the corresponding winning node are associated with the same node.

Therefore, a node will be represented by several multilingual terms that are often synonymous. In this way, conceptual-related multilingual terms are organized into term clusters within a common semantic space. The problem of feature incompatibility among multiple languages is, thus, overcome.

Development of a Concept-Based Multilingual Text Classifier

The objective of constructing a concept-based multilingual text classifier is to reveal the conceptual content of arbitrary multilingual web documents by organizing them into concept categories in accordance with their meanings. Sorting document collections by the self-organizing map algorithm depends heavily on the document representation scheme. To form a map that displays relationships among document contents, a suitable method for document indexing must be devised. Contextual contents of documents need to be expressed explicitly in a computationally meaningful way.

In information retrieval, the goal of indexing is to extract a set of features that represents the contents, or the 'meaning' of a document. Among several approaches suggested for document indexing and representation, the vector space model (Salton, 1989) represents documents conveniently as vectors in a multidimensional space, defined by a set of language-specific index terms. Each element of a document vector corresponds to the weight (or occurrence) of one index term. However, in a multilingual environment, the direct application of the vector space model is infeasible due to the feature incompatibility problem. Multilingual index terms characterizing documents of different languages exist in separate vector spaces.

To overcome the problem, a better representation of document contents incorporating information about semantic/conceptual relationships among multilingual index terms is desirable. Toward this end, the multilingual concept space obtained in Section 3 is applied.

On the multilingual concept space, conceptually-related multilingual terms are organized into term clusters. These term clusters, denoting language-independent concepts, are used to index multilingual documents in place of the documents' original language-specific index terms. As such, a concept-based document vector that explicitly expresses the conceptual context of a document, regardless of its language, is obtained. The term-based document vector of the vector space model, which suffers from the feature incompatibility problem, can now be replaced with the language-independent, concept-based document vector. The transformed concept-based document vectors are then organized using the self-organizing map algorithm to produce a concept-based multilingual text classifier.

To do so, each document of the parallel corpus is indexed by mapping its text, term by term, onto the multilingual concept space, whereby statistics of its 'hits' on each multilingual term cluster (i.e., concept) are recorded. This is done by counting the occurrence of each term on the multilingual concept space at the node to which that term is associated. These statistics of term cluster occurrences can be interpreted as a kind of transformed 'index' of the multilingual document. The concept-based multilingual text classifier is formed with the application of the self-organizing map algorithm, using the transformed concept-based document vectors as inputs.

Let $\mathbf{y}_i \in R^G (1 \leq i \leq H)$ be the concept-based document vector of the ith multilingual document, where G is the number of nodes existing in the multilingual concept space, and where H is the total number of documents in the parallel corpus. In addition, let $\mathbf{m}_j = [m_{jn} \mid 1 \leq n \leq G] (1 \leq j \leq J)$ be the G-dimensional model vector of the jth node on the map. The algorithm for forming the concept-based multilingual text classifier is given below.

Step 1: Select a training concept-based document vector $\mathbf{y}_i$ at random.

Step 2: Find the winning node s on the map with the vector $\mathbf{m}_s$ which is closest to document $\mathbf{y}_i$ such that:

$$\|\mathbf{y}_i - \mathbf{m}_s\| = \min_j \|\mathbf{y}_i - \mathbf{m}_j\| \tag{4}$$

Step 3: Update the weight of every node in the neighborhood of node s by:

$$\mathbf{m}_t^{new} = \mathbf{m}_t^{old} + \alpha(t)(\mathbf{y}_i - \mathbf{m}_t^{old}) \tag{5}$$

where $\alpha(t)$ is the gain term at time $t (0 \leq \alpha(t) \leq 1)$ that decreases in time and converges to 0.

Step 4: Increase the time stamp t and repeat the training process until it converges.

After the training process, multilingual documents from the parallel corpus that describe similar concepts are mapped onto the same node, forming document clusters on the self-organizing map. Each node, thus, defines a concept category of a concept-based multilingual text classifier and its corresponding browsing interface. The concept-based multilingual text classifier is then used to classify incoming multilingual web documents.

To do so, the text of every multilingual web document is, first, converted into a concept-based document vector using the multilingual concept space as the linguistic knowledge base. This document vector is then input to the multilingual text classifier to find the winning concept category which is closest to it on the self organizing map. Consequently, every multilingual web document is assigned to a concept category on a concept-based browsing interface, based on the conceptual content it exhibits. Based on a predefined network of concepts associating correlated multilingual web documents, the purpose of concept-based explorative browsing in multilingual web content mining is achieved.

Personalization of the Concept-Based Browsing Interface

With the overwhelming amount of information in the multilingual WWW, not every piece of information is of interest to a user. In such circumstances, a user profile, which models the user's information interests, is required to filter out information that the user is not interested in.

Common approaches to user profiling (see Lieberman et al., 1999; Lang, 1995; Mukhopadhyay et al., 1996) build a representation of the user's information interests based on the distribution of terms found in some previously seen documents which the user has found interesting. However, such representation has difficulties in handling situations where a user is interested in more than one topic. In addition, in a multilingual environment, the feature incompatibility problem resulting from the vocabulary mismatch phenomenon across languages makes a language-specific, term-based user profile insufficient to represent the user's information interest that spans multiple languages.

To overcome these problems, we propose a concept-based representation for building user profiles. Using language-independent concepts rather than language-specific terms implies that the resulting user profile is not only more semantically comprehensive but also independent from the language of the documents to be filtered. This is particularly important for multilingual web content mining, where knowledge relevant to a concept in significantly diverse languages has to be identified.

To understand the user's information interests for personalizing multilingual web content mining, the user's preference on the WWW is used. Indicators of these preferences can be obtained from the user's bookmark file. To generate a concept-based user profile from a user's bookmark file, web documents pointed to by the bookmarks are first retrieved. Applying the multilingual concept space as the linguistic knowledge base, each web document is then converted into a concept-based document vector using the procedure described in Section 4. Each concept-based document vector representing a bookmarked web page is input to find its winning node on the multilingual text classifier. All bookmarked multilingual web pages for which a node is the winning node are associated with the same concept category. After mapping all bookmarks' document vectors onto the multilingual text classifier, the concept categories relevant to the user's bookmark file are revealed.

As such, these concept categories can be regarded as the user profile representing a user's information interest in multiple topics. By highlighting these concept categories on the concept-based browsing interface, multilingual web content mining is, thus, personalized. This task of user-oriented concept-focused information filtering is particularly important for user who wants to keep track of global knowledge that is relevant to his personal domain of interest over the multilingual WWW.

TOWARD INTELLIGENT PERSONAL MULTILINGUAL WEB MINING AGENT

Intelligent agent has been a well-known technology for relieving people from the burden of information overload by facilitating personal web information access (see Chen & Sycara, 1998; Mladenic, 1996; Han et al., 1998). Intelligent agents all rely on a user profile to filter incoming information as relevant or irrelevant to a user's information need. The user-oriented, concept-based multilingual web content mining approach introduced in this chapter will, thus, be applied to develop an agent-based personal multilingual web mining system for facilitating web multilingual information access. This personal multilingual web mining agent, guided by the concept-based user profile and incorporating the multilingual text classifier, should provide an effective mechanism for automatic personalized knowledge discovery over the multilingual web. Given such development, multilingual web content mining targeting useful knowledge specific to a user's personal domain of interest can be realized. As such, a user's information need for personalized global knowledge discovery can be effectively satisfied.

CONCLUSION

This chapter has presented a user-oriented, concept-based approach for multilingual web content mining using self-organizing maps. The multilingual concept space is constructed to enable an automatic and unsupervised discovery of the multilingual linguistic knowledge from a parallel corpus. A concept-based multilingual text classifier is developed to realize a language-independent, concept-based classification of multilingual web documents onto a single browsing interface. A concept-based user profile is generated from the user's bookmark file to model a user's multilingual information interests comprising multiple topics. This approach to user profiling increases the semantic comprehensiveness, and the resultant user profile is independent of the language of the web documents to be filtered. As a result, multilingual web content mining activities, ranging from explorative browsing to personalized information filtering, can be effectively personalized.

REFERENCES

Carbonell, J. G., Yang, Y., Frederking, R. E., Brown, R. D., Geng, Y., & Lee, D. (1997). Translingual information retrieval: A comparative evaluation. In *Proceedings of the 15th International Joint Conference on Artificial Intelligence (IJCAI'97)* (pp. 708-714).

Chakrabarti, S. (2000). Data mining for hypertext: A tutorial survey. *ACM SIGKDD Exploration*, *1*(2), 1-11.

Chang, C., Healey, M. J., McHugh, J. A. M., & Wang, J. T. L. (2001). *Mining the World Wide Web: An Information Search Approach*. London: Kluwer Academic.

Chen, L. & Sycara, K. (1998). WebMate: A personal agent for browsing and searching. In *Proceedings of the 2nd International Conference on Autonomous Agents and Multi-Agent Systems (Agents '98),* (May, pp. 132-139). New York: ACM.

Davis, M. (1996). New experiments in cross-language text retrieval at NMSU's computing research lab. In *Proceedings of the 5th Retrieval Conference (TREC-5)* (pp. 447-454). Gaithersburg, MD: National Institute of Standards and Technology.

Han, E. et al. (1998). WebACE: A web agent for document categorization and exploration. In *Proceedings of the 2nd International Conference on Autonomous Agents and Multi-Agent Systems (Agents '98),* (May, pp. 408-415). New York: ACM.

Kohonen, T. (1995). *Self-Organising Maps*. Berlin: Springer-Verlag.

Kosala, R. & Blockeel, H. (2000). Web mining research: A survey. *ACM SIGKDD Exploration*, *2*(1), 1-15.

Landauer, T. K. & Littman, M. L. (1990). Fully automatic cross-language document retrieval. In *Proceedings of the 6th Conference on Electronic Text Research* (pp. 31-38).

Lang, K. (1995). NewsWeeder: Learning to filter news. In *Proceedings of the 12th International Conference on Machine Learning,* Lake Tahoe, California (pp. 331-339). San Francisco, CA: Morgan Kaufmann.

Lieberman, H., Van Dyke, N. W., & Vivacqua, A. S. (1999). Let's browse: A collaborative browsing agent. In *Proceedings of the 1999 International Conference on Intelligent User Interfaces, Collaborative Filtering and Collaborative Interfaces* (pp. 65-68).

Mladenic, D. (1996). *Personal webwatcher: Implementation and design.* Ljubljana, Slovenia: University of Ljubljana, J. Stefan Institute, Department of Intelligent Systems. (Technical Report IJS-DP-7472, October 1996)

Mukhopadhyay, S., Mostafa, J., Palakal, M., Lam, W., Xue, L., & Hudli, A. (1996). An adaptive multi-level information filtering system. In *Proceedings of the 5th International Conference on User Modelling* (pp. 21-28).

Salton, G. (1989). *Automatic Text Processing: The Transformation, Analysis, and Retrieval of Information by Computer.* Boston, MA: Addison-Wesley.

Soergel, D. (1997). Multilingual thesauri in cross-language text and speech retrieval. In *Working Notes of the AAAI Spring Symposium on Cross-Language Text and Speech Retrieval,* Stanford, California (pp. 164-170).

Tan, A.-H. (1999). Text mining: The state of the art and the challenges. In *Proceedings of the PAKDD'99 Workshop on Knowledge Discovery from Advanced Databases,* Beijing, China (pp. 65-70).

Chapter VII

A Textual Warehouse Approach:
A Web Data Repository

Kaïs Khrouf, University of Toulouse III, France

Chantal Soulé-Dupuy, University of Toulouse III, France

ABSTRACT

An enterprise memory must be able to be used as a basis for the processes of scientific or technical developments. Indeed, it was proven that information useful to these processes is not found solely in the operational bases of companies; it is also found in textual information and exchanged documents. For that reason, we propose the design and implementation of a documentary memory for business document warehouses. Its main characteristic is to allow the storage, retrieval, interrogation and analysis of information extracted from disseminated sources and, in particular, from the Web.

INTRODUCTION

An enterprise must allow for the sharing of knowledge and information between its employees in order to optimize their tasks. However, the volume of information contained in documents represents a major concern for these companies. Indeed, companies must be fully reactive to any new information and must follow the fast evolution and spread of information. So, a business memory which stores this information and allows end-users to access or analyze it is necessary for every enterprise.

This memory aims to:

- merge information from several sources, such as the World Wide Web, intranets, etc.;
- take the information evolution into account;
- allow end-users to view and analyze information according to their needs;
- facilitate decision-making.

These objectives can be reached by using the concept of textual warehouses, which allows the storage of documents and their exploitation through the techniques of information retrieval, factual data interrogation, and multidimensional analysis of information.

This chapter is organized as follows. First, we outline some work devoted to document querying through information retrieval or database techniques. Then, we propose an architecture and a generic model of textual warehouses. The next section describes the information extraction to feed the warehouse. Finally, we present the techniques we propose to exploit information contained in the warehouse. We describe the information retrieval process and the multidimensional analyses.

BACKGROUND

IRS (Information Retrieval Systems) were initially introduced to exploit non-structured documents, i.e., documents which contain no information about their logical structure. These documents were analyzed to represent their textual content and, therefore, their relevance in response to a non-structured query (free natural language). During the last 20 years, several theoretical models were proposed, and several systems based on those models have been implemented. The most well-known of these systems are: the Boolean model [STAIRS (IBM, 1982)], the vector-space model [SMART (Salton, 1971)], the probabilistic model (Turtle & Craft, 1990), the bayesian models (Van Rijsbergen, 1986), the linguistic models [RIME (Chiaramella & Nie, 1990)], and the connectionist model [MERCURE (Boughanem et al., 1999)].

Since then, attempts have been made to apply the IRS techniques to structured or semi-structured documents for the use of logical structures during the evaluation of a query. Among these works, we can quote:

- Textriever system (Burkowski, 1992), a search engine for a collection of structured documents;
- Personal Daily News (Fourel et al., 1998), an integrated environment for the management and retrieval of structured documents.

The approach of DBMS (DataBase Management Systems) allows for the quick treatment of a set of data. So, the idea is to apply this technique to documents. For structured documents, i.e., those whose logical structure is specified, many works were realized. Among these works, we can quote:

- e-XML Media Repository (Gardarin et al., 2002), a software component for the storage and query of XML documents;
- Xyleme (Abiteboul et al., 2001), describing a project that integrates XML data from the Web into a database.

For the semi-structured documents, i.e., those whose logical structure is partially defined, much work has been done despite the difficulties presented by these types of documents. Among these works, we can quote:

- HyWEB (Gardarin & Yoon, 1996), whose finality is the construction of an HTML (HyperText Markup Language) document base, and where the goal is to be able to interrogate a class of documents;
- WIND (Faulstish et al., 1997), which builds a data warehouse from specific information (about a particular domain) extracted from the Web.

As regards analysis, the works are very recent and mainly based on data mining techniques, not on a multidimensional approach. Concerning document storage and interrogation, all these works manipulate structured documents, or semi-structured documents, but not non-structured documents. In fact, in each case, only one standard is chosen, which implies a predefined database schema (predefined structure). Moreover, this work is devoted to the interrogation of documents starting from their factual descriptions; it does not involve the analysis of their textual content. In the information retrieval process, a query results in a collection of documents, which obliges the user to consult the content of a great number of documents to find the specific information he is looking for.

Contrary to this previous work, we propose a generic model of textual warehouses able to contain any type of document (structured, semi-structured and non-structured) and able to perform information retrieval, data interrogation, and multidimensional analysis. Moreover, our approach is generic because no restriction is imposed for the documents to be integrated.

DEFINITION AND ARCHITECTURE OF TEXTUAL WAREHOUSES

From the definition of data warehouses (Inmon, 1994), we define the textual warehouses as a source of information that is subject-oriented, filtered, integrated, archived (versions), and organized for a process of retrieval, interrogation or analysis.

The information contained in a document warehouse must be organized as follows:

- subject-oriented: the data of a warehouse must be organized by subject, thus allowing for the collection of all relevant information for analysis;
- filtered: the warehouse must contain only the documents that can be useful for facilitating the task of decision-makers (Chevalier et al., 2003);
- integrated: the content of the warehouse results from the integration of heterogeneous information from multiple sources;
- archived: the warehouse must allow for the historization of the documents in order to preserve their various evolutions.

The architecture we propose for the definition of the textual warehouses is presented in Figure 1. This architecture includes two stages: warehouse storage and warehouse exploitation.

The first stage involves extracting the structure and content from each document in order to store them in the warehouse. Each textual element of content must be indexed to extract information that will be used afterward by techniques of information retrieval.

The second stage manipulates the information contained in the warehouse. For that task, we propose three techniques:

Figure 1. Architecture of Textual Warehouses

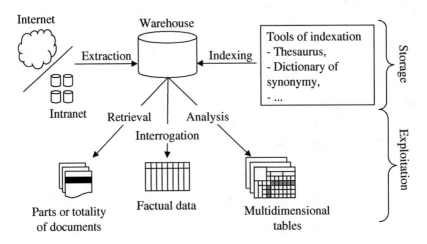

- *information retrieval*: retrieve documents or passages of documents (from their textual content) that are considered relevant for a user query formulated by simple keywords (non-structured queries);
- *data interrogation*: use a DBMS language to interrogate the warehouse (structured queries) and retrieve factual data (specific information);
- *multidimensional analysis*: analyze information by constructing textual marts (specific views) according to OLAP (On-Line Analytical Processing) techniques.

Such textual warehouses then become the basic tool for company employees who wish to exploit information which they need for their daily professional tasks (e.g., administrative intranet, digital libraries, technical documentation, etc.).

GENERIC MODEL OF
TEXTUAL WAREHOUSES

Textual warehouses (Khrouf et al., 2001) must constitute a source of synthetic and homogeneous information, just like data warehouses. Nevertheless, if the data sources of data warehouses are generally structured according to the relational model, then the sources of the textual warehouses are strongly-

Figure 2. Generic Model of Textual Warehouses

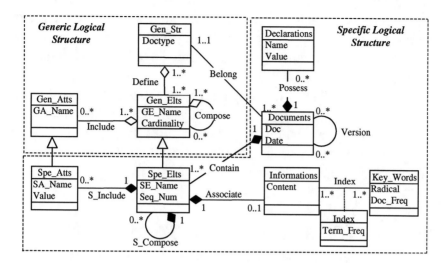

structured complex objects. The generic model we propose must, on the one hand, accept any type of document and, on the other hand, facilitate the retrieval, interrogation and analysis of documents (structure and content). The idea is to identify logical classes of documents in order to gather them according to these classes, therefore making it possible for users to focus on the classes which interest them (e.g., books, newspapers, proceedings, etc.).

With this goal in mind, we distinguished two types of logical structures (Khrouf & Soulé-Dupuy, 2001): the generic logical structure (i.e., the common structure of a document set) and the specific logical structure (i.e., the structure of one document). Figure 2 describes the generic model of textual warehouses we propose by respecting UML (Unified Modelling Language) formalism.

The generic logical structure is characterized by three meta-classes: "Gen_Str" (Generic Structures), "Gen_Elts" (Generic Elements), and "Gen_Atts" (Generic Attributes). In our generic model, a generic logical structure is defined by a set of generic elements, which can be composed of other generic elements. Each of these elements can also be described by generic attributes.

The specific logical structure is characterized by the other classes. In our generic model, a document is characterized by a set of declarations. It contains from 1 to *n* "Spe_Elts" (Specific Elements). For each element, we associate 0 or 1 information and/or 0 or *n* "Spe_Atts" (Specific Attributes). Each information is indexed by a set of keywords (stemmed word "Radical") extracted from its textual content. Each keyword is associated with its frequency in the concerned information "Term_Freq" and with its absolute frequency "Doc_Freq" (i.e., the frequency of the stemmed word in the whole collection of information).

This object model was implemented in the DBMS Oracle 8. The design was realized by an object-oriented modelling (UML) and the implementation carried out in an object-relational DBMS (Oracle 8). To ensure this translation, we used the transformation rules described in Soutou (2001). An extract of the object-relational diagram obtained is schematized in the appendix.

INFORMATION EXTRACTION

The information extraction must determine the different parts of a document whose every part presents a coherent idea. To achieve this stage, we define three types of documents:

- documents with tags having a *semantic vocation* (e.g., SGML, XML documents);
- documents with tags having a *presentation vocation* (e.g., HTML documents);
- *non-structured documents* (e.g., TXT documents).

We present, in what follows, an extraction method that can be applied to every type of document.

Documents with Tags Having a Semantic Vocation

For this type of document, we distinguish two sub-families: well-formed documents, i.e., those which obey syntactical rules; and valid documents, i.e., well-formed documents which also obey a structure (Data Type Description or DTD).

The logical structure of well-formed documents is determined as follows:

Stage 1: Restitution of document tags (create a new file that contains the document tags) and restitution of attributes. The attribute name is prefixed by "A_".

Figure 3. Example of Logical Structure Determination for Well-Formed Documents

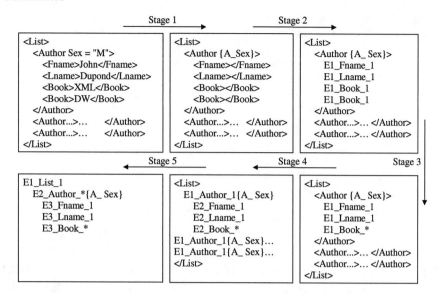

Stage 2: Every start tag followed by its end tag is replaced by a defined element (the level is 1, and the cardinality is 1). *Note:* The element name is prefixed by "Ex_" (where *x* constitutes the number of its level) and followed by its cardinality.

Stage 3: If consecutive elements have the same name, they are replaced by only one element, whose cardinality becomes * instead of 1.

Stage 4: Every start tag, followed by the defined elements and by its end tag, is replaced by a new defined element. The level of this new element takes the value of 1, and the level of its sub-elements must be incremented by 1.

Stage 5: Repeat the process (stages 1 to 4) until we obtain a file which contains only defined elements.

The logical structure of valid documents is determined by their DTD in the following ways:

- the keyword "!DOCTYPE" corresponds to the logical structure name;
- the keyword "!ELEMENT" corresponds to an element of the logical structure;
- the keyword "!ATTLIST" corresponds to the attributes of the concerned element;
- the element level is determined according to the appearance order.

Figure 4. Example of Logical Structure Determination for Valid Documents

< !DOCTYPE List
< !ELEMENT List (Author *)>
< !ELEMENT Author (Fname, Lname, Book *)>
< !ATTLIST Author Sex… >
< !ELEMENT Fname Cdata>
< !ELEMENT Lname Cdata>
< !ELEMENT Book Cdata>]>
	E1_List_1
	  E2_Author_*{A_Sex}
	    E3_Fname_1
	    E3_Lname_1
	    E3_Book_*

Once the logical structure is determined, it is necessary to check if this structure already exists among the generic logical structures of the warehouse. If the generic logical structure already exists, the system must store the document in the warehouse by attaching its specific logical structure to the corresponding generic logical structure. If the system finds a similar structure among the generic logical structures, it checks whether it is possible to modify this structure. The similarity between two structures depends on the common elements and their order. Otherwise, the system creates a new generic logical structure.

We assume that the logical structures of documents are represented as tree structures. A tree structure is characterized by a root r (doctype of the DTD), which is connected to all other nodes (elements of the DTD) by a single way, whose r is the origin. The arcs of tree structures are oriented.

To compare two generic logical structures, we decompose every structure into several sub-trees with two levels (the root and their ordered sons). So, we can compare the corresponding sub-trees (having the same root) as follows: The system must determine the state of every element of both sub-trees. We distinguish two states: 'o' for an element found in both structures and 'n' for an element not found in a structure. Later, we must apply the following formal specification.

X: The ordered list of elements of the first sub-tree (that of the document);

Y: The ordered list of elements of the second sub-tree (that of the warehouse);

State(e): return the state of the element e;

Pos(e): return the position of the element e in the ordered list of the sons of the same root;

Length(E): return the number of elements in the ordered list E.

Case 1: Both first elements of both sub-trees must not have the state 'n'.

$\exists x \in X$ / $Pos(x)=1$, $State(x)=$ 'n' and $\exists y \in Y$ / $Pos(y)=1$, $State(y)=$ 'n' $\Rightarrow$ Failure

Case 2: Both last elements of both sub-trees must not have the state 'n'.

$\exists x \in X$ / $Pos(x)=Length(X)$, $State(x)=$ 'n' and $\exists y \in Y$ / $Pos(y)=Length(Y)$, $State(y)=$ 'n' $\Rightarrow$ Failure

Case 3: If all the elements of the first sub-tree have the state 'o', then success.

$\forall x \in X$ / $State(x)=$ 'o' $\Rightarrow$ Success

If one of the previous cases was not discovered, the system must apply these rules:

Rule 1: $\forall x_1, x_2 \in X$ / $State(x_1)=$ 'n', $State(x_2)=$ 'n' and $Pos(x_2)=Pos(x_1)+1 \Rightarrow X \leftarrow X-\{x_2\}$

Rule 2: $\forall x_1, x_2, x_3 \in X$ / $State(x_1)=$ 'o', $State(x_2)=$ 'n', $State(x_3)=$ 'o', $Pos(x_3)=Pos(x_2)+1$, $Pos(x_2)=Pos(x_1)+1$ and $x_1 x_3 \not\subset Y \Rightarrow$ Failure

Example 1

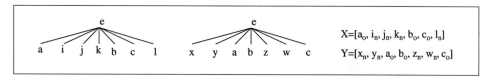

The result after applying **Rule 1:** $X=[a_o, i_n, b_o, c_o, l_n]$ et $Y=[x_n, y_n, a_o, b_o, z_n, w_n, c_o]$.

The result after applying **Rule 2:** Success. Because $[a_o, b_o] \subset Y \Rightarrow$ these two sub-trees can be merged.

The list of the element *e* is $Z=[x, y, a, i, j, k, b, z, w, c, l]$

Example 2

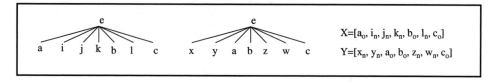

The result after applying **Rule 1:** $X=[a_o, i_n, b_o, l_n, c_o]$ et $Y=[x_n, y_n, a_o, b_o, z_n, w_n, c_o]$.

The result after applying **Rule 2:** Failure. Because $[b_o, c_o] \not\subset Y \Rightarrow$ these two sub-trees cannot be merged. The order cannot be determined.

Documents with Tags Having a Presentation Vocation

The logical structure extraction of this document type is difficult because the tags are used especially for the presentation. Indeed, this language does not define a generic logical structure in a simple way (contrary to other DTDs, such as those of the SGML or XML languages which are more expressive).

Because it is more ambiguous, a rewriting stage for HTML semi-structured documents is necessary to add more semantics to tags of this document type. We established rules for tag rewriting:

- all presentation tags are deleted because they present no information about the organization of document elements (e.g., <B>, <HR>);
- structural and reference tags are preserved because they constitute hypertextual information;
- informative tags are deleted. These tags are inserted by the authors to comment their sources, and they do not influence the document structure;
- presentation tags of structural elements are replaced by the classic structural tags, e.g., a tag <Cite> that highlights a quotation is replaced by a simple paragraph.

We rename the HTML tags that we preserve with more explicit names for a better legibility, whose extract is presented in Table 1. We also preserve the attributes, which are likely to bring some semantic information.

Since we have a document where the structural elements were detected, we must identify the generic and specific logical structures in the same way we do for structured documents.

Non-Structured Documents

For the non-structured documents, we use the segmentation technique (Lallich & Ouerfelli, 1998). This technique decomposes a text into fine and coherent documentary units. We distinguish different methods of segmentation:

Table 1. HTML Tags

HTML Tag	Use	New Tag
<P>	Definition of paragraph	<PARAGRAPH>
<OL>	Ordered list	<LIST Type = "Ordered">
<UL>	Unordered list	<LIST Type = "Unordered">
<LI>	List item	<LISTITEM>
<TABLE>	Definition of table	<TABLE>

segmentation by a sequence of words, segmentation by sentences, and segmentation by paragraphs. These methods of segmentation are not reliable because they ignore the syntactical and semantic aspects of text. Indeed, our objective, then, is to identify documentary units according to more semantic criteria. This unit must be separated and characterized by formal indicators.

The basic idea of our segmentation method is to begin with a minimal unit, i.e., the typographic paragraph (separated by carriage returns), to find the documentary unit that presents the required properties (linguistic autonomy, syntactic and semantic cohesion), thus forming a homogeneous "thematic" passage. We indicate by paragraph a text block separated by two carriage returns. The carriage return, in our work, is considered as a typographic sign that separates the paragraphs. The text block separated by the carriage returns can have different forms (title, element list, and paragraph). To associate paragraphs in the same documentary unit, we use some linguistic markers that we find between the paragraphs:

- presence of linear integration markers (e.g., if, then, so, furthermore, etc.) at the start of the paragraph;
- presence of connection words (e.g., for example, for this, etc.) at the start of the paragraph;
- resumption anaphoric at the start of the paragraph: by a demonstrative (e.g., it, this, etc.) or by a personal pronoun (e.g., it, him, etc.);
- presence of markers (below, above) which refer to textual or not textual objects.

Once the documentary units of a document have been defined, we perform the extraction of the generic and specific logical structures in the same way we do for structured documents.

We presented the different techniques for the extraction of information contained in the documents. In what follows, we describe the mechanisms we used to handle the content of the document warehouse by the processes of information retrieval and multidimensional analyses.

INFORMATION RETRIEVAL

An information retrieval process implies the development of mechanisms that allow a user, who is not necessarily specialist, to retrieve the documentary information which corresponds best to his needs. According to this approach, information retrieval is intended to facilitate information restitution from a documentary collection. The problem, then, is the representation and organization of document content. The technique used to solve this problem is the indexing process (Soulé-Dupuy, 2001).

The indexing process extracts a set of information characterizing a document. This information can be keywords extracted from the document textual content, or it can be information concerning the documents, which is called metadata (e.g., the author name, the abstract, the edition date). These metadata can also constitute the elements of structure used during the identification of the logical structures of the documents. The information indexing in the generic model is then based on the classic techniques of automatic text indexing. It is made, generally, following two fundamental stages:

- *indexing term identification*;
- *indexing term evaluation and weighting*.

During the first stage, i.e., indexing term identification, it is necessary to determine all the words that will be used for indexing. It is also necessary to define the element that will be chosen to unite the indexing, such as stem, single word, or word group. The determination of indexing terms is done through several methods, including thesaurus, dictionary of synonymy, location of word groups, and parsing (see Salton et al., 1983; Frakes & Yates, 1992).

For the indexing term evaluation, we can, by studying the term occurrence frequency in the documents, determine the terms necessary for indexing. Indeed, the weighting of a term corresponds to its frequency of occurrence in the document. We distinguish two frequencies:

- *term frequency* "Term_Freq" corresponds to the number of term occurrences in the concerned information;
- *absolute frequency* "Doc_Freq" corresponds to the stemmed word's frequency in the whole collection of information.

We notice then:

- terms having a high frequency correspond, generally, to the articles, pronouns, propositions, etc., and they must be excluded because of their semantic lack;
- terms having a weak frequency are not representative of the document content. The most significant terms are those whose frequency is intermediate.

To evaluate the representativeness of terms in an instance of object "Information," we adapted the formula of Sparck Jones (1972):

$$TermWeight_{ij} = TF_{ij} \left(1 + \log \left(\frac{N \cdot TF_{ij}}{AF_i} \right) \right)$$

TF_{ij} : frequency of the term i in the concerned specific element j,

N: number of specific elements in the collection of documents (in the warehouse),

AF_i : absolute frequency of a term i in the collection of documents.

The information retrieval process adapted for our generic model presents several advantages. First, it does not flood the user with an important number of documents. Second, it presents a more efficient retrieval. So, instead of calculating the similarity between a query and totality of text, we measure the similarity between this query and each part (specific elements) constituting the text. This allows more specific and more localized access to the information (one of our objectives). *Note:* The information retrieval techniques based on indexes of terms do not exploit the logical structure of documents. They restitute documents or parts of documents, but they do not obtain specific information, such as the edition year of a book. The idea, then, is to use a DBMS and structured languages.

MULTIDIMENSIONAL ANALYSIS

The textual warehouse must allow decision-making, which implies the ability to implement new processes for textual information analysis. The multidimensional model is an option which is better adapted to data analysis than a relational model. Indeed, it considers a subject to be analyzed as a point in a space with several dimensions. The data are organized so as to implement the analyzed subject and the different perspectives of the analysis. Several formalisms for the multidimensional model have been proposed: hypercube (Agrawal et al., 1995), multidimensional table (Gyssens & Lakshmanan, 1997), cube (Thomas et al., 1997), f-tables (Cabibbo & Torlone, 1998), etc. In what follows, we detail, multidimensional tables, which are the basic concept of our contribution. The multidimensional table is the logical model commonly used in multidimensional analysis. Its representation in tabular form is well-suited for any user, insofar as he is already accustomed to interpreting this common type of representation.

A *multidimensional schema* is defined by a schema and instances. The schema is defined by (D, A, Param):
– $D = <d_1, d_2\ldots, d_n>$ is the list of the dimensions, – $A = \{A_1, A_2\ldots, A_p\}$ is the set of the attributes, – Param is a function $D \rightarrow 2^{\{A1, A2, \ldots, Ap\}}$ associating the dimensions and the attributes. – With $\forall i, j = 1\ldots, n; i \neq j; param(d_i) \cap param(d_j) = \varnothing$. – (A parameter is associated to one dimension).

The attributes belonging to the set $P = \cup_{1 \le i \le n} param(d_i)$ are the parameters of the analysis. The attribute A_m belonging to the set $M = A - \cup_{1 \le i \le n} param(d_i)$ is called the *measures of the analysis* (they are the attributes other than those of the parameters). Figure 5 represents a multidimensional table. The symbol * indicates that there is no value.

Conceptual Modeling of the Textual Marts

The multidimensional model represents data in a mart in the form of a schema grouping, which is a set of facts and dimensions. A textual mart is specialized for an activity type, an analysis type, and a user group.

Figure 5. Visualization of a Multidimensional Table

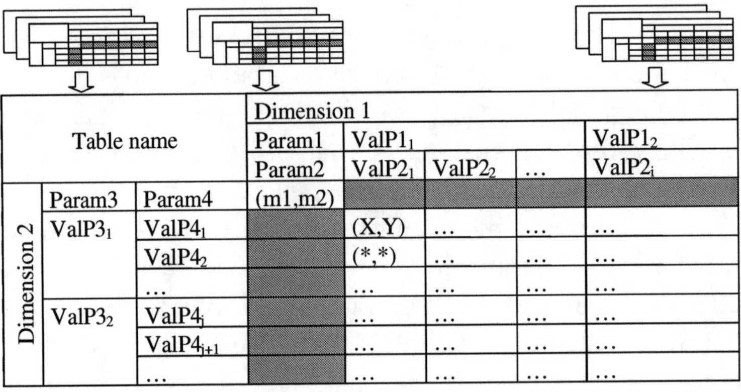

Table name			Dimension 1				
			Param1	$ValP1_1$			$ValP1_2$
			Param2	$ValP2_1$	$ValP2_2$	...	$ValP2_i$
Dimension 2	Param3	Param4	(m1,m2)				
	$ValP3_1$	$ValP4_1$		(X,Y)	...	...	...
		$ValP4_2$		(*,*)	...	...	...
		...		...	...	...	...
	$ValP3_2$	$ValP4_j$		...	...	...	...
		$ValP4_{j+1}$		...	...	...	...
		...		...	...	...	...

The documents implemented in the warehouse are organized according to their DTD. These last ones organize the elements among them according to a hierarchy dependence.

A *hierarchy dependence* between two elements A_i and A_j,
noted $A_i \Rightarrow A_j$, implies that the element A_i belongs to the element A_j.

By basing itself on these dependencies, it is possible to define a hierarchy.

A *hierarchy H* is defined on a set of elements by:
$H_i = <A_1, A_2 \ldots \quad , A_n>$ where $A_1 \Rightarrow A_2 \Rightarrow \ldots \quad \Rightarrow A_n$.

A textual mart contains one or more facts. A fact constitutes a subject of analysis (the different measures of activity that must be analyzed).

A *fact* is defined by ($Name^F$, E_Mes^F, Fct^F, H^F):
– $Name^F$ is the fact name,
– E_Mes^F is the measure element,
– Fct^F is the aggregation function applied by the fact,
– H^F is the fact hierarchy.

The measures of an activity can be observed according to different perspectives. Every perspective is represented by a dimension.

A *dimension D* is defined by ($Name^D$, E_Par^D, H^D):
– $Name^D$ is the dimension name,
– $E\_Par^D = <P_1, P_2, \ldots \quad , P_n>$ is the element set that constitutes analysis parameters,
– H^D is the dimension hierarchy.

Every textual mart is characterized by its multidimensional schema. We define a multidimensional schema as a model composed of facts and dimensions.

A *multidimensional schema S* is defined by ($Name^S$, Dim^S, $Fact^S$):
– $Name^S$ is the multidimensional schema name,
– $Dim^S = <D_1, D_2, \ldots \quad , D_n>$ is the dimension list,
– $Fait^S = \{F_1, F_2, \ldots , F_n\}$ is the fact set.

Graphic Construction of Textual Marts

In this section, we present the stages involved in building textual marts that perform multidimensional analyses.

Stage 1: Automatic display of generic logical structures and documents.
Stage 2: The user must choose a generic logical structure or a document.
- if the user chooses a generic logical structure, then the analysis concerns all the documents belonging to this structure;
- if the user chooses a document, the analysis concerns only this document.

Stage 3: The system must automatically display the generic logical structure:
- if the user chose a generic logical structure, the system displays the elements of this structure;
- if the user chose a document, it is necessary to refer to the corresponding generic logical structure to display its elements.

Stage 4: The user must specify the role (i.e., dimension or fact) of some elements to build the textual mart by using contextual menus. The elements chosen by the user are highlighted by using different shapes and colors for the dimensions and facts.

Figure 6. Generic Logical Structure Chosen by the User

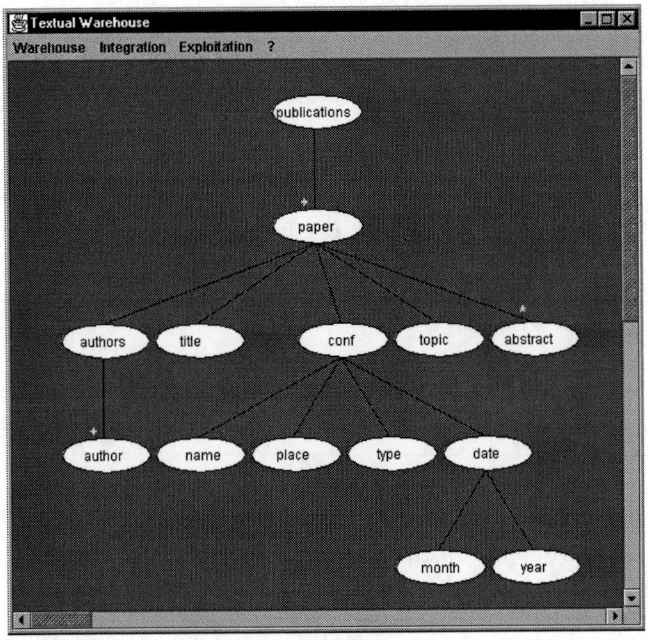

Figure 7. Generic Logical Structure Modified by the User

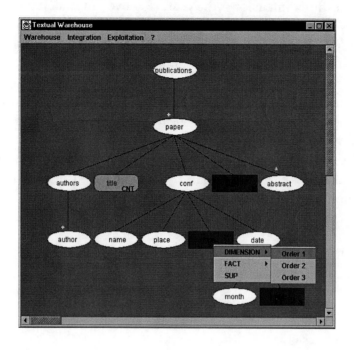

Figure 8. Schema of Textual Mart

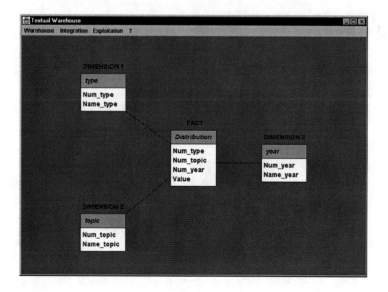

In this example, the first dimension is the type, the second dimension is the topic, and the third dimension is the year. However, the fact is the number of papers. This textual mart, then, determines the number of papers by type, topic and year. At this time, the user task is finished. The result will be a multidimensional table. Figure 8 presents the schema of textual mart.

Stage 5: Automatic generation of views: for every element *e* chosen by the user, the system must generate a view containing several attributes:

- the first attribute corresponds to the document number of the element *e*;
- the second attribute is the number of the element constituting the ancestor common to all the elements chosen by the user;
- the last attribute corresponds to the information of the element *e*.

```
CREATE VIEW Dimension_n (Doc, Anc, Inf) AS                          (1)
SELECT    e.s_compose ... s_compose.itsdoc.num,                     (2)
          e.s_compose ... s_compose.num,                            (3)
          e.content                                                 (4)

FROM      Spe_Elts e
WHERE     e.s_compose ... s_compose.itsdoc.doc = "Name_Doc"         (5)
          e.s_compose ... s_compose.itsdoc.belong.doctype = "Name_SL"  (6)
AND       e.inherit.ge_name="Elt_m" ;
```

```
(1) Or Fact_n (Doc, Anc, Inf)
(2) Attribute 1: number of the document
(3) Attribute 2: number of the element constituting the ancestor common to all the
    chosen elements
(4) Attribute n : content of the chosen element
(5) If the user chose a document
(6) If the user chose a logical structure
```

Note: The number of "s_compose" for the attributes is determined by calculating the level number between the corresponding element (document or ancestor element) and the chosen element *e*.

For the first dimension, the view that the system must generate is the following:

```
CREATE VIEW Dimension_1 (doc, paper, type) AS
SELECT   e.s_compose.s_compose.s_compose.itsdoc.num,
         e.s_compose.s_compose.num,
         e.content
FROM     Spe_Elts e
WHERE    e.s_compose.s_compose.s_compose.itsdoc.belong.doctype = "publications"
AND      e.inherit.ge_name = "Type" ;
```

In the same way, the system must generate all the other views. We will then have four views: Dimension_1 (doc, paper, type), Dimension_2 (doc, paper, topic), Dimension_3 (doc, paper, year), and Fact_1 (doc, paper, title).

From these views, the system must then generate another view by a joint on the first two attributes (in our example "doc" and "paper"):

```
CREATE VIEW Joint (type, topic, year, title) AS
SELECT   d1.type, d2.topic, d3.year, f1.title
FROM     Dimension_1 d1, Dimension_2 d2, Dimension_3 d3, Fact_1 f1
WHERE    d1.paper = d2.paper     AND     d2.paper = d3.paper
AND      d3.paper = f1.paper     AND     d1.doc = d2.doc
AND      d2.doc = d3.doc         AND     d3.doc = f1.doc ;
```

To generate a last view, the system must apply the aggregation operation by grouping the dimensions:

```
CREATEVIEW Distribution (type, topic, year, number) AS
SELECT      j.type, j.topic, j.year, count (j.title)
FROM        Joint j
GROUP BY j.type, j.topic, j.year ;
```

Figure 9. Multidimensional Table "Distribution"

topic/type	international conference	national conference	other conferences
data minin	26	9	1
information retrieval	14	5	4
interaction and autonomy	16	10	4
modeling and algorithms	3	*	4
reasoning and decision	40	10	12
software development	4	*	4
systems and networks	9	4	6

The view generated by the system must be visualized according to a multidimensional table "Distribution."

CONCLUSION

The concept of textual warehouses we propose allows manipulating the documents of a heterogeneous collection by their structures and their contents, contrary to other systems that impose a predefined structure. Indeed, the proposed generic model is suitable for storing heterogeneous documents according to their logical structures and for applying the techniques of information retrieval (restitution of passages but not the whole documents), data interrogation (restitution of factual information), and multidimensional analysis (analyzing data according to several dimensions by using a graphic language that offers a great simplicity for the users).

Several experiments have been carried out on two aspects — first on the integration of large collections of heterogeneous documents issued from the Laboratory Intranet, and then on the analysis and use of this warehouse content by several non-experimented users. The distinction between the generic and the specific structures improved the expressiveness of a large document collection in the way to retrieve, exploit and analyze its content. The graphic language is also open enough to allow any user to construct any query, even a complex one.

At present, our main goal is to continue the merging of the techniques developed within the framework of the information retrieval and the data warehouses. Indeed, the specifications of the document warehouse need to be extended in order to:

- define an interrogation language appropriate for the warehouse instead of using SQL language to facilitate query syntax;
- apply the multidimensional operators to textual marts in a textual way, according to a formalism or in a graphic way;
- extract statistical information and knowledge to explain the behaviors of users and the definition of user profiles.

Let us assume that the document warehouse is the base for the definition of a business memory; it is intended for any person in an organization who must quickly access and analyze any useful information. This memory must contain any knowledge extracted from document content (i.e., from structure and textual parts). Our future work will aim to extend the process of textual analysis to integrate personalization criteria and metadata (by the user himself or by an automatic process).

ACKNOWLEDGMENTS

We would like to acknowledge M. Franck Ravat, assistant professor at Toulouse I University, for his helpful comments and discussions on this research. We also thank M. Mohamed Mbarki (Master student) for his contribution to the implementation of the system.

REFERENCES

Abiteboul, S., Cobena, G., & Mignet, L. (2001). Change-centric management of versions in an XML warehouse. In *Proceedings of VLDB'01*, Rome, Italy (pp. 581-590).

Agrawal, R., Gupta, A., & Sarawagi, S. (1995). *Modelling multidimensional database*. San Jose, CA: IBM Almaden Research Center. (Technical Report)

Boughanem, M., Chrisment, C., & Soulé-Dupuy, C. (1999). Query modification based on relevance back propagation in ad hoc environment. *Information Processing & Management Journal*, *35*(2), 121-139.

Burkowski, F. J. (1992). Retrieval activities in a database consisting of heterogeneous collection of structured text. In *Proceedings of ACM SIGIR'92*, Copenhagen, Denmark (pp. 112-125).

Cabibbo, L. & Torlone, R. (1998). A logical approach to multidimensional databases. In *Proceedings of EDBT'98*, Valencia, Spain (pp. 183-197).

Chevalier, M., Christine, J., & Khrouf, K. (2003). Towards a documentary memory: Building a document repository for companies. In *Proceedings of ICEIS'03*, Angers, France (pp. 213-218).

Chiaramella, Y. & Nie, J. (1990). A retrieval model based on an extended model logic and its application to the RIME experimental approach. In *Proceedings of SIGIR'90*, Brussels, Belgium (pp. 25-44).

Faulstich, L. C., Spilopoulou, M., & Linnemann, V. (1997). WIND: A warehouse for Internet data. In *Proceedings of BNCOD 15: Advances in databases*, London (pp. 169-183).

Fourel, F., Mulhem, P., & Bruandet, M. (1998). A generic framework for structured document access. In *Proceedings of DEXA'98*, Vienna, Austria (pp. 521-530).

Frakes, W. B. & Yates, R. B. (1992). *Information Retrieval Data Structures & Algorithms*. Boston, MA: Addison-Wesley.

Gardarin, G. & Yoon, S. (1996). HyWEB: Un système d'interrogation orienté-objet pour le Web. In *Proceedings of BDA '96,* Cassis, France (pp. 205-224).

Gardarin, G., Mensch, A., & Tomasic, A. (2002). An introduction to the e-XML data integration suite. In *Proceedings of EDBT'02,* Prague, Czech Republic (pp. 297-306).

Gyssens, M. & Lakshmanan, L. V. S. (1997). A foundation for multidimensional database. In *Proceedings of VLDB'97*, Bombay, India (pp. 106-115).

IBM World Trade Corporation. (1982). *Storage and information retrieval (STAIRS) reference manual*. Amsterdam: IBM Netherlands. (Technical Report)

Inmon, W. H. (1994). *Building the Data Warehouse*. New York: John Wiley & Sons.

Khrouf, K. & Soulé-Dupuy, C. (2001). Decisional textual dataweb design. In *Proceedings of ISE'01,* Las Vegas, Nevada (pp. 40-43).

Khrouf, K., Soulé-Dupuy, C., & Zurfluh, G. (2001). Exploitation d'une mémoire d'entreprise à partir d'entrepôts textuels. *ISI Journal, 6*(3), 87-117.

Lallich, G. & Ouerfelli, T. (1998). La segmentation pour l'indexation d'un document technique: Principe et méthodes. *Proceedings of EFRA '98,* Sfax, Tunisia.

Salton, G. (1971). *The SMART Retrieval System: Experiment in Automatic Document Processing*. Englewood Cliffs, NJ: Prentice Hall.

Salton, G., Fox, E. A., & Wu, H. (1983). *Introduction to Modern Information Retrieval*. New York: McGraw-Hill.

Soulé-Dupuy, C. (2001). Bases d'informations textuelles: Des modèles aux applications. *HDR memory*. Toulouse, France: Paul Sabatier University - Toulouse III.

Soutou, C. (1999). *Relationel-objet sous Oracle8: Modélisation avec UML*. Paris: Editions Eyrolles.

Sparck Jones, K. (1972). A statistical interpretation of term specificity and its application in retrieval. *Journal of Documentation, 28*(1), 11-20.

Thomas, H., Datta, A. & Viguier, I. (1997). *A conceptual model and algebra for online analytical processing in decision support databases*. Tucson, AZ: University of Arizona. (Technical Report)

Turtle, H. & Craft, B. (1990). Inference networks for document retrieval. In *Proceedings of SIGIR'90*, Brussels, Belgium (pp. 1-24).

Van Rijsbergen, C. (1986). A new theoretical framework for information retrieval. In *Proceedings of RDIR'86*, Pisa, Italy (pp. 194-200).

APPENDIX

Extract of the Warehouse Relational-Object Diagram

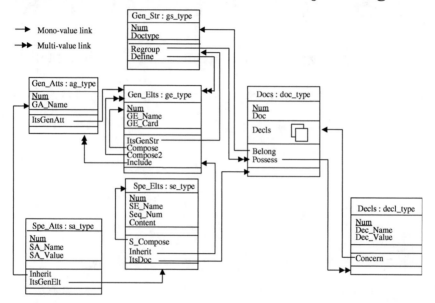

Chapter VIII

Text Processing by Binary Neural Networks

T. Beran, Czech Technical University, Czech Republic

T. Macek, Czech Technical University, Czech Republic

ABSTRACT

This chapter describes a rather less traditional technique of text processing. The technique is based on the binary neural network Correlation Matrix Memory. We propose using the neural network for text searching tasks. Two methods of coding input words are described and tested. Further, we discuss the problems of using this approach for text processing.

INTRODUCTION

With more and more people becoming familiar with computers, the amount of information stored in electronic formats is quickly increasing. The consequence of that is the need to be able to search large amounts of data for particular information. Various techniques have been developed for the text searching task. Many techniques are very fast and sophisticated. Speed is one of the most important criteria, but it is not the only one. The other one is the ability to deal with somehow corrupted text. Text could be corrupted, for example, when we do not know exactly what we are searching for, or if the text is the result of OCR or speech recognition.

In this chapter, we describe a rather less traditional technique for the text searching task. The technique is based on a binary neural network called CMM (Correlation Matrix Memory). We have tested CMM on the problem of finding a particular word in a single text document. Searching gives all occurrences of the word. Although the technique is able to search approximately, here we focus on exact searching.

This chapter is divided as follows: "Technique Description" explains our approach and describes CMM; "Text Coding and Experiments" explains the importance of input patterns coding, proposes two new methods, and shows initial experiments; "Discussion" discusses some problems that arise when this technique is applied to real text.

TECHNIQUE DESCRIPTION

In this section, we describe the principle of the technique based on binary neural network as well as on CMM itself. Usually, a fast conventional technique is used for text searching tasks, e.g., Boyer-Moor or Shift-or algorithms. Conventional techniques go through text and compare it with a searched pattern. Our technique is based on storing associations between words and their location in the text. The association is stored in CMM. This approach is similar to techniques such as inverted file lists or hash tables (Hodge & Austin, 2001).

Our approach is shown in Figure 1. It operates in two phases — the learning and the recalling. The *learning phase* stores associations between words and their positions in the text document. The *recalling phase* searches for a query word. In fact, there is no search during the recalling phase; it simply recalls a proper association.

In the learning phase, the parser goes trough the text and cuts off the words. All words are coded and pass their code word to the input of the CMM. Coding input words significantly influences properties of CMM and the recall process. It checks whether the input word has been already learned. If it has, the word is learned no more; but its position in the text is added to a proper entry of the position table. Otherwise, a code for this word is produced and put at the output of CMM. Then, a new association is learned, and a new entry in the position table is added. The position table contains entries for all learned words.

Figure 1. Learning (left side) and Recalling (right side) Phase of the Technique

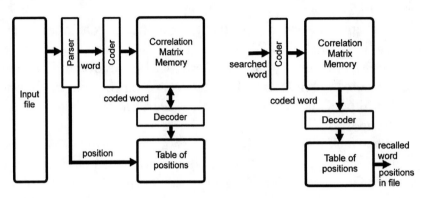

Each entry in the table consists of positions for the particular word. The code addresses the proper entry in the position table.

In the recalling phase, an input word is coded in the same way as it is during the learning phase, and the result is applied to the input of CMM. CMM then recalls the association or answers that there is no association for this pattern. If CMM gives a represent code, it is then decoded to obtain the address in the position table. The entry contains all positions of the query word in the text document.

Correlation Matrix Memory

Correlation Matrix Memory is an associative memory. It allows information to be stored in a content-addressable way. The information that memory stores are the associations between an input and an output. The associative memory has similar properties to other forms of neural networks: the ability to learn, the ability to generalize, inherent parallelism. We use the correlation matrix memory with binary elements. This type of CMM is called weightless, or binary, CMM. It means that both the inputs and the weights of the network are binary (0 or 1). Because of binary processing, CMM is a fast neural network. While some other neural networks require a long time for training, its learning process is not iterative (it uses so-called "one shot" learning process).

The learning process starts with all elements of the matrix set to 0. The matrix is formed by the superposition of the outer product matrices created from the training pairs. Superposition means applying the logical *or* of the matrices.

Learning is evaluated as follows (see also Figure 2):

$$w_{ij} = \bigvee_{m=1}^{p} a_i^{(m)} b_j^{(m)},$$ (1)

where the operator $\vee$ means logical *or* over its arguments (of binary type), a is the input pattern, b is the output pattern, and p is the number of associations. For a more detailed description (see O'Keefe, 1997).

The recalling process is done in two steps. First, an integer vector is evaluated from the summation of some rows of the matrix. Then, the integer vector is thresholded to obtain an output binary vector. Those rows of the matrix are chosen for the summation, which correspond to the ones in the input vector. The integer (accumulating) vector is given by:

$$r_j = \sum_{\forall i} M_{i,j} t_i, \forall j,$$ (2)

where M is the binary matrix and r is the integer vector. Then, the thresholding process is applied to the integer vector. Thresholding evaluates the binary vector. Thresholding influences the ability of CMM to reject noise—to answer correctly to an incomplete input pattern. Thresholding also adds a nonlinear aspect to the recalling process. There are several types of thresholding. In our tests, we use so-called *L-max thresholding*.

Figure 2. Learning (left side) and Recalling (right side) Phases of CMM

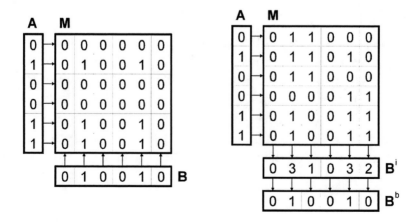

Table1. An Example of L-Max Thresholding for L = 2

Integer vector	Output binary vector and its alternatives		
3 3 2 1	1 1 0 0	-	-
3 1 2 0	1 0 1 0	-	-
3 3 2 3	1 1 0 0	0 1 0 1	1 0 0 1

L-max thresholding is based on a presumption that all output vectors have a constant number of ones. It implies that we do not need to care about the values in the summation vector. We simply choose L biggest values in the integer vector and set the corresponding bits in the output binary vector to 1.

Table 1 shows an example of L-max thresholding for $L = 2$. We can see from the table that the technique could produce an uncertain output in special cases. In such cases, we choose a random one. An appropriate coding of output vectors could distinguish correct patterns.

There is a mechanism commonly applied to an input vector before it is put to the matrix. It processes input binary vectors and converts them into a form with more manageable properties. This mechanism is called *n-tuple prepro-cessing*. It divides the input vector into n parts (called tuples), which are independently coded. The coded tuples are concatenated to produce the whole input vector of the matrix. The tuples have the same length. They are coded by the "1 of N" code. This code has two useful properties for behavior of the correlation matrix. Firstly, it transforms the arbitrary number of ones in the input vector into the constant number of ones (equal to number of tuples). Secondly, it produces a vector that is sparser then the original one.

Capacity of CMM

As mentioned above, CMM associates pairs of input and output vectors. Clearly, it is able to associate just a certain number of the associations. After that limit, CMM starts recalling incorrectly. This limit depends on the size of matrix as well as on the character of trained pairs. The capacity of CMM can be defined in several ways. We adopt the definition of O'Keefe (1997), which measures capacity as the number of trained pairs when the probability of correct output is 0.5. For this probability, the number of trained associations is given by:

$$T = \ln(-\ln\frac{\ln 2}{H})/(NI \cdot \ln(1 - \frac{N \cdot NI}{H \cdot R})) ,$$ (3)

where T is the number of trained associations, R is the number of elements in the input vector, NI is the number of bits set in the input vector, H is the number of elements in the output vector, and N is the number of bits set in the output vector.

TEXT CODING AND EXPERIMENTS

This section explains the influence of word coding on the properties of CMM. Two proposed method of coding are also defined. Experiments comparing those coding methods are shown.

The important part of the described technique is transforming input words into a binary form. We need to impose some restrictions on input data in order to improve the behavior of the matrix. The input data should be sparse and orthogonal. It allows for filling the matrix regularly (with uniform distribution). It increases the capacity of CMM and also improves its ability to deal with corrupt patterns. The real text without any preprocessing does not have these optimal properties.

Simple Text Coding

Figure 3 shows the frequencies of letters in English text where word duplicities are omitted. That is more suitable for CMM, because each word is trained just once. The simple text coding could not be efficient. For example, the most frequent letter 'e' is 81 times more frequent then the letter 'z'. Simple

Figure 3. Histogram of Letters for Non-Repeated English Words

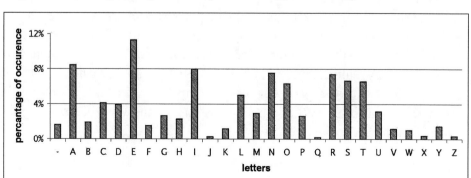

coding does not take into account this fact. Therefore, it generates saturated locations in the matrix during the learning process. These locations consequently cause faults when recalling.

In our experiments, we have tested three types of coding. The first one is a simple coding. It divides input words into letters that are then coded independently. Each letter on a particular position is assigned with only one logical 1 in the binary vector. This simple coding does not provide for changes to the distribution of the letters so it does not have good properties for the matrix.

Proposed Text Coding

In this subsection, we describe two codes for the real text. The aim is to eliminate the inappropriate properties of the real text. The name of the first coding is "coding by equal intervals." The idea of this coding method is the division of the trained set into several intervals of equal, or almost equal (differs at most by one), parts. The intervals are produced for each symbol (a letter) of the patterns. Each position generates a sub-code that is given by putting the letter under the particular interval. These sub-codes are then concatenated to obtain the whole code word for CMM.

In order to get intervals for the first letter, we sort the patterns in lexicographic order. We divide this list into intervals of equal length. The second group of intervals we achieve in a similar way. The only difference is that we sort the patterns starting from the second letter. The first letter of patterns is moved after the last letter, etc. The code word for the first letter is then determined by the interval (of the first group) to which the letter belongs.

For the recalling process, we need to remember the words on the boundaries of the intervals. So, we need the additional information stored in a memory (apart from storing the associations to CMM). We find out which interval belongs to the word by comparing the word with the boundary of the intervals. We can use the binary search method, particularly for more intervals. This type of coding partly eliminates the inappropriate character of the real text — big frequency differences among individual letters. Therefore, we code equal intervals, instead of letters. The drawback of this method is that it takes a lot of time to create the intervals. For words of length D, we need to sort all set of words D-times. But, the advantage of this coding is that it maintains the ability of the matrix to recall incomplete corrupt patterns. We will use this ability for approximate searching.

Figure 4. The Comparison of Three Methods of Coding

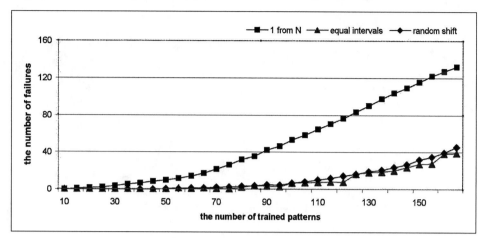

The second proposed coding is called "coding with random shift" (Tregner, 1999). This method adds a pseudorandom number to each letter in the pattern. The operation module (with the size of the alphabet) is then applied on the summation. The result is then processed by the 1 of N code. This coding gives us nearly uniform distribution over the patterns passing to CMM. We need the same pseudorandom numbers to get the same code for the recalling process. Thus, the random numbers for letters in a word should be generated from the word.

We use the summation of ASCII codes of letters in the word as the seed for a pseudorandom series. This summation is the only linking point of a particular pattern for both the training and recalling processes. This coding is simple and efficient. Unfortunately, this method cannot work with a corrupt word. If there is only one letter modified in the input word, we obtain an incorrect seed for the pseudorandom series. That will cause all the letters to be decoded to incorrect numbers, and the recalling pattern will be completely different from the original one. The solution could be in getting the seed in another way. We can obtain it, for example, from the first two letters of the words. Then, the value of the seed will be sensitive only to the first two letters of words. However, this way loses the desired uniform distribution.

The graph (in Figure 4) shows a big difference between simple text coding and the two proposed methods of coding. The simple text coding does not provide uniform distribution of code words in the alphabet. Words containing more frequent letters cause locally oversaturated places in the matrix. These

Figure 5. The Comparison of Speed of Conventional Techniques and CMM

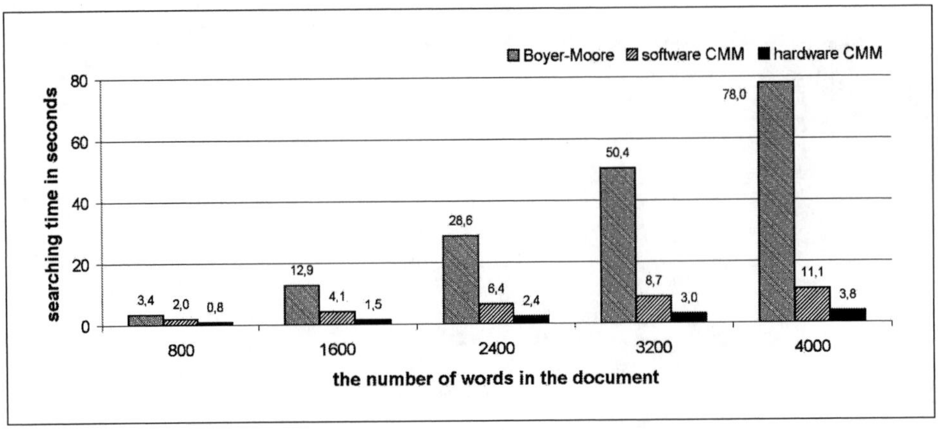

locations result in more faults during the recalling process (capacity drops). The method of "equal intervals" gives almost the same result (slightly better) with the method of "random shift."

In order to obtain more uniform distribution of ones in the matrix, we tried coding two neighboring letters as one symbol. The distribution of code words for two letters is much better compared to the one-letter coding. However, it is still far from the uniform distribution.

Speed Comparison

We have compared the speed of the CMM technique to the Boyer-Moore algorithm (Mraz, 2000). Figure 5 illustrates the results of this test. We also tested the CMM technique on a dedicated CMM hardware accelerator. This board was developed at the University of York (Austin & Kennedy, 1995).

We used the following parameters for the CMM technique: word length was 6, the number of ones in the input vector was 6, the matrix size was 192 x 192 bits, and we used L-max thresholding. For a more detailed description, (see Mraz, 2000). The test shows that the conventional technique, Boyer-Moore, is significantly slower for use with more words in text documents. The reason is the linear processing of Boyer-Moore algorithms. Using a hardware accelerator of CMM is approximately three-times faster than using a software simulation of CMM.

DISCUSSION

Here, we discuss some aspects of using CMM for text processing tasks. First, we discuss the ability of CMM to reject noise. Then, we analyze the applicability of CMM for the approximate matching task. Next, we propose how we can deal with different lengths of words.

Ability to Reject Noise

The key property of CMM is its ability to deal with noisy input data. That means it can respond correctly when the input pattern is corrupt. The question is how far the recalling pattern can be from the originally trained one. The difference is measured by the Hamming distance (the number of different bits) between them. Simple CMM is not able to deal with shifted patterns.

The ability to reject noise significantly depends on the characteristics of trained data. The probability of answering correctly depends on how similar the corrupt pattern is to the trained one; it depends on their Hamming distance. The input method of coding should be designed with this aspect in mind. For example, it could correspond to the typical mistakes we make by typing text on a keyboard. So, the coding method could consider the layout of the keyboard. Neighboring letters would have a smaller Hamming distance because it is more probable that we overstrike a neighboring letter on the keyboard.

There is also another characteristic of real text we should take into account. The real text contains a lot of similar words that differ only by one letter (light-night, among-along, etc.). It contrarily affects the matrix because it causes many overlaps of patterns that reduce capacity.

Approximate Searching

Conventional techniques for approximate matching work when the distance is defined exactly. They use several types of distances, e.g., the Levenshtein distance, Hamming distance, etc. They work exactly because they give all words with a given distance as the result.

On the other hand, CMM is not capable of exactly measuring the distance between patterns. The recalling process tries to find the most similar pattern. CMM does not ensure that it responds correctly to every pattern with a certain Hamming distance from the trained pattern. So, we cannot say that CMM is able to correct patterns with a certain Hamming distance. It depends on several aspects. First, it depends on the used input code that gives similar binary patterns for similar input words. It also depends on the distances of other trained patterns. Similar patterns tend to make saturated locations in the matrix.

Traditional pattern matching techniques produce a set of words (and their positions in the text) that satisfies a given distance as their result. Contrary to these techniques, CMM finds only the one nearest pattern. One possibility is to take more responses before the thresholding process chooses the only one.

Different Length of Words

The correlation matrix has a constant size, while words in text have different lengths. In our experiments, we have tested only words with a constant number letters. The solution could be to use several matrices. Each matrix would store words of a particular length. Another solution is to use one matrix and complete the words to the length of the longest one.

CONCLUSION

The conventional techniques used for pattern matching are designed to solve many types of text searching problems. The technique based on CMM has some limitations, and it is suitable only for some types of text searching problems. CMM is suitable for tasks where we need an efficient search tool in cases where the precision of the answer is not critical. The advantage of CMM is its ability to work with noisy data. The other advantage of the technique is fast processing.

We have shown that the coding of input patterns significantly affects the capacity of correlation matrix memory. Simple "1 of N" coding does not give good results. We have proposed two coding schemes. Both give good results because of their nearly uniform distribution. However, the method of "random shift" does not keep the ability of CMM to deal with corrupt patterns. The speed experiments show promising results when compared to traditional fast techniques, such as Boyer-Moore. The reason is another approach to searching the patterns. The technique based on CMM recalls only the pattern from the associative memory and takes the position of a pattern from the position table. On the other hand, the CMM technique needs to be trained before recalling. Training processes text linearly with the size of the text.

In the future, we want to study and improve the coding of input patterns. Next, we want to apply this technique to the approximate searching problem. We also want to use more advanced architecture (more CMM) to get better results of processing.

ACKNOWLEDGMENTS

The authors thank the students of Czech Technical University, V. Tregner and L. Mraz, for their significant contribution to the project. We also want to thank to Prof. J. Austin, from the University of York, who allowed us access to the hardware simulator of CMM, and A. Turner, who provided support for our use of the accelerator.

REFERENCES

Austin, J. & Kennedy, J. (1995). The design of a dedicated ADAM processor. *Proceedings of the IEEE Conference on Image Processing and Its Applications.*

Hodge, V. J. & Austin, J. (2001). An evaluation of standard retrieval algorithms and a binary neural approach. *Neural Networks* (vol. 14, pp. 287-303). Cambridge, UK: Elsevier.

Mraz, L. (2000). *Fast text searching by neural nets.* Prague, Czech Republic: Czech Technical University. (MSc Thesis)

O'Keefe, S. (1997). *Neural-based content analysis of document images.* York, UK: University of York, Department of Computer Science. (PhD Thesis)

Tregner, V. (1999). *Searching in text using correlation matrix memory.* Prague, Czech Republic: Czech Technical University. (MSc Thesis)

Chapter IX

Extracting Knowledge from Databases and ANNs with Genetic Programming:
Iris Flower Classification Problem

Daniel Rivero, University of A Coruña, Spain

Juan R. Rabuñal, University of A Coruña, Spain

Julián Dorado, University of A Coruña, Spain

Alejandro Pazos, University of A Coruña, Spain

Nieves Pedreira, University of A Coruña, Spain

ABSTRACT

In this chapter, we present an application of Genetic Programming (GP) in the field of data mining and extraction of Artificial Neural Networks (ANN) rules. To do this, we will use its syntactic properties to obtain high level expressions that represent knowledge. These expressions will have different types as there is the need at each moment: we will obtain different expressions like IF-THEN-ELSE rules, mathematical relations between variables or boolean expressions. In this chapter, we will not only apply GP to solve the problem, but we will try different modifications and different ways to apply it to solve the problem. We will show how making a data pre-processing we can obtain better results than using the original values. That is, by adding a little knowledge from the problem we can improve the performance of GP.

INTRODUCTION

In the world of Artificial Intelligence (AI), the extraction of knowledge has been a very useful tool for many different purposes, and it has been tried with many different techniques. Here, we will show how we can use Genetic Programming (GP) to solve a classification problem from a database, and we will show how we can adapt this tool in two different ways: to improve its performance and to make it possible to detect errors. Results show that the technique developed in this chapter opens a new area for research in the field, extracting knowledge from more complicated structures such as Artificial Neural Networks (ANNs).

BACKGROUND
Genetic Programming and Artificial Neural Networks

Genetic Programming (GP) (Koza, 1992) is an evolutionary method used to create computer programs that represent approximate or exact solutions to a problem. This technique allows for the finding of programs with the shape of a tree, and, in its most common application, those programs will be mathematical expressions combining mathematical operators, input variables, constants, decision rules, relational operators, etc.

All of these possible operators must be specified before starting the search. So, with them, GP must be able to build trees with the objective of finding the desired expression which models the relation between the input variables and the desired output. This set of operators is divided into two groups: the *terminal set* contains the operators which cannot accept parameters, like variables or constants; and the *function set*, which contains the operators, such as add or subtract, which need parameters. Once the terminal and non-terminal operators are specified, it is possible to establish types. Each node will have a type, and the construction of child expressions needs to follow the rules of the nodal type (Montana, 1995).

GP creates automatic program generation by means of a process based on the evolution theory of (Darwin, 1864), in which, after subsequent generations, new trees (individuals) are produced from old ones by means of crossover, copy and mutation (see Fuchs, 1998; Luke & Spector, 1998), based on natural selection; the best trees will have more chances of being chosen to become part of the next generation. Thus, a stochastic process is established which, after successive generations, obtains a well-adapted tree.

As the programs we are obtaining with GP have the shape of trees, GP can be adapted to many different kinds of problems. The problem proposed in this chapter is extracting knowledge from databases. We will show how we can solve it with GP in two different ways in a classification problem: by extracting a rule (with the shape of an IF-THEN-ELSE rule) that makes classifications, and by extracting different rules, one for each classification class.

In the field of knowledge discovery from databases, one of the most successful applications of GP is in the development of fuzzy rules (see Fayyad et al., 1996; Bonarini, 1996), mixing its ability to develop rules and using the technique of Automatically Defined Functions (ADF), described in Koza (1994), for obtaining fuzzy rules.

In a recent work done by Wong and Leung (2000), GP is applied as a knowledge extraction technique from databases, and they present LOGENPRO (Logic Grammar Based Genetic Algorithm). They combine GP and representation of knowledge in first order logic. This first approximation shows the advantages of GP as a KDD (Knowledge Discovery in Databases) extraction technique.

GP was also used as a rule extraction technique in combination with decision trees, where the functions in the nodes of the trees use one or more variables (Bot, 1999), but this combination makes the algorithm design very complicated. More recently, Engelbrecht et al. (2001) applied GP and decision trees to extract knowledge from databases, designing an algorithm called BGP (Building-Block Approach to Genetic Programming). In this algorithm, GP is combined with decision trees, but, in this case, it is centered in the concept of a building block, which represents a condition or a node of the tree. A building block has three parts: an attribute, a relational operator, and a threshold. Rules are obtained by combining different values of the parts of the building blocks in the shape of decision trees.

A new research area is the use of GP to extract knowledge from Artificial Neural Networks (ANNs). An ANN (see Lippmann, 1987; Haykin, 1999) is an information-processing system based on generalizations of human cognition or neural biology. An ANN consists of many simple computational neural units connected to each other. An input is presented to its input units, this input vector is propagated through the whole network, and finally, some kind of output is spit out. The most common type of ANN (and the one used in this chapter) consists of different layers with some neurons on each and connected with feed-forward connections (i.e., the exit of one neuron cannot go to the entrance of a neuron of the same or previous layer) and trained with the backpropagation algorithm (Johansson et al., 1992).

ANNs have proven to be a powerful tool in many different applications, but they have a big problem. The reasoning process they follow cannot be explained, i.e. there is no clear relationship between the inputs presented to the network and the outputs they return. To solve this problem, GP can be applied to perform rule extraction on these pairs of given inputs/returned outputs in order to be able to understand the behavior of ANNs.

Description of the Problem

The iris flower data (SAS Institute, 1988) were originally published by Fisher (1936) as examples of discriminant analysis and cluster analysis. Four parameters, *sepal length, sepal width, petal length* and *petal width*, were measured in millimeters on 50 iris specimens from each of three species, *Iris setosa, Iris versicolor* and *Iris virginica*. Given the four parameters, one should be able to determine which of the three classes a specimen belongs to. There are 150 data points listed in the database.

One of the reasons for applying this problem is the physical situation of the classes in the four-dimensional space. Figure 1 shows the space distribution for variables X_1 and X_2 (petal length and petal width). As shown in Duch et al. (2000), with these two variables, we can get a higher discrimination for the three classes, a fitness of a 98 percent success using only these two variables. So, they are an important reference point for comparing the results graphically.

In this chapter, we will show how we can use GP and ANNs to solve the iris flower problem. When we use GP, we will see two different points of view. In the first, we will use GP to obtain a rule classifier system (one-tree classification); in the second, we will try to find a Boolean expression for each of the three species to determine if the data belongs to that class (three-tree classification).

We will also use an ANN to solve this problem and, in order to understand the network obtained, we will use GP to extract the rules that explain its behavior. We will see how GP seems to be a suitable technique, not just for classifying problems, but also for extracting knowledge from databases and ANNs and data mining in general.

Figure 1. Distribution of the Three Classes

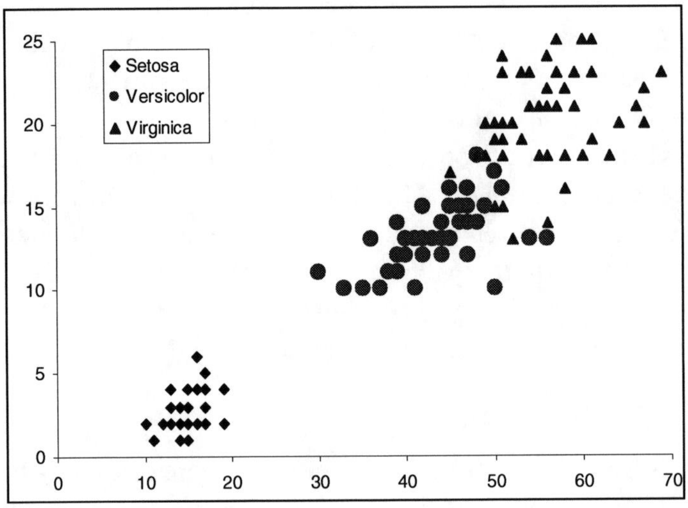

RULE EXTRACTION FROM DATABASE WITH GP

In this section, we will show how we can apply GP to extract knowledge from databases. In particular, we will apply it to extract rules to solve the iris problem in two different ways: with one rule that makes the classifications, or with three rules, one each for determining whether a sample belongs to a class or not.

One-Tree Classification

In this part, we will configure and run GP to obtain a single tree that makes a classification of the data points. Here, we will show how we can improve the performance of GP by pre-processing the data and, this way, obtain better results.

Classification with No Pre-Processing

Here, we will solve the problem with the data taken as is, with no modification at all.

Configuration

As explained in earlier, to make it possible to run GP, we need to specify the terminal and function sets.

Since we want to obtain a flower classification, we will need to make trees with a concrete structure. We will use the typing properties of GP to do this. We will ask GP to make trees with a special type: FLOWER_TYPE.

To have the trees as classifier rules, we need three terminals and one function returning that type. These terminals are *Setosa*, *Virginica* and *Versicolor*, one for each type of flower. The function is IF-THEN-ELSE, which accepts, as first input, a Boolean expression and, as second and third inputs, expressions with FLOWER_TYPE type, whether they are one of the three terminals or other IF-THEN-ELSE expressions.

So, the resulting trees will have the shape of a decision rule. For example:

IF <boolean expression>
THEN
    IF <boolean expression>
    THEN **Virginica**
    ELSE **Versicolor**
ELSE
    IF <boolean expression>
    THEN **Setosa**
    ELSE **Versicolor**

To build the Boolean expressions, we will use as terminals the variables X_1, X_2, X_3 and X_4, which stand for *petal width*, *petal length*, *sepal width* and *sepal length*, respectively (all four variables real numbers); and we will use the random constants, extracted from the real interval between 1 and 80. We chose this interval because it contains the maximum and minimum values those four variables can have.

We also have the traditional arithmetic operators +, -, * and %, standing % for the division-protected operator, which returns a value of 1 if the denominator is equal to 0.

For building Boolean expressions, relational and Boolean operands are required; relational for establishing relations between the real expressions (containing those four variables and constants) and Boolean operators for joining other Boolean expressions, if necessary.

The complete set of terminals and functions, with their types and their children types, in case of being functions, can be seen in Table 1.

Table 1. Terminal and Function Sets Used for the One-Tree Classification

	Name	Returning type	Parameter type
Terminal set	X_1, X_2, X_3, X_4	REAL	
	[1, 80]	REAL	
	Setosa, Verginica, Versicolor	FLOWER_TYPE	
Function set	IF-THEN-ELSE	FLOWER_TYPE	BOOLEAN, FLOWER_TYPE, FLOWER_TYPE
	+, -, *, %	REAL	REAL, REAL
	<, >,>=,<=	BOOLEAN	REAL, REAL
	AND, OR	BOOLEAN	BOOLEAN, BOOLEAN
	NOT	BOOLEAN	BOOLEAN

Results

For solving this problem, different combinations of parameters were used. The set with which we obtained better results can be seen in Table 2.

The result is a classification rule with a fitness of 99.33 percent success: it fails in one case out of a possible 150. The rule obtained, after 23 hours of computing in an AMD K7 at 1 GHz and 128 MB of RAM, is the following:

IF (X_2 < 25.370) THEN SetosaELSEIF ((((X_2-40.959)%X_2)<(X_2-(X_3-(X_1%(X_1-(X_4-23.969))))) AND ((X_2 % (X_2 - 42.760) <(X_2-(23.969%(X_2-(X_4-(X_2-34.507)))))) AND (((X_1-10.856)%(X_2-40.959))<(X_2-(X_3-((X_2-42.760)% (X_1-21.777))))))) AND (((X_2-X_3 < (X_4-(X_2 % (X_2 - (X_4 - (X_2 - (X_4 - (X_2 - (X_3-((X_2-40.959)%(X_1-21.777)))))))))))) AND (((X_2 % (X_2-(X_4-(X_2-(X_3-(X_1 % (X_2-40.959))))))) % (X_2-40.959))<X_2-(X_3-(X_1%(X_1-21.777))))) AND ((23.969 % (X_1 - 10.856)) < ((X_2- (23.969 % (X_2- (X_4- (X_2-(X_3-((X_2-40.959) % (X_2-X_3-21.777)))))))))-(X_2% (X_2-(X_4-(X_2-40.959))))))))))) AND ((X_3- ((X_2-40.959)%(X_1-21.777)))>21.777))

Table 2. Best Parameters for Solving with GP

Selection algorithm	Tournament
Crossover rate	95%
Mutation rate	4%
Population size	500 individuals
Parsimony level	0.0001

THEN Virginica
ELSE Versicolor

Classification with Pre-Processing

Now we will see how we can improve the performance of GP by pre-processing the data. What we will do is normalize the data to make all four parameters be in the interval [0,1]. We do this to make these four variables be in the same rank. So, for GP, it will be easier to make and combine mathematical expressions including constants, because these will be in similar ranks. We won't be combining expressions with out-of-rank values.

Configuration

Since we still want to obtain one tree with the shape of an IF-THEN-ELSE classifier rule, we will use a terminal set and a function set similar to the ones explained in the previous section and shown in Table 1. The only exception is the use of random constants: now they will not be within the rank [1,80], but in the rank [0,1] because, as we have the data normalized in that rank, we need the constants to be in the same rank, too.

Results

The best set of parameters found for solving this problem is the same as described in the previous section, shown in Table 2. With these parameters, the best expression found, with a fitness of 100 percent, computed with the same machine and after seven hours, is the following:

IF (X_2 < 0.373)
THEN **Setosa**
ELSE IF ((((0.483>((X_4-0.799)*(0.483%(X_1-X_2)))) AND (X_3> 0.701)
OR (X_4>(X_1-(0.182+X3)*(0.483%(X_1-X_2)))))) OR ((((-0.132) * ((X_1
* X_2) % ((0.821 * (0.721-(X_1 - (0.182+X_3)))) - (0.182+X_3)))) >
(0.483%(X_1-0.701)))))
THEN
IF ((((X_4>(-0.132*((X_1*X_1)%(0.721-(0.182+X_3))))) AND (X_4 > ((-
0.132) * (0.483 % (0.721 - (((X_1-((0.182+X_3) * 0.877))*(0.483%(X_1-
X_2)))*(0.483 %(0.182+X_3))))))))
AND (0.821>((-0.132)* (0.483%(X_1-0.701)))))) AND (X_4>(-
0.132*(X_4 % (0.721-(((X_1-(0.182+X_3)) *(0.483%(X_1-X_2))) *
(0.483%(0.182+X_3)))))))))) OR ((X_3>(X_1-(-0.132))) OR

$((X_2>0.721)$ AND $(X_4>((-0.132)*(0.483\%(X_1-$
$((0.182+X_3)*0.877))))))))$
THEN
      IF $((((0.721>(X_2*X_4))$ AND $(X_4>X_2))$ OR $(((X_1<0.877)$ OR
      $(0.799>X_4))$ OR $(X_3>0.799)))$
      THEN **Verginica**
      ELSE **Versicolor**
   ELSE **Versicolor**
ELSE **Versicolor**

Note that the second expression (obtained with pre-processing) has better fitness (100%), and has been found in less time. So with a small pre-processing of the data, we improved the performance of GP in both the fitness obtained and in the time taken to develop the desired expression.

Three-Tree Classification

In this section, we will solve the problem from a different point of view. We will use GP, not for making a simple classification into one of the three classes, but to extract three Boolean rules to determine whether a particular data point belongs to each species of flower.

As we have three decision rules, it will have an additional advantage: if, for the same data point, none of the rules determines an output as true, or if more than one makes an output as true, then we can conclude that this point is not well classified by the system. We can detect some errors made by the system.

Table 3. Terminal and Function Sets Used for the Three-Tree Classification

	Name	**Returning type**	**Parameter type**
Terminal set	X_1, X_2, X_3, X_4	REAL	
	[0, 1]	REAL	
Function set	IF-THEN-ELSE	BOOLEAN	BOOLEAN, BOOLEAN, BOOLEAN
	+, -, *, %	REAL	REAL, REAL
	<, >,>=,<=	BOOLEAN	REAL, REAL
	AND, OR	BOOLEAN	BOOLEAN, BOOLEAN
	NOT	BOOLEAN	BOOLEAN

Table 4. Expressions Obtained for Classifying into the Three Different Classes

Flower type	Expression obtained	Fitness
Setosa	$(X_1 < 0.3141)$	100%
Versicolor	$((((0.677 > X_3)$ OR $(0.526 < X_2 < (0.736)))$ AND $((((0.610 < X_1 < 0.721)$ OR $((0.3360 < X_1 < 0.526)$ OR $(0.526 < X_2 < 0.721)))$ AND $((X_3 > X_1)$ OR $(0.677 > X_1))))$	100%
Virginica	$(((X_1 > X_2)$ OR $(X_2 > 0.718))$ AND $((X_2 > X_4)$ OR $((((0.739 < X_2 < 0.765)$ OR $(X_4 > 0.902))$ OR $(X_1 > X_3))))$	99.33%

Configuration

To obtain these Boolean rules, we configure GP to obtaining Boolean expressions. The resulting type will be BOOLEAN. As Boolean elements, we will have the IF-THEN-ELSE classifier rules (accepting three children with BOOLEAN type), the relational operators needed to establish relations between variables and constants, and Boolean operators.

We will also need the four variables and random constants now inside the interval [0,1] because now we are working directly with normalized values. The complete terminal and function sets are shown in Table 3.

Table 5. Comparison Between the Method Proposed Here and Other Methods

Method	Type	Fitness	Reference
Proposed here	Rules	100%	
ReFuNN	Fuzzy	95.7%	(Kasabov, 1996)
C-MLP2LN	Crisp	98.0%	(Duch et al, 2000)
SSV	Crisp	98.0%	(Duch et al, 2000)
ANN	Weigths	98.67%	(Martinez and Goddard, 2001)
Grobian	Rough	100.0%	(Browne et al, 1998)
GA+NN	Weigths	100.0%	(Jagielska et al, 1996)
NEFCLASS	Fuzzy	96.7%	(Nauck et al, 1996)
FuNe-I	Fuzzy	96.0%	(Halgamuge and Glesner, 1999)

Figure 2. Distributions Obtained for the Three Classes

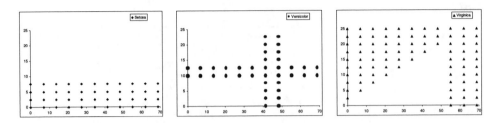

Results

The set of parameters which gave better results is the same as described in the previous section and shown in Table 2. With these elements, the results obtained, with the inputs already normalized, can be seen in Table 4. Note that the third expression (used for *Iris Virginica*) has a fitness of 99.33 percent success, i.e., it fails in one case out of the 150. This case is classified by the system as both *Virginica* and *Versicolor* (false, true, true), which is an invalid exit and it is detected. So, we can say that the system doesn't have any failures and gets a fitness of 100 percent success.

The comparison with other techniques can be seen in Table 5.

The distributions obtained from these three rules can be seen in Figure 2. In this graph, and in the one following, the X axis references petal width (X_1) and the Y axis references petal length (X_2).

Figure 3. Distributions Obtained from the Rules and from the Training Set

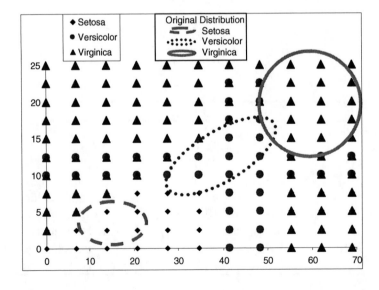

We can put these three distributions together in the same graph and compare them with the training set. This is shown in Figure 3.

In this figure, we can see that the rule extraction system tries to join those values which depend on each classification and tries to isolate them from those values which are dependent on other classifications. The intersection areas are those in which the system makes incorrect outputs, indicating that the given output is not correct and that an individual analysis is necessary for those values to determine to which class they belong.

RULE EXTRACTION FROM ANNS

In this section, we will solve the iris problem with an ANN, and then we will use GP to obtain the mathematical equations that explain the relation between the inputs and outputs of the ANN.

Martinez and Goddard (2001) proved that a maximum adjustment of 98.67 percent correct answers (two errors) is achieved with six neurons in the

Figure 4. Obtained ANN

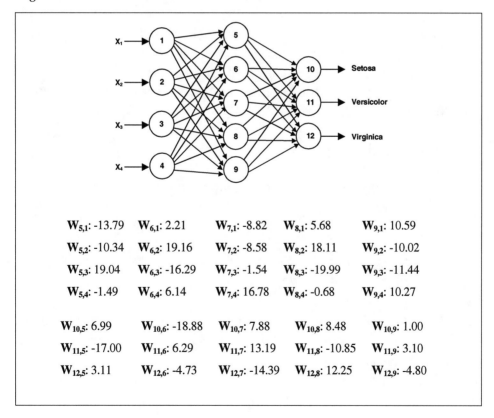

$W_{5,1}$: -13.79	$W_{6,1}$: 2.21	$W_{7,1}$: -8.82	$W_{8,1}$: 5.68	$W_{9,1}$: 10.59
$W_{5,2}$: -10.34	$W_{6,2}$: 19.16	$W_{7,2}$: -8.58	$W_{8,2}$: 18.11	$W_{9,2}$: -10.02
$W_{5,3}$: 19.04	$W_{6,3}$: -16.29	$W_{7,3}$: -1.54	$W_{8,3}$: -19.99	$W_{9,3}$: -11.44
$W_{5,4}$: -1.49	$W_{6,4}$: 6.14	$W_{7,4}$: 16.78	$W_{8,4}$: -0.68	$W_{9,4}$: 10.27
$W_{10,5}$: 6.99	$W_{10,6}$: -18.88	$W_{10,7}$: 7.88	$W_{10,8}$: 8.48	$W_{10,9}$: 1.00
$W_{11,5}$: -17.00	$W_{11,6}$: 6.29	$W_{11,7}$: 13.19	$W_{11,8}$: -10.85	$W_{11,9}$: 3.10
$W_{12,5}$: 3.11	$W_{12,6}$: -4.73	$W_{12,7}$: -14.39	$W_{12,8}$: 12.25	$W_{12,9}$: -4.80

hidden layer. With the system put forward by Rabuñal (1999) and five hidden neurons, tangent hyperbolic Activation functions and threshold function of 0.5 in the output neurons, the previous register has improved (with regard to the number of hidden neurons), reaching also a 98.67 percent of correct answers. In the cases with *Iris setosa*, no error is obtained; in the cases with *Iris versicolor* and *Iris virginica*, two errors are made, which are not detected because the ANN produces a valid classification (only one true output), but an erroneous one.

The architecture and connection weights obtained may be observed in Figure 4.

Now we have a network trained to solve the problem. However, the problem now is to understand how this network works. This is a problem present in the world of ANNs that has made many experts reluctant to use them because they need, not only to solve their problems, but also to know how the system solves them.

To understand how the ANN solves this problem, we will apply GP as we did before (this time, we will use the three-tree classifier system) to the pairs' input/ANN output. Now, the desired outputs will not be those of the problem, but the ones returned by the ANN to the inputs. So, we will obtain rules that explain the behavior of the ANN when it produces those outputs. If we apply this rule-discovery system with the same parameter configuration that we have previously seen, the following rules have been obtained.

The following rule has been obtained from the inputs-outputs of the ANN corresponding to the classification of *Iris setosa, and* produces an adjustment of 100 percent correct answers:

$$(X_1 < 0.3116)$$

The rule obtained from the inputs-outputs of the ANN corresponding to the classification of *Iris versicolor* produces an adjustment of 100 percent correct answers, being the following:

$$((0.2892 < X_1 < 0.5316) \text{ OR } (((X_3 > X_2) \text{ OR } ((X_4 > 0.7643) \text{ AND } (X_2 > X_1)))$$
$$\text{AND } (0.5316 < X_2 < 0.7268)))$$

The rule obtained from the inputs-outputs of the ANN corresponding to the classification of *Iris virginica* produces an adjustment of 100 percent correct answers, being the following:

Figure 5.   Distribution Obtained of the Three Classes Produced by the Rules from the ANN

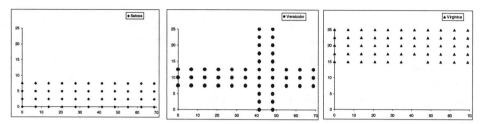

$$(((X_1 > X_3) \text{ AND } (X_1 > X_2)) \text{ OR } (((0.5497 < X_1) \text{ AND}$$
$$((0.5497 > X_3) \text{ OR } (0.7279 < X_2))) \text{ AND } (0.6787 < X_2)))$$

If we analyze the results obtained, we may observe the distributions carried out by the ANN and the rules obtained by using the analysis file. It is shown in Figure 5.

FUTURE WORKS

Once we explain the reasoning process of the ANN with the training patterns, the next step is to carry out this explanation process with a complete set of patterns, not only those used for training. For this purpose, it will be necessary to create a system that produces new patterns, gives them to the network, and runs GP with the produced outputs. This process should be continuous, changing the patterns as needed while the explanation process goes on.

CONCLUSION

As shown in the results, GP seems to be a powerful technique for extracting knowledge from different systems. In this chapter, it has been applied to two systems, a database and an ANN, using a well-known problem, the iris flower data. We achieved good results with the additional advantage of having as results presented as mathematical expressions which show the relationships among the parameters.

When we used GP to extract knowledge from databases, we saw two different points of view, using one expression or three different expressions to make the classification.

In the first attempt, the one-tree classifier, we show how we can adapt GP to produce decision rules with the desired shape, and, therefore, how we can obtain high-level explicit knowledge about the system. In this part, we can also see that it is better to do a pre-processing of the data to improve the performance of GP. This is so because we gave all of the parameters the same rank; so, the system finds it easier to work with all variables and constants in the same rank (i.e., it does not find problems in combining constants and values with much different values). We can conclude that, with a minimum analysis of the data, we can improve the process in two ways: in the final success and in the time needed to obtain it.

The second attempt, the three-tree classifier, gave additional knowledge. With the construction of three different Boolean expressions, one for each class, we obtained an additional knowledge. Now we can detect errors made by the system.

GP, then, is shown to be a suitable technique for extracting knowledge from databases, not only in classification problems. Its ability to adapt to many different environments (the user selects which operator is needed to be included in the sets) allows for the extraction of mathematical relations, decision rules, etc.

But we also used GP to extract knowledge from a more complicated system, an ANN. The extraction of the knowledge contained in it has made it possible to understand the network. This rule extraction process for ANNs can be used on any network, therefore, making possible their use in many other application areas where the ability to explain the reasoning processes is important.

REFERENCES

Bonarini, A. (1996). Evolutionary learning of fuzzy rules: Competition and cooperation. In W. Pedrycz (Ed.), *Fuzzy Modelling: Paradigms and Practice.* Norwell, MA: Kluwer Academic.

Bot, M. (1999). *Application of genetic programming to induction of linear classification trees.* Amsterdam, Netherlands: Vrije Universiteit. (Final Term Project Report)

Browne, C., Düntsch, I. & Gediga, G. (1998). IRIS revisited: A comparison of discriminant and enhanced rough set data analysis. In L. Polkowski & A. Skowron (Eds.), *Rough Sets in Knowledge Discovery* (vol. 2, pp. 345-368). Heidelberg, Germany: Physica Verlag.

Darwin, C. (1864). *On the Origin of Species by Means of Natural Selection or the Preservation of Favoured Races in the Struggle for Life.* Cambridge, UK: Cambridge University Press.

Duch, W., Adamczak, R. & Grabczewski, K. (2000). A new methodology of extraction, optimisation and application of crisp and fuzzy logical rules. *IEEE Transactions on Neural Networks, 11*(2).

Engelbrecht, A. P., Rouwhorst, S. E., & Schoeman, L. (2001). A building block approach to genetic programming for rule discovery. In H. Abbass, R. Sarkar & C. Newton (Eds.), *Data Mining: A Heuristic Approach.* Hershey, PA: Idea Group.

Fayyad, U., Piatetsky-Shapiro, U. G., Smyth, P., & Uthurusamy, R. (1996). *Advances in Knowledge Discovery and Data Mining.* Menlo Park, CA: AAAI/MIT Press.

Fisher, R. A. (1936). The use of multiple measurements in taxonomic problems. *Annals of Eugenics* (pp. 179-188).

Fuchs, M. (1998). Crossover versus mutation: An empirical and theoretical case study. In *Proceedings of the 3rd Annual Conference on Genetic Programming.* San Francisco, CA: Morgan Kauffman.

Halgamuge, S. K. & Glesner, M. (1994). Neural networks in designing fuzzy systems for real world applications. *Fuzzy Sets and Systems, 65*, 1-12.

Haykin, S. (1999). *Neural Networks* (2nd ed.). Englewood Cliffs, NJ: Prentice Hall.

Jagielska, I., Matthews, C. & Whitfort, T. (1996). The application of neural networks, fuzzy logic, genetic algorithms and rough sets to automated knowledge acquisition. In *Proceedings of the 4th International Conference on Soft Computing (IIZUKA'96), Japan.* (vol. 2, pp. 565-569).

Johansson, E. M., Dowla, F. U., & Goodman, D. M. (1992). Backpropagation learning for multi-layer feed-forward neural networks using the conjugate gradient method. *International Journal of Neural Systems, 2*(4), 291-301.

Kasabov, N. (1996). *Foundations of Neural Networks, Fuzzy Systems and Knowledge Engineering.* Cambridge, MA: MIT Press.

Koza, J. (1992). *Genetic Programming: On the Programming of Computers by Means of Natural Selection.* Cambridge, MA: MIT Press.

Koza, J. (1994). *Genetic Programming II: Automatic Discovery of Reusable Programs.* Cambridge, MA: MIT Press.

Lippmann, R. P. (1987). An introduction to computing with neural nets. *IEEE ASSP Magazine.*

Luke, S. & Spector, L. (1998). A revised comparison of crossover and mutation in genetic programming. In *Proceedings of the 3rd Annual Conference on Genetic Programming.* San Francisco, CA: Morgan Kauffman.

Martínez, A. & Goddard, J. (2001). Definición de una red neuronal para clasificación por medio de un programa evolutivo. *Mexican Journal of Biomedical Engineering, 22,* 4-11.

Montana, D. J. (1995). Strongly typed genetic programming. *Evolutionary Computation, 3*(2), 199-200.

Nauck, D., Nauck, U. & Kruse, R. (1996). Generating classification rules with the neuro-fuzzy system NEFCLASS. *Proceedings of the Biennal Conference of the North American Fuzzy Information Processing Society (NAFIPS'96),* Berkeley, California.

Rabuñal Dopico, J. R. (1999). *Entrenamiento de redes de neuronas artificiales mediante algoritmos genéticos.* A Coruña, Spain: Universidad da Coruña, Facultad de Informática. (Graduate Thesis)

SAS/STAT user's guide (Release 6.03 ed.). (1998). Cary, NC: SAS Institute Inc.

Wong, M. L. & Leung, K. S. (2000). *Data Mining Using Grammar Based Genetic Programming and Applications.* Norwell, MA: Kluwer Academic.

Chapter X

Social Coordination with Architecture for Ubiquitous Agents — CONSORTS

Koichi Kurumatani, AIST, Japan

ABSTRACT

We propose a social coordination mechanism that is realized with CONSORTS, a new kind of multi-agent architecture for ubiquitous agents. By social coordination, we mean mass users' decision making in their daily lives, such as the mutual concession of spatial-temporal resources achieved by automatic negotiation of software agents, rather than by verbal and explicit communication directly done by human users. The prerequisite infrastructure for such an electronic negotiation mechanism is a multi-agent architecture for ubiquitous agents that are grounded in the physical world, by which software agents can trace users' moving history, understand their intentions and preferences, and negotiate each other, all while protecting users' privacy through temporal identifiers. The functionality of social coordination is realized in the agent architecture, where three kinds of agents work cooperatively, i.e., a personal agent that serves as proxy of the user; a social coordinator working as a service agent; and a spatio-temporal reasoner. We also summarize some basic mechanisms of social coordination functionality, including stochastic distribution and market mechanisms.

INTRODUCTION

Social coordination is observed in many scenes in our daily lives. People give way to each other when they happen to pass in a corridor or on the road even if they have not met before. And, when purchasing a train or plane ticket, people often give up their position in line to a really hurrying person. In this chapter, we handle the problem of how such social coordination can be realized as an information service by cooperative software agents that are embedded in social infrastructure.

Based on the rapid development of information technology, we can expect that highly-distributed information processors and sensors will be linked by a network. And, in the near future, they will be grounded to the physical world and embedded in social infrastructure, e.g., rooms, buildings, streets, and roads. In such environments, called ubiquitous or pervasive computing environments, one of the keys to providing several kinds of services for people and society is software agent technology.

The purpose of this research is to show a way to realize a social coordination mechanism in daily life through cooperating agents. By social coordination, we mean automatic negotiation by software agents working as a proxy for users, as opposed to the explicit and verbal communication done directly by human users. We have to pay attention to the difference between social coordination and collaboration. Collaboration means highly-organized activity by human users in order to achieve goals that have not been solved, which usually takes long time to obtain a solution. In contrast, social coordination requires real-time responses, e.g., we have to react rapidly to give a traffic lane to others. On the other hand, the best solution cannot be necessarily acquired through social coordination. Even if the best solution is not obtained, if we can reduce just one percent of the traffic in a city or in a country, it will bring much benefit to the economy and environment.

Reflecting the nature of the problem, social coordination requires different approaches from the ones developed for collaboration, e.g., CSCW (Computer-Supported Cooperative Work), Collaborative Multiagent (Grosz & Kraus, 1996), conventional web-based meeting site, and so on.

EXAMPLE: MASS USER SUPPORT
IN THEME PARK

One of the examples of social coordination is mass user navigation in a theme park (see Kurumatani, 2002; Kurumatani, 2003). At present, services such as information providing and reservations for attractions are made possible through conventional web-based agent technology. Our intention is to provide more sophisticated services by using the user's situation. One such service is mass user navigation (Figure 1). People tend to make reservations for a popular attraction regardless of the crowd in front of it, and they might ignore less-crowded despite a fair amount of interest. By coordinating users' intentions and preferences, there is a possibility of controlling resource coordination, such as congestion, while keeping users' satisfied. In other words, mass user navigation means coordinating resources to exchange users' intentions and preferences in order to keep them happy.

In the following sections, we explain the underlying architecture, called CONSORTS, for ubiquitous agents, and we give the formalization of the mass user navigation. The architecture CONSORTS is designed to provide mass user support, in addition to conventional personal support services, in a ubiquitous computing environment.

Figure 1. Theme Park Problem

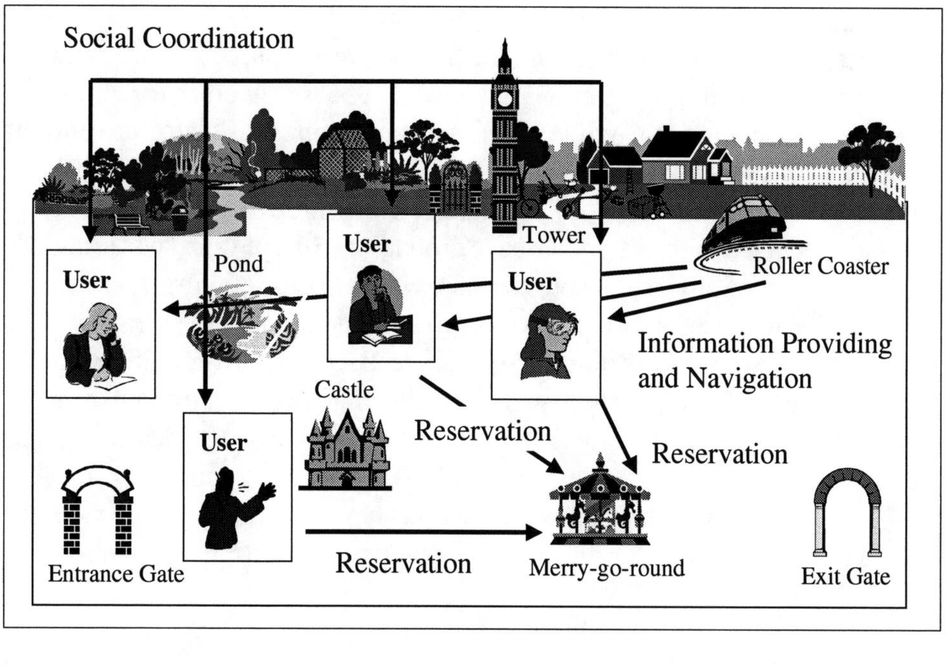

Figure 2. CONSORTS: Architecture for Ubiquitous Agents

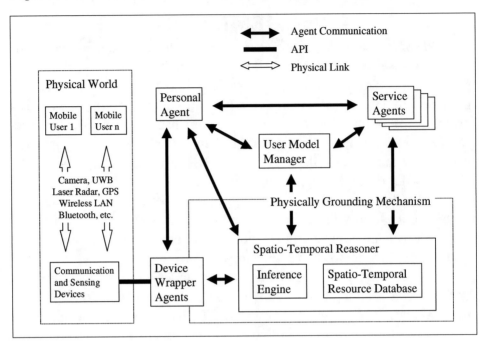

CONSORTS: ARCHITECTURE FOR UBIQUITOUS AGENTS

CONSORTS (an architecture for COgNitive reSOurce management with physically-gRounding agenTS) is a new kind of architecture for ubiquitous agents. It is designed to realize mass user support in addition to conventional personal assistance. The key concepts in CONSORTS are "semantic grounding" and "cognitive resources." By using sensory information brought through a ubiquitous environment, agents have grounding to the physical world and they are conscious of physical resources (especially spatio-temporal resources) in a cognitive way, i.e., they can recognize, reorganize, and operate raw physical resources as cognitive resources. Services realized in CONSORTS include (1) extension of conventional personal services using information about the physical world, such as position; and (2) mass user support that provides information and social coordination for mass users beyond personal support.

In the architecture, we assume that users have mobile information devices such as PDAs or cellular phones, and that users' positions are captured by sensors, such as cameras or wireless LANs. We also assume that their history of moving is tracked by sensors and registered in a spatio-temporal reasoner. Service agents provide situation-based services that use information about a user's position and moving history. One such situation-based service provides information according to a user's position. For example, when a user happens to get near an attraction that he might be interested in, a navigation agent gives the user directions on how to get there.

Mass user navigation consists of two parts. The first part is *personal service*, which directs users to their favorite places according to their intentions and preferences. In other words, it maximizes the number of places they want to visit, and it minimizes moving distance and time while obtaining needed guidance information. The second part is *social coordination service*, which tries to decrease congestion and total moving distance and time for all users by making plans for all the users by coordinating their intentions and preferences. Another important part in this architecture is a *user model* which describes the user, i.e., (1) Intention: Goals that the user should achieve in a period, such as a day; (2) Preference: Goals that the user expects to visit in the period; and (3) Attribute: A static description about the user that can be used to retrieve suitable information.

FORMALIZATION OF THE PROBLEM: RESOURCE SPACE, PLAN, UTILITY

In this section, we formalize the problem of mass user navigation in order to deal with it by computational methods. The formalization is as follows. The symbol U denotes the set of all users, while u denotes each user, i.e.:

$$U = \{u_i \mid i \in [1, n_u]\}, \quad n_u = |U|. \quad T = \{t_i \mid i \in [1, n_t]\}, \quad n_t = |T|.$$

$$S = \{s_i \mid i \in [1, n_s]\}, \quad n_s = |S|. \quad R = T \times S = \{r_{ij} = (t_i, s_j)\}.$$

The set T is given as temporal segments in the form of a simple discrete representation of time. The set S is given as spatial segments in the form of a qualitative representation of space, e.g., a region corresponding to the neighborhood of an attraction in a theme park, or a region in which users can access a specific wireless LAN access point (see Kurumatani, 1995; Kurumatani & Nakamura, 1997). Social resource set R is defined as the direct product of the temporal segments and spatial segments. The capacity of resources is represented as a function: $cap(r) : R \rightarrow \Re$.

A plan is a point sequence in the resource set R along time, where there is no same temporal segment in the resource sequence of any plan. Therefore, a user cannot be in two or more spatial segments at a time. When there is no common temporal segment that belongs to some pair of plans selected from the original ones, more than one plan can be connected to become a longer one, i.e.:

$$plan_{new} = connect(plan_1, ..., plan_n) = \cup \, plan_i, \quad i \in [1,n],$$

$$\text{if} \quad \forall \, plan_i \, (\forall \, plan_j \, (\neg \exists \, t_k \, (plan_i = (t_k,*) \wedge plan_j = (t_k,*)))), \quad i \neq j,$$

$$* \text{ is any of spatial segments.}$$

This connection process is mainly used to generate a new candidate of plans from simple short ones. From the viewpoint of search in artificial intelligence, the search space has the complexity of the number of S to the number of T: $O(Plan) = |S|^{|T|}$, where $Plan$ is the set of all possible plans.

The resource space where plans are generated and verified is shown in Figure 3. The vertical axis shows the time flow represented by temporal segments; the horizontal axis shows the spatial segments. A plan for an individual user is shown as a broken line, and congestion (resource conflict) occurs on the place shown by circles. If the capacity of resources at the place is less than the number of total plans crossing there, congestion occurs at the place in the resource set.

Another important element in the formalization is the utility of plans, which is used to measure their effectiveness for individual users and society. Basically, both of the utilities can be defined arbitrarily to control the reasoning process. In our formalization, as a utility for individuals, we use (1) the linear addition of the evaluation of each resource, and (2) the evaluation of special sequences appearing in the plan. As a utility for society, we use macro-attributes of the society, e.g., degree of congestion, use ratio of resources, environment pollution, and so on. It is difficult to balance two kinds of utilities for individuals and society. The criteria for the balance are deeply connected with the policy of what kind of social coordination we want to realize. For the present, we use linear addition for both types of utilities.

Figure 3. Plans and Congestion in Resource Space

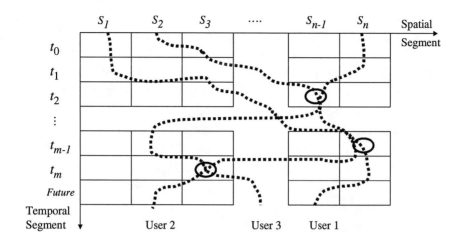

APPROACHES TO THE PROBLEM

We can take many kinds of approaches to the problem. At first sight, it seems a kind of planning or scheduling problem in an artificial intelligence sense. Although determining a plan for an individual user can be executed by planning, social coordination cannot be handled well by conventional planning and scheduling techniques that lack real-time response.

Genetic algorithm (GA) or reinforcement learning works well because of its ability to generating new, flexible plans, but it also lacks real-time response. Stochastic distribution, e.g., CSMA/CD used in Ethernet (IEEE802.3) for packet collision avoidance, works fast, but it cannot generate good plans because it doesn't take the user's intention or preferences into consideration.

Another approach is to introduce some kind of market or auction mechanism by preparing a kind of bulletin board where a part of plan linked to users' intention or preferences is exchanged among users. Market or auction mechanisms reflect an individual user's model and generate good plans faster than planning, GA, and reinforcement learning, but it is slower than stochastic distribution.

To summarize the candidates for social coordination mechanism, each candidate has merits and demerits as follows:

(1) **Combinatorial Optimization.** Coordination problem can be formalized as combinatorial optimization problem (e.g., Lawler et al., 1985) in many

cases, which can generally be solved by genetic algorithm (Goldberg, 1989). This approach can give the most optimal solution, but real-time response is difficult.

(2) **Stochastic Distribution.** Stochastically distributing resources among users is a time-efficient approach (e.g., Floyd et al., 2001), which can be analyzed by a queuing network (e.g., Chao et al., 1999). The solutions obtained by this approach usually lack accuracy, i.e. obtained solutions are far from optimal ones.

(3) **Market Mechanism.** Methods based on market mechanism (see Wellman et al., 2001; Prado & Wurman, 2002) can reflect the flexibility of users' motivations and intentions, and it keeps real-time response. Basically, fluctuations are observed in market mechanisms, by which the behavior of the whole system can become unstable.

(4) **Planning and Scheduling.** Conventional AI planning and scheduling (e.g., Miyashita, 2000) are flexible methods that can control spatial and/ or temporal complexity and the accuracy of the solution by using heuristics. Unfortunately, preparing good heuristics for all kinds of problems is nearly impossible.

We are now designing an algorithm for mass user navigation based on the generation, connection, and evaluation of plans, with stochastic distribution and exchange in market and auction mechanism. The basic idea is that, first, we generate element plans for individual users, and then we connect the plans to increase both types of utilities. If congestion occurs in this process, we modify each user's plan by stochastically distributing its elements in the resource place. This algorithm itself seems to work well and fast, but it does not generate good candidates because it does not take the user's intention or preferences into consideration. We then introduce an exchange mechanism, by using a market-like bulletin board, in order to decrease the number of the applications of stochastic distributions.

CONCLUSION

In this chapter, we have proposed the concept of social coordination in daily life, which is a mutual concession mechanism for social resources, e.g., space, time, and reservations, through automatic negotiation among software agents rather than through the explicit and verbal communication of human users.

We have also proposed a new kind of architecture, called CONSORTS, for ubiquitous agents in which mass user support services are provided in addition to conventional personal supports.

As an example of social coordination, we have proposed, formalized and analyzed mass user navigation. Although mass user navigation seems to be a planning or scheduling problem at first sight, we have pointed out that conventional problem-solving mechanisms, such as planning, scheduling, GA, reinforcement learning, or stochastic distribution itself, do not work well. To solve the problem, we have proposed a method based on the generation, connection and evaluation of plans, with plan modifications by stochastic distribution and market/auction mechanism, i.e., a kind of bulletin board where users' intentions and preferences are exchanged among users.

Social coordination is not a part of social collaboration. It requires real-time response, although it cannot necessarily generate the best solutions. Real-time response does not seem to be crucial in the theme park problem, but it is really important in other applications, such as social coordination in traffic control, because we do not have much time for decision making in traffic and for navigation guidance when we drive a car. In addition, if we can reduce the amount of traffic in a city or country by just one percent, it will bring much benefit to the economy and environment.

Social coordination is working as an underlying mechanism in our daily lives. Our intention is to enhance such mutual concession mechanisms in a sophisticated way by using software agent technologies. Because this research is just beginning, we will examine and refine the definition of the problem and the algorithm to solve it, first by multi-agent simulation and later by applying it to real situations.

ACKNOWLEDGMENT

The author would like to thank Hidenori Kawamura, Akio Sashima and Noriaki Izumi for their comments and suggestions on social coordination and architecture for ubiquitous agents.

REFERENCES

Chao, X., Miyazawa, M., & Pinedo, M. (1999). *Queuing Networks*. New York: John Wiley & Sons.

Floyd, S., Gummadi, R., & Shenker, S. (2001). *Adaptive RED: An algorithm for increasing the robustness of RED*. To appear, http://citeseer.nj.nec.com/floyd01adaptive.html (Technical Report)

Goldberg, D. E. (1989). *Genetic Algorithms in Search, Optimization and Machine Learning*. Boston, MA: Addison-Wesley.

Grosz, B. & Kraus, S. (1996). Collaborative plans for complex group action. *Artificial Intelligence, 86*(2), 269-357.

Kurumatani, K. (1995). Generating causal networks for mobile multi-agent systems with qualitative regions. In *Proceedings of IJCAI'95, Montreal, Canada* (pp. 1750-1756).

Kurumatani, K. (2002). User intention market for multi-agent navigation - An artificial intelligent problem in engineering and economic context. In *Working notes of the AAAI-02 workshop on multi-agent modeling and simulation of economic systems (MAMSES-02)*.(pp. 1-4). Menlo Park, CA: AAAI Press. (Technical Report WS-02-10)

Kurumatani, K. (2003). Mass user support by social coordination among users. In *Working notes of the IJCAI'03 workshop on multiagent for mass user support* (pp. 58-59).

Kurumatani, K. & Nakamura, M. (1997). Qualitative analysis of causal graphs with equilibrium type-transition. In *Proceedings of IJCAI'97, Nagoya, Japan* (pp. 542-548).

Lawler, E. L., Lenstra, J. K., Rinnooy Kan, A. H. G., & Shmoys, D. B. (eds.). (1985). *The Traveling Salesman Problem: A Guided Tour of Combinatorial Optimization*. New York: John Wiley & Sons.

Miyashita, K. (2000). Learning scheduling control knowledge through reinforcements. *International Transactions in Operational Research, 7*(2), 125-138.

Prado, J. E. & Wurman, P. R. (2002). Non-cooperative planning in multiagent, resource-constrained environments with markets for reservations. In *Working notes of the AAAI-02 workshop on planning with and for multiagent systems* (pp. 60-66). Menlo Park, CA: AAAI Press. (Technical Report WS-02-12)

Wellman, M. P., Walsh, W. E., Wurman, P. R., & MacKie-Mason, J. K. (2001). Auction protocols for decentralized scheduling. *Games and Economic Behavior, 35*, 271-303.

Chapter XI

Agent-Mediated Knowledge Acquisition for User Profiling

A. Andreevskaia, Concordia University, Canada

R. Abi-Aad, Concordia University, Canada

T. Radhakrishnan, Concordia University, Canada

ABSTRACT

This chapter presents a tool for knowledge acquisition for user profiling in electronic commerce. The knowledge acquisition in e-commerce is a challenging task that requires specific tools in order to facilitate the knowledge transfer from the user to the system. The proposed tool is based on a hierarchical user model and is agent-based. The architecture of the tool incorporates four software agents: processing agent maintaining the user profile, validating agent interacting with the user when information validation is needed, monitoring agent monitoring the effects of the changes made to the user profile, and a filtering agent ensuring the safe information exchange with other software.

INTRODUCTION

In the past few years, Internet shopping has been growing rapidly. Most companies now try to offer a web service for online purchase and delivery in addition to their traditional sales and services. For consumers, this means a broader range of online stores from which to buy products. At the same time, this also means that users face more complexity in using these online services. This complexity, which arises due to factors such as information overloading or lack of relevant information, reduces the usability of e-commerce sites.

This fact is supported in a study presented by Schaffer and Sorflaten (1999) that revealed serious usability problems with e-commerce sites. In this study, respondents gave the following top three reasons for abandoning a web site during personal shopping: inability to find the sought item (56%); the site is disorganized or confusing (54%); and low speed in downloading the pages (53%).

Usability is a prerequisite for the success of e-commerce. If people cannot easily find a product, then they cannot buy it. It does not matter how cheap the products are (Nielsen Norman Group, 2001a). Besides that, customer loyalty depends on positive branding, which is associating a logo or a product with a positive emotional experience. When someone has a negative experience with a web site, being unable to find a product or navigate the site, they associate that negative experience with the brand. Firsthand experience is much more powerful in determining whether a customer will remain loyal to a brand, and no amount of marketing can overcome a negative experience such as being unable to use or find information on a web site (Rohn, 1998).

Since its very beginning, the Internet has been growing in popularity and complexity; the largeness makes it difficult for the user to find the information he needs. Often, it is more difficult for users to shop on the Internet than by conventional means. On the Internet, the user finds himself either "flooded" with irrelevant information mixed with some relevant information, or lacking relevant information altogether. In the context of B-to-C e-commerce type, we note the following:

- User interfaces play an important role in achieving user acceptance.
- Queries usually return more matches than the user can consult or fewer matches than expected.
- The user is "flooded" by unwanted and sometimes unsolicited information (e.g., advertisement banners that pop-up or appear as part of the main window of the browser).

- The information is sometimes very badly organized, which makes it difficult to read and scan through.
- Some of the cultural and ethical values of shopping in stores are missing when shopping through the Internet (trust, honesty, negotiation, policy, etc.)
- Some of the sites target a global clientele without adapting the site to the local needs — e.g., supporting multiple currencies (Nielsen Norman Group, 2001b), offering the information in multiple languages, and using universal metaphors or ones that are not specific to a given region or group of people (Hershlag, 1998). Examples of such metaphors can be found in Haque et al. (2001).

One possible way to help solve these problems is to personalize interactions and content between the user and the e-commerce system based on an appropriate user model. User modelling implies incorporating certain knowledge about the user. This knowledge describes what the user "likes" or what the user "knows" (Chin, 1986). It can help us to decide what kind of information he/she is interested in as well as how to present this information. For e-commerce, user modelling can be useful in four different ways (Lu, 1999):

- Providing personalized services to a particular user. For example, filtering out the information that does not correspond to the user's center of interest.
- Disambiguating the user's search input based on his user model. For example, filling in missing fields by anticipation in a query form.
- Providing proactive feedback to assist the user. For example, a hint message that pops up when the user is taking too long to perform a task.
- Presenting the information in a way suitable to the user's needs. For example, presenting the information in an appropriate language.

Many e-commerce sites (e.g., amazon.com and garden.com) already incorporate user-modelling capabilities for the purpose of personalizing the interactions. Major commercial software packages for e-commerce sites and portals developers often provide personalization capabilities as a standard feature [e.g., IBM Net Commerce (www-3.ibm.com/software/webservers/commerce/wcs_pro/), ATG Dynamo (www.atg.com), BroadVision (www.broadvision.com), and others]. The previous user models have been used to predict the user's preference in narrow and specific domains. The results of such work have been limited to suggesting novels or movies to the user, personalizing the navigation of catalogues, or adapting the information presentation (Ardissono & Goy, 2000). These models have been applied in bookstores, music stores and video stores. The main purpose of this personalization was to keep customers in the store longer or to attract more visitors to the site.

As shown by IBM High-Volume Web Site Team (2000) and Colkin (2001), we are currently witnessing a new shift in personalization toward catering to the needs of repeat customers, as well. Encouraging shoppers to return to an e-commerce web site is beneficial and challenging. One may use special promotions and discounts for this purpose or show tailored contents (i.e., information about specific products deemed to be interesting for this particular customer, different level of details for different users, etc.).

Our ultimate goal is to be able to deal with multiple domains while fulfilling the four tasks mentioned[1]. We explore the concepts of dynamic personalization and agent support. We describe a user-model named PIE[2] that is ontology-based and parameter driven and that can be helpful in broad domains, such as a shopping mall or a department store, as well as in narrow domains, such as bookstores. The second part of the chapter discusses methods for acquiring knowledge about the user's preferences.

AGENT-SUPPORTED DYNAMIC PERSONALIZATION

Dynamic personalization, or user profiling, can be understood as "matching customers and content in real time" (ILOG Press Release, 2000). But this definition is very general and, as further analysis shows, it gives rise to various interpretations. The study of several systems demonstrates that the term *dynamic personalization* is used in several ways. We describe three cases that are not mutually exclusive.

Case 1: In this case, dynamic personalization means that the content and/or parts of the user interface are dynamically generated according to a (static) user profile (e.g., http://www.interactivesites.com/pdfs/DARTmail_dynamicpers.pdf). Such systems are mostly commercial products for CRM (customer relationship management) activities, such as email campaigns, targeted advertisement, etc. Most commercial products claiming to provide dynamic personalization belong to this type.

Case 2: In the second case, there may be some a priori stored information about the user, but it is augmented by the dynamically varying "current context" of the user (e.g., http://www.indasea.com/dyper.htm or MIT media lab research in the domain of context-aware computing).

Case 3: In the third case, the user profile, or user's interest itself, is dynamic. The changes over time are captured through a chosen set of factors pertinent to the user. This approach is described in Hannigan and Palendrano (2002), and it is gaining popularity although it is still at the research stage (e.g., IBM Dynamic Personalization research project[3]). It can be combined with data about current user contexts when applicable. For example, a system of this kind has been suggested by Goto and Kambayashi (2001) for mobile passenger support systems in the use of public transportation.

In most cases, described in the e-commerce literature, dynamic personalization serves as a means to better target marketing campaigns. It is applied in refining the profile of an "ideal" customer to whom the advertisement and other promotional materials should be addressed, based on the mining logs of customers' acceptance or rejection of offers. Applying dynamic personalization to the maintenance of individual profiles of repeat customers in a store is a more challenging task that has not been given the attention it deserves, despite the popularity of the concept of one-to-one marketing. Most likely, this is due to the complexity of the task.

Creating and especially maintaining a dynamic user profile is a time-consuming, complex task that puts considerable load on the end-user and the knowledge engineer. To reduce the amount of effort required, software agents could possibly be employed at different stages of the process.

Software agents have been around for about two decades and have gained a considerable popularity in different areas of human-computer interaction[4]. There is no universally accepted definition of the term "agent" or "intelligent agent" (see Bradshaw, 1997; multiple references can be found in Terpsidis et al., 1997; Moukas et al., 1998; Negroponte, 1997). Software agents possess certain qualities that are common to this technology: they are autonomous, proactive, and knowledge-based; they assist the user and manifest social behavior[5]. E-commerce has been among the domains where agents play the most important role, ranging from "search-bots" to "auction-bots."

Most of the applications of agent technology to e-commerce have been centered in assisting sellers in web-service maintenance and monitoring, or helping buyers in the process of searching, auctioning and price negotiations (Desharnais, 2000). User modelling in the context of agent technology has been mostly interpreted in terms of building user profiles as part of an agent's knowledge base. However, in this chapter we are concerned with knowledge acquisition for personalization of the interaction between a virtual store and a customer rather than simply for transaction support in e-commerce (even though it is true that these two aspects influence each other).

Two distinct approaches to KA can be identified with regard to the knowledge about the individual user:

(a) "Knowledge capturing" by monitoring the dialog between the user and the system and intercepting the relevant data. This approach is useful for data mining operations that create new knowledge about the user. In this approach, the user does not contribute explicitly to the KA process. The captured data is used in 'data mining,' and the mined information is reviewed by knowledge engineers or by other specialists before it is used. A variant of this approach would be to apply the traditional AI-based machine learning techniques with no human intervention.

(b) "Knowledge elicitation" by a KA tool. This is a stand-alone phase in which the user contributes explicitly and directly to the building of a knowledge base about that individual.

It is possible to use agent technology in both of these approaches to reduce the burden on the human participants. Let us consider the following aspects of agent assistance that are labeled Assist-1, Assist-2, etc. These aspects will be illustrated through a wellness products store that will be our running example throughout the rest of the chapter.

The wellness store is a specialized boutique that sells healthy products such as organic food, vitamins and minerals, food supplements, etc. This kind of store has been growing in popularity in both brick-and-mortar and click-and-order versions. It has a specific customer base: people who shop there are health-conscious individuals who are willing to spend more for the perceived benefits of a healthy life-style. At the same time, their concerns and interests are very different, and there exists a large variety of products to cater to these diverse needs. Selecting the right kind of product is a complex task. A system that has information about a user's needs and constraints can considerably facilitate that task.

In the following, we will show how agents can assist in gathering and using user information in this case. The system under consideration has a product database, a user database containing individual user profiles, and a product taxonomy.

Assist-1: Agent assists in the initial profiling stage. Setting the initial profile will influence the further updates and usage of it; therefore, special care should be taken at this stage to assist the user in completing the questionnaire, as well as in selecting the most suitable stereotypes for filling in the missing values. At this stage, the agent will use stored knowledge about typical user characteristics to set missing values in the user model or to explain to the user how the parameter values might affect the system performance. The goal is to make a new user, just registering into the system, comfortable and informed about the questions asked in the building of the 'initial user profile' that is individualized.

For example, a first-time user who is registering in a wellness store can provide the system with some personal information, such as health concerns, age, etc. At this stage, the user input is the main source of information supplied to the agent. At the same time, this source has a priority over other sources — a parameter values set based on this input should have highest certainty and should overwrite any system's inferences. To ensure the reliability of this information, the agent will help the user

(a)   understand the implications of the supplied information,
(b)   make correct choices, and
(c)   alleviate privacy concerns related to the use of information given to the system.

At the same time, we cannot ask the user to complete a really long questionnaire; and, due to privacy concerns or a lack of time, the user might not want to give all the information during the first visit to a new store. The information that the user supplies can go directly in the user profile, but many parameter values will remain empty because of the lack of direct user input. To fill the missing slots of the user profile, the agent can apply a set of rules based on stereotypes.

Assist-2: The agent can process the information supplied by the web log mining module and make changes to the user profile when necessary. The agent will autonomously complete the task of collecting information from these sources and decide if there is a need for modification. The agent can also assist the user in clarifying the changes before committing to them. The goal is to provide the ultimate control to the user in deciding how his/her interests are represented in the system through appropriate user models.

For example, suppose the user has told the system at profile initialization that she is vegetarian but she is now buying meat. As we have noted in Assist-1, the information from these two sources has different weight — values directly based on data supplied by the user get highest certainty; values inferred by the system have lower certainty and should not overwrite user-supplied data. The agent detects the inconsistency between the initial constraints and the results of observations that seem to violate these constraints. It asks the user if any changes to the profile should be made.

The goal of the agent is to create a profile that will maximize the satisfaction of the user. Therefore, the agent wants to relax the existing constraints in order to give the user immediate access to necessary information. Before making these changes, the agent explains that, by making the adjustment, the user may get access to the list of meat products at the login time without doing a special search for them because this information is usually not displayed to vegetarians.

Assist-3: The agent can assist in tracking the effects of the changes made to the user profile and report back to the user at a suitable point so that the user may revoke the changes (or modify them). The goal is to enhance the user's confidence by knowing whether the changes made in the model are yielding better performance or not. Since the ultimate goal is maximal performance of the system and maximum customer satisfaction, the agent can help in the tedious process of adjusting the profile and monitoring the results of these adjustments for the overall trend as well as for particular constraints.

For example, after a change to the profile has been made — e.g., preferred brand of yogurt has been changed from Danone to Yoplait — the products of the former producer have been moved from the first browsing screen to the second. The user might not realize that the new constraint was too rigorous and might be frustrated by not finding familiar products at the usual place. The agent should then volunteer information about this change and let the user know about its effects. The user can then either choose to keep the constraints as they are and make extra effort to browse more categories or relax the constraint and get easier access to the desired information. Using such a feedback loop, the agent will achieve faster convergence of the profile to the desired performance level.

Assist-4: The agent can assist the user in trust-related issues. For example, it could proactively warn about certain vendors, or products. This case is similar to Assist-3, but here, the agent deals with external knowledge about the world. The agent's task is twofold — it finds information relevant to the user (e.g., sources of in-depth knowledge, facts relevant for the user's decision-making) in the "outside world" and, at the same time, it filters the requests coming for user information (e.g., by filtering out queries that violate the user's privacy). The knowledge about the user can be kept locally by the user agent. Other agents or software can ask questions to this user-agent using a standard interface, such as KQML (http://www.cs.umbc.edu/kqml/) or FIPA (http://www.fipa.org/). The user agent may answer such queries on its own, when permitted by the user, or after getting the approval of the user.

In all four cases mentioned above, the knowledge engineer's task will be limited to setting up the agents and testing and fine-tuning their behavior instead of making decisions in every single case. Building such an agent to assist the KE would require a very clear understanding of the knowledge acquisition process. When such agents are in operation, they are expected to reduce the amount of time and effort required by the end-user in making the profile reflect the dynamic changes in his/her lifestyle or circumstances. Instead of manually resetting the profile and answering questions every time when significant changes occur, the agent-supported approach should reduce the human effort.

Finding a perfect balance between providing transparency and sense of control to the user on one side, and minimizing the user's time and annoyance on the other side is a major issue when it comes to user agents. One of the possibilities for solving this problem, particularly when it is due to the mode of interaction, is to provide the user with a choice of different modes of interaction with the agent; the user can select one that suits him/her best. We suggest providing three modes of user-agent interaction:

- *Maximal user involvement.* The agent should report to the user and get his/her approval for any decision (e.g., changes made to user profile). It will ensure maximum transparency and control, but will also require a significant investment of time and effort by the user;

- *Intermediate user involvement.* The agent initiates the dialog only when in doubt (e.g., when observed behavior strongly contradicts previously set values). It is a challenge to design an algorithm to detect when an agent is in doubt.
- *Minimal user involvement.* The agent does not initiate any interaction with user. Instead, the user asks the agent in cases when he/she wants to have system behavior explained or changed. In this mode, the actions of the system are less transparent but, by the same token, the user saves the time and effort needed for constantly monitoring the agent's actions.

The choice of the mode of interaction should be a part of the user profile. The value for this characteristic can be set in two ways:

(1)   Manually, by the user (e.g., the user can be provided with a menu with the three choices that he/she can access any time);
(2)   Automatically, by the processing agent. In this case, the starting value would be *maximal user involvement*, which corresponds to high degree of interaction, because a novice user not familiar with the system might need considerable support from the agent during the registration process. When the profile is initialized, the certainty for this value will decrease slightly; it will decrease considerably if the user chooses not to pay attention to the agent's advice (e.g., closes the dialog box). If the user, on the contrary, seems to need more help (e.g., accesses the help very often), the value can be increased.

There will be two thresholds that separate three modes of interaction: T1 will serve as a boundary between high and intermediate involvement; T2, between intermediate and minimal. For example, when the value drops below T1 (e.g., 0.5), the interaction mode is switched to *intermediate*. If the value becomes even smaller (e.g., close to 0), the mode is set to *minimal* interaction. The exact values for thresholds should be validated empirically and may differ, depending on the kind of characteristics of the customer base of a particular shop/boutique (e.g., customers in a virtual computer store might rely more on the agent than visitors of a cosmetic store; people who shop for computer games are more likely to prefer *maximal user involvement* interaction, while grocery shoppers don't want to spend extra time communicating with the agent when doing routine shopping).

PROPOSED USER MODEL

The user's shopping behavior is classified as comparative shopping, planned shopping, or browsing-based shopping (Lu, 1999). In each of these behaviors, the needs of the user are different. During comparative shopping, the user's task is the selection of one item out of many. The user model can assist the user in the selection process. Filtering the results of the query posed to the database is a task that could be assisted. We do this filtering based on selected features. For example, suppose the user is looking for a motorcycle, and we know from his profile that he prefers Honda products. Then, we can eliminate all other motorcycles from other manufacturers. We can also disambiguate a query by filling in missing fields with values inferred from the user model.

In the case of planned shopping, we do another kind of information filtering. The filtering here is at a higher level of abstraction and more flexible because the user might have a "rough idea" about what he wants to buy in the future (e.g., a bicycle or a roller blade as next summer's sports hobby). In this case, we want to filter among a hierarchy such as departments, shelves and categories, before narrowing down to specific products.

Browsing-based shopping denotes shopping with a casual objective (window-shopping). Here, the main interaction problem is the limited size of the screen, since the user is looking for a panoramic view. Also we want to be able to identify the user's needs in this case and give interesting, personalized suggestions. In all the cases, the language, the content, and the presentation of the information should be adapted to the user's specific needs.

The model proposed by Abi-Aad (2001) contains three main types of information about the user:

- The categories and subcategories of products the user is interested in. This knowledge can help filter information or personalize browsing on a general level. We refer to this as PIE (Preference Indication by Example).
- The features of those products or categories. This knowledge can help compare items and predict the user's interests on a more specific level.
- Any additional information about the user concerning these products, such as the reason for the user's interest in the product or his expertise in the domain. This knowledge about the user can help determine how to present the information. And, it can also help detect when an opportunity is interesting for the user. The user-centered additional information is also domain-dependent (e.g., expert in cars, professional skier); therefore, it is associated with products. We call it "user additional information."

Figure 1. A Fragment of a User Model

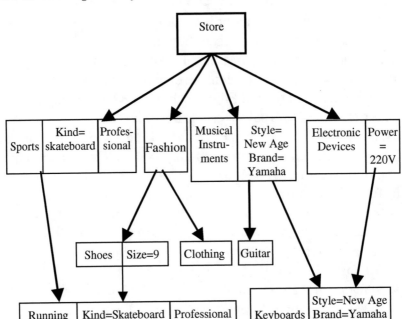

A value denoting the degree of interest, ranging from –5 to 5, is associated with each of these types of information. In addition, a degree of certainty of each value is also included. Figure 1 shows the relationships among these three types of information as well as a part of the navigation graph. In the diagram, we have shown only the nodes with a value higher than a threshold. The PIEs form a natural hierarchy among themselves that is best represented as a DAG (Directed Acyclic Graph). It is not a tree because some products can belong to more than one category. This hierarchy helps build and refine the user model. It can help propagate information up-and-down the DAG and, thus, vary the relative notions of generic and specific. The information (values, features, and user additional info) can be inherited from general categories to their subcategories. The information can also be overridden in specific categories to correct inaccuracies inherited from general categories.

The second advantage of this hierarchy is being able to filter information on different levels, since the user's preferences might vary in precision. For example, consider the following PIEs hierarchy: "store → department →

category → shelf → item." Each of these levels is, in fact, a subcategory of its parent category. When we are relatively sure of a "category" of product that the user would be interested in, then we compare values of PIEs at the following lower level in the hierarchy, the "shelf" level, in order to filter the information.

The features are represented by giving them values. So, the features are stored as attribute-value pairs (e.g., 'color = red,' 'height = 5 inches,' 'wrinkle-free = yes'). Also, features can be compared to values such as 'height > 5 inches.' Or, features are prohibited from having a certain specific value (e.g., 'color red'). Features are associated with the products and, therefore, we associate a list of features with each PIE — details about the car engine to someone who is an expert in cars - and only show external details, such as color, to a person who doesn't know much about car mechanisms.

During comparative shopping, item-wise comparison is usually made at a very low level, based on the features. During planned shopping, comparison is made at an intermediate level, based on the values of the PIEs. And, during browsing-based shopping, comparison based on the values of the PIEs is made at high and low levels, switching appropriately between them.

KNOWLEDGE ACQUISITION
FOR USER MODEL

Knowledge Acquisition (KA) has been an area of active and extensive research since the 1970s, but none of the existing KA systems seems directly applicable to capturing information about the user in the context of e-commerce. There exist several interactive KA tools that allow an end-user with limited experience in the knowledge acquisition process, and with minimal training, to enter or update a knowledge-base. An overview of several such tools can be found in Gil and Kim (2002). Some of these tools [PC PACK (Speel et al., 1999)[7]; KSSn and WebGrid (Gaines & Shaw, 1998)[8]; EXPECT (Blythe et al., 2001)[9]; and PROTÉGÉ-2000 (Grosso et al., 1999)[10]] possess a user-friendly interface and allow creation of sophisticated knowledge bases, ontologies, or conceptual models. But, they all require at least some training, and they are relatively slow.

In the case of user modelling for e-commerce, we need to find another approach that would make the KA tool intuitive to use, even for a naïve user with no previous knowledge. In order to gain this advantage, we can sacrifice granularity because the user model does not need to make very subtle distinctions in attribute values, as is done, for instance, by WebGrid and other

KSSn tools. Knowledge capture for user profiling on the web can benefit from a combination of techniques that will take some load off the user and put it on the system that will extract information from observation (activity logs, browsing behavior, shopping history, etc.).

There exist two major approaches to data collection for user profiling (Colkin, 2001):

(1) *Explicit profiling* occurs when users enter data themselves by filling in forms and answering questionnaires. This approach is good because the user has control over the information he/she supplies to the system; that builds trust. This approach puts less load on the system. On the other hand, the time and effort users spend on entering their data into the system should be minimized. An average customer wants convenience and speed at all stages of his/her interaction with the system, not just the promise of future enhancements. Therefore, another approach becomes necessary for fine-tuning and maintaining the user model.

(2) *Implicit profiling and use of legacy data* can fill that gap between the amount of information desirable for the system and the amount of user involvement. This method consists of tracking the user's behavior and using various machine learning techniques to make conclusions based on that behavior. The major downside of this approach is the unreliability of the algorithmically obtained inferences (there will be a lot of noise that is difficult to interpret).

We use explicit profiling as the first step in KA for user modelling in e-commerce. Based on this information, an initial user profile is built during the customer's first visit to the store. If the customer returns, this initial profile is updated, based on the shopping history.

To make the creation of the user model easy and pleasant for a user, we propose to provide him/her with an intelligent assistant to help in the task. Such an agent will be proactive and relatively autonomous. In the proposed system, this role is played by a community of agents which gets the data from the user via user interface, captures the information from the observation of the user's actions, processes this data, and performs data verification, if needed, with minimal load on the user's time and effort.

The proposed architecture incorporates all four agent's tasks (described on pages 170-172 as Assist 1 to Assist 4). Agent A1 takes care of the initialization of the profile (Assist-1) and dynamically updates it based on transaction data (Assist-2). Agent A2 takes care of interaction with the user when explanation or validation of results is necessary (Assist 2 and 3). The user profile is stored locally, and a KB-U agent ensures the safe information exchange between the user and other agents and the system software by filtering incoming queries (Assist-4). The agents are organized into a KA subsystem that also contains other modules, as shown in Figure 2.

The KA subsystem's goal consists of transforming raw input data received from the dialogue with the user, through observation or event tracking, into a standardized format that can be used by the rest of the e-commerce system.

The KA subsystem tasks include:

- receiving data from the user;
- processing of data;
- validating and fine-tuning of information about the user; and
- storing the information about the user.

The KA subsystem gets the input from two sources: directly from the user, via User Interface (Type-1 interaction), and from the system (i.e., the Web Server Log Mining module), based on transaction history (Type-2 interaction). There are two kinds of data coming directly from the user:

(a)   The results of filling forms with personal data (it can range, depending on the specifics of the e-store, from limited amount of personal data typically required for any registration and credit card transactions, to different sorts of additional information, such as color preferences, dietary restrictions, etc.);

(b)   The elicited knowledge from the user through the dialogue between user and agents aimed at clarifying or validating the system's reasoning. Type-2 interaction occurs inside the system when different modules and agents exchange information in order to dynamically update the profile.

In the first stage of the process of building the user model, Agent A1 gets raw user data from the user interface and transforms it into a format defined by node frame slots, using agent's knowledge base that includes such information as market definition, product domain ontology, consumer typology, etc. The agent compares the user information to the facts stored in the system and produces values for the user profile in a format required by the user model. This process results in setting initial values for frame slots (features). Thus, even with a limited amount of information available, the user model is not empty when the customer returns after the initial registration.

Figure 2. Architecture for Knowledge-Acquisition Sub-System

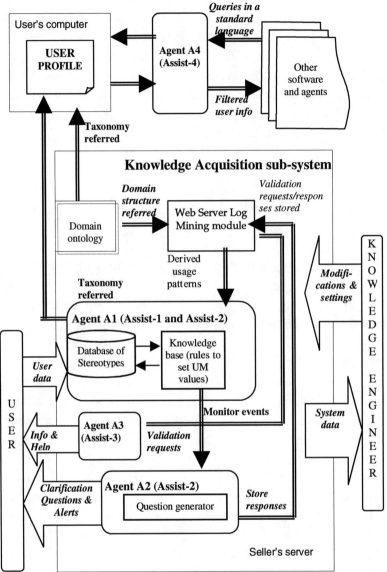

For example, at the root of the tree, the system has stored information about name, age, and some other characteristics of the user. Immediate results of the availability of such information in the user profile would be customized presentation or advertisement (e.g., a teenager will not be exposed to content or visual presentations designed for seniors). Some values can be inferred for internal nodes (e.g., if the user Ms. X mentioned "weight control" as a main reason for shopping in the wellness store, the system can expect that the user will prefer fat-free varieties of all products).

Suppose that the system later collects information about the user by observation (browsing logs, purchase history) and updates previously set fillers of the frame slots.

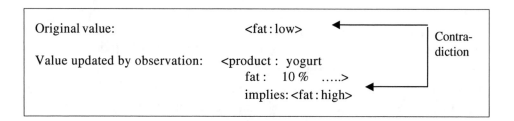

The monitoring agent will detect the contradiction and create a dialogue with the user to confirm if the profile needs to be updated or if the violations against the profile are intentional and should be left alone.

Agent A1 also has a special set of rules that oversees the modifications made to the profile in order to detect problems. This includes detecting cases where the current user's actions contradict the information stored in the profile, as well as alerting the user if the modified value gets close to the threshold. When a problem has been detected, Agent A1 may call Agent A2, which initiates a clarification dialogue with the user. Or, Agent A1 may start a trial period during which it monitors the trend to decide whether the observed deviation in user behavior was occasional and should be ignored or whether it was persistent and should be incorporated into the user model.

Agent A3 monitors the effects of changes made to user profile on system behavior (for example, by analyzing system logs) and supplies the user with appropriate information and advice at a suitable moment.

The following four typical use cases are used to test a prototype that we have developed for KA purposes. These use cases are developed based on the overall operation of a typical system and its services.

Use Case 1: First-Time Registration and Profile Initialization

This use case involves Type-1 interaction and corresponds to Assist-1, described above. The typical scenario for this use case develops as follows:

At registration, the user keys in relevant information (personal data and appropriate additional facts related to the current domain). At this stage, the knowledge acquisition tool uses the information that is typically supplied by the user to a system for transaction authorization (thus, the user does not have to put extra effort into creating the profile and is not required to give the system additional personal data). Some of the stereotype-based values can be set even before any interaction with user. For example, the system may know that there is a 60 percent chance that a shopper would give preference to organic products, and the user normally shops in specialized small shops rather than in supermarkets.

This user data goes to Agent A1. The agent uses a set of rules that compares the user's values to the information stored in the database of stereotypes, consults the domain hierarchical organization (ontology), and arrives at values to be assigned to the slots of frames stored at PIE nodes. A certainty factor is calculated for each value. Certainty factors of leaf values of the PIE DAG influence the degree of belief in the facts stored in internal nodes higher in the hierarchy. For example, if the user states his/her interest in a vitamin-enriched vegetable juice used as dietary supplement, the certainty factor is increased for juices as well as for dietary supplements.

At this point, the user model available in the system is stereotype-based. It reflects typical characteristics of people of a certain age, sex, family situation, etc. (the values were assigned based on population statistics and marketing research data). Results of this stage allow the system to start the next session equipped with enough knowledge to be able to attempt the customization of the presentation, advertisement or search.

Use Case 2: Second Time Visitor Profile Update

This case describes the process of dynamic adaptation of the user profile based on activity logs. It involves Type-2 interaction and corresponds to Assist-2, described on page 170. The typical scenario for this use case develops as follows:

When a user who is already registered returns, his/her actions (time spent viewing, suggestions based on initial profile, browsing sequences, shopping cart decisions, etc.) are recorded in a user activity log. These data are later analyzed by Agent A1 in order to extract relevant information about the user's preferences. Results of the analysis are compared to values originally stored in the user model. In case of minor changes, new, individual values have preference over those based on stereotypes. If the difference is very significant (e.g., while filling the questionnaire, the user informed the system that he is vegetarian, which resulted in giving the slot "food-preferences" value "not meat" with highest certainty 1; but, while shopping, the user showed particular interest in deli products and even bought some ham), Agent A1 can not make a decision and calls Agent A2 to clarify the problem. Then, the system might ask the user about his/her preference (in this particular case, in a form of a simple yes/no question (see Use Case 3)). The user's answer to the question overwrites previously set values. Now the user model built upon the values of slots in the frames is more individualized — wherever possible, stereotypes are replaced by individual user preferences — and now, the customer's profile is different from a typical profile for the same demographic segment of the population.

Use Case 3: Repeat Customer Profile Maintenance

This use case is a variation of the previous one which occurs when the user model has been set, based on stereotypes as well as on the user's activity logs, and the system has to prove or disprove its conclusions based on additional data coming from the user's activity logs. This use case corresponds to functions Assist-2 and Assist-3; it also makes use of both Type-1 and Type-2 interactions. One of the possible scenarios of this use case would be the following:

While a customer makes repeated purchases in the store, Agent A1 keeps analyzing his/her activity logs in order to change the values of certainty factors (e.g., if a user is buying some high-fiber products at every visit, then the certainty factor associated with high fiber will increase accordingly; on the contrary, if the user, at first, purchased herbal supplements but, some time later, started ignoring all such products suggested by the system and did not buy any more such supplements, the system will decrease the certainty factor for herbal supplements).

Agent A1 also monitors the logs for typical patterns in the user's shopping behavior (e.g., typical contents of the shopping basket, brand loyalty, etc.). Significant changes in the user's behavior are registered and validated by Agent A2 (e.g., the system would ask the user about the change in his/her preferences if, after having avoided any product containing cocoa, the customer starts buying chocolate bars at every visit). Minor changes can be validated by the system itself. In this case, Agent A1 sets a trial period during which the validation agent monitors the particular trend in the user behavior in order to distinguish between occasional deviation from typical pattern and consistent change of behavior.

Confirmed patterns are also reflected in the user model. After several visits to the store, the profile of the user becomes highly personalized and mostly reflects the user's individual preferences. Constant monitoring of the user's activity allows the system to perform dynamic updates of the user model in order to reflect changes in the user's preferences and to detect his/her typical shopping patterns.

Use Case 4: Information Exchange with the Outside World

This use case is served by Agent A4 and involves Type-2 interaction, but it can also be initialized by the user (Type-1 interaction). There are two main scenarios for this use case, depending on the direction of communication.

In the first scenario, the user or his agents request the information that is not available in the system. In this case, Agent A4 initializes a search for other sources of information. These sources include different forms of documents as well as other systems and agents. For example, if the user is looking for information on the possible side-effects of a particular weight-loss product, Agent A4 can extract the necessary data from the product monograph, request this information from the vendor's or producer's agents, or find people who used this product and are willing to share their experience. In the last case, A4 can supply the user with available contact information.

In the second scenario, the query comes from outside, and Agent A4 plays the role of a gate-keeper by filtering the incoming requests and limiting the amount of information to be supplied in response to a query, based on constraints set by the user (e.g., a list of friendly agents) and on world knowledge (e.g., information can be given to a reliable long-term partners but not to an unknown company).

CONCLUSION

In this chapter, we have described a model-based knowledge acquisition tool for user profiling for electronic commerce applications. The tool aims to reduce the burden on the user's side while providing a sense of control and trust. The tool is based on a selected user model and is agent-mediated.

Based on the customer's shopping behavior, the user's personalization needs are identified, and an appropriate user model is described. The user model presented in this chapter consists of a directed acyclic graph of PIEs (Preference Indication by Example). This model is motivated by the perceived need to broaden the coverage of the domain of products while dealing with a virtual or electronic shopping mall.

Knowledge about the consumer is acquired using different techniques, ranging from fill-in forms and dialogue to the observation of user actions and machine learning. Analysis of user data is done by the processing Agent A1 and by the Web log mining module. The validation Agent A2 deals with conflict resolution and interacts with the user via dialogues.

Our tool is domain-dependent. If the domain is changed, the ontology and other related data have to be changed, but the overall structure of the system remains the same. The tool allows dynamic user profiling that goes through a constant monitoring, validation, and upgrade cycle. Our ongoing research is still focusing on this last issue.

REFERENCES

Abi-Aad, R. (2001). *A new user model to support electronic commerce.* Montreal, Canada: Concordia University. (Unpublished Master's Thesis)

Abi-Aad, R., Andreevskaia, A., & Radhakrishnan, T. (2001). Capturing the knowledge about the user for e-commerce applications. In *Proceedings of the Workshop on Knowledge in E-Business, K-CAP 2001, 1st International Conference on Knowledge Capture* (pp. 15-21).

Ardissono, L. & Goy, A. (2000). Tailoring the interaction with users in web stores. *User Modeling and User-Adapted Interaction, 10*(4), 251-303.

Blythe, J., Kim, J., Ramachandran, S., & Gil, Y. (2001). An integrated environment for knowledge acquisition. *Proceedings of the Conference on Intelligent User Interfaces (IUI'01),* (pp. 13-20).

Bradshaw, J. (1997). Introduction to software agents. In J. Bradshaw (Ed.), *Software Agents*, (pp. 1-46) Menlo Park, CA: AAAI Press.

Chin, D. (1986). User modeling in UC: The UNIX consultant. In *CHI'86 Proceedings* (pp. 24-28).

Colkin, E. (2001, August 23). Personalization tools dig dipper. *InternetWeek.com.* Retrieved September 29, 2001, from: http://www.internetweek.com/story/IWK20010823S0003

Desharnais, P. (2000). *Agent-assisted price negotiation for electronic commerce.* Montreal, Canada: Concordia University (Unpublished Master's Thesis)

Etzioni, O. & Weld, D. S. (1995). Intelligent agents on the Internet: Fact, fiction, and forecast. *IEEE Expert, 10*(4), 44-49.

Franklin, S. & Graesser, A. (1996). Is it an agent or just a program? A taxonomy for autonomous agents. *Proceedings of the 3rd International Workshop on Agent Theories, Architectures, and Languages,* (pp. 21-35).

Gaines, B. R. & Shaw, M. L. G. (1998). *WebGrid II: Developing hierarchical knowledge structures from flat grids.* Retrieved May 27, 2003, from: http://repgrid.com/reports/KBS/WG/WG.pdf

Gaines, B.R. & Shaw, M.L.G. (n.d.). *Knowledge acquisition tools based on personal construct psychology.* Retrieved May 27, 2003, from: http://ksi.cpsc.ucalgary.ca/articles/KBS/KER/

Gil, Y. & Kim, J. (2002). Interactive knowledge acquisition tools: A tutoring perspective. *Proceedings of the 24th Annual Meeting of the Cognitive Science Society,* (pp. 357-362).

Goto, K. & Kambayashi, Y. (2001). Dynamic personalization and information integration in multi-channel data dissemination environments. In *Proceedings of the 2nd ACM International Workshop on Data Engineering for Wireless and Mobile Access* (pp. 104-109).

Grosso, W. E., Eriksson, H., Fergerson, R. W., Gennari, J. H., Tu, S. W., & Musen, M. A. (1999). *Knowledge modeling at the millennium (The design and evolution of protege-2000),* (pp. 16-21).

Hannigan, T. & Palendrano, C. (2002). Personalization can be quite dynamic. *DM Review.* Retrieved May 10, 2003, from: http://www.dmreview.com/master.cfm?NavID=198&EdID=5798

Haque, R., Ying, Z. J., & Seffah, A. (2001). *Make it easy to shop online: Investigation on web-design for simplifying online applications to satisfy users' context-of-use.* (IBM Conference Papers)

Hershlag, M. (1998, July). Shopping the net. *Time Magazine.*

IBM High-Volume Web Site Team. (2000). *Web site personalization.* Retrieved September 29, 2001, from: http://www7b.boulder.ibm.com/wsdd/library/techarticles/hvws/personalize.html#resources

ILOG. (2000). *Open market and ILOG collaborate to bring highest level of "dynamic personalization" to e-merchandising customers.* Retrieved May 27, 2003, from: http://www.ilog.com/corporate/releases/us/ (ILOG Press Release)

Lu, J. (1999). *User interface agents in electronic commerce applications.* Montreal, Canada: Concordia University. (Unpublished Master's Thesis)

Moukas, A., Guttman, R., & Maes, P. (1998). Agent-mediated electronic commerce: An MIT Media Laboratory perspective. In *Proceedings of the International Conference on Electronic Commerce (ICEC),* Seoul, Korea (April 6-9, pp. 9-15).

Negroponte, N. (1997). Agents: From direct manipulation to delegation. In J. Bradshaw (Ed.), *Software Agents.* (pp. 57-66). Menlo Park, CA: AAAI Press.

Nielsen Norman Group. (2001a). *E-commerce user experience: High-level strategy guidelines.* Retrieved May 15, 2001, from: http://www.nngroup.com/reports/ecommerce/strategy.html

Nielsen Norman Group. (2001b). *E-commerce user experience: Design guidelines for international users.* Retrieved May 21, 2001, from: http://www.nngroup.com/reports/ecommerce/international.html

Rohn, J. A. (1998). Creating usable e-commerce sites. *StandardView, 6*(3), 110-115.

Schaffer, E. & Sorflaten, J. (1999). Web usability illustrated: Breathing easier with your usable e-commerce site. *The Journal of Economic Commerce, 11*(4).

Speel, P., Shadbolt, N. R., de Vries, W., van Dam, P., & O'Hara, K. (1999). Knowledge mapping for industrial purposes. *Proceedings of the 12th Workshop on Knowledge Acquisition, Modelling Management (KAW'99).*

Terpsidis, I. S. et al. (1997). The potential of electronic commerce in re-engineering consumer-retailer relationships through intelligent agents. In J.-Y. Roger, B. Stanford-Smith & P. Kidd. (Eds.), *Advances in Information Technologies: The Business Challenge.* Amsterdam: IOS Press.

ENDNOTES

[1] Preliminary work and first version of the system was described in Abi-Aad et al. (2001).

[2] The term *Preference Indication by Example* was introduced in Abi-Aad (2001).

[3] http://www.trl.ibm.com/projects/mrm/dp/index_e.htm

[4] Information about various aspects of agents' development and use can be found at http://agents.umbc.edu/

[5] Other attributes often considered pertinent for agents include reactivity, temporal continuity, personality, and mobility (see Etzioni & Weld, 1995; Franklin & Graesser, 1996).

[6]   These approaches correspond to two kinds of modern knowledge acquisition tools described in the previous chapter: knowledge elicitation tools and knowledge capture tools.

[7]   http://www.epistemics.co.uk/products/pcpack/

[8]   http://tiger.cpsc.ucalgary.ca/WebGrid/WebGrid.html

[9]   http://www.isi.edu/expect/

[10]   http://protege.stanford.edu/index.html

Chapter XII

Development of Agent-Based Electronic Catalog Retrieval System

Shinichi Nagano, Toshiba Corporation, Japan

Yasuyuki Tahara, Toshiba Corporation, Japan

Tetsuo Hasegawa, Toshiba Corporation, Japan

Akihiko Ohsuga, Toshiba Corporation, Japan

ABSTRACT

Heavy electric machinery industry is currently developing electronic market places of product and parts. PLIB is the standard of dictionary model and content model for describing both commercial specifications and technical specifications of the parts and products used in the heavy electric machinery industry. This chapter represents development of an agent-based electronic catalog retrieval system using a multi-agent framework Bee-gent, in order to exchange PLIB catalog data between existing heterogenous electronic catalog servers. This chapter also gives qualitative discussion of the developed system.

INTRODUCTION

As Internet technologies develop rapidly, companies are shifting their business activities to e-Business on the Internet. Worldwide competition among corporations accelerates the reorganization of corporate sections and partner groups, resulting in a break of the conventional steady business relationships. For instance, a marketplace would lower the barriers of industries and business categories, and then connect their enterprise systems.

Electronic catalogs contain the data of parts and products information used in the heavy electric machinery industry. They contain not only the commercial specifications for parts (manufacturer name, price, etc.), but also the technical specifications (physical size, performance, quality, etc.). The ISO13584 Parts Library, called PLIB for short, is the standard dictionary model and content model for describing both specifications (see Pierra, 1997, 1998).

Currently, software vendors are developing electronic catalog servers. The electronic catalog server is intended to realize marketplaces of catalog data in a PLIB scheme, thus enabling us to retrieve catalog data and integrate it into our own procurement and CAD systems. However, the following issues must be resolved in order to exchange PLIB catalog data among electronic catalog servers. (1) The time it takes to retrieve the desired catalog data from millions of catalog servers over the Internet must be reduced. (2) Because heterogeneous electronic catalog servers have distinctly different retrieval and inquiry interfaces, the complexity of integrating them must be overcome. (3) A variety of retrieval requirements must be promptly realized.

This chapter represents the development of an electronic catalog retrieval system which uses the multi-agent framework Bee-gent™ (see Kawamura, 2000; Bee-gent, 1999) to exchange PLIB catalog data among existing catalog servers. The proposed system agentifies the electronic catalog servers implemented by distinct software vendors. A mediation mobile agent migrates among the servers to retrieve electronic catalog data and then brings them back to the departure server. Thus, an integration of heterogeneous electronic catalog servers can be realized. This agent-based integration system has the following advantages. (1) A mobile mediation agent can retrieve catalog data more effectively than a way of message passing. (2) A coordination procedure among electronic catalog servers can be flexibly defined according to changes in the system environment. (3) Various requirements for retrieving catalog data can be promptly realized.

This chapter is organized as follows. We first describe the integration issues for electronic catalog servers. Then, we introduce a multi-agent frame-

Figure 1. Examples of PLIB Catalog Dictionary and Content

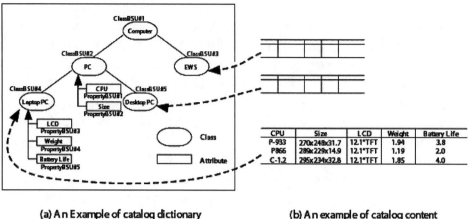

(a) An Example of catalog dictionary   (b) An example of catalog content

work, Bee-gent. Next, we show the development of the proposed system integrated by Bee-gent, and discuss its advantages. Finally, concluding remarks are given.

ELECTRONIC CATALOG RETRIEVAL SYSTEM

Electronic Catalog

Electronic catalogs contain data of parts and products information used in the heavy electric machinery industry. They contain not only the commercial specifications of parts (manufacturer name, price, etc.), but also the technical specifications (physical size, performance, quality, etc.). The ISO13584 Parts Library, called PLIB for short, is the standard dictionary model and content model for describing both specifications (see Pierra, 1997, 1998).

The dictionary model is a framework for defining the classification and hierarchy of a parts library. A class of parts is characterized by a variety of the attributes of parts, such as manufacturers, product types, performance, etc., and a lower class inherits attributes from its upper classes. On the other hand, the content model is a data scheme for describing both the commercial and technical specifications of parts. The content of each catalog is associated with a class in the dictionary model. Each class and attribute is identified by a unique code called a BSU (Basic Semantic Unit).

Figure 1 shows an example of PLIB catalog dictionaries and contents. A dictionary can be represented in a tree form, as shown in Figure 1(a). Each oval denotes a class, and each edge between ovals stands for an inheritance relation between classes. Each rectangle denotes an attribute, which is associated with a class. For instance, three attributes, LCD, Weight and Battery Life, are associated with the Laptop PC class. The bottom table, shown in Figure 1(b), represents three contents associated with the Laptop class. The contents are defined using five attributes: CPU, Size, LCD, Weight, and Battery Life. The former two attributes are inherited from the PC class, and the latter three attributes come from the Laptop class.

An electronic catalog server is an implementation which realizes a marketplace for exchanging catalog data in a PLIB scheme. It is intended to let us retrieve catalog data from electronic servers and then integrate the retrieved data into our own servers, procurement systems, and CAD systems. Currently, major heavy electric machinery companies are building up their own electronic catalog servers with the aim of enclosing their customers, partner groups, and industries.

Integration Problems

This section presents the issues to be resolved for integrating electronic catalog servers.

(1) *Retrieval time:* There are millions of parts in the heavy electric machinery industry. Catalog service providers have public catalog data for general customers and private catalog data for their specific customers on electronic catalog servers. Thus, it is impossible to manage all the catalog data in a unified way. Although a server should retrieve catalog data in a certain class from other servers if it does not have the data, it generally takes an extremely long time to retrieve the desired catalog data from the mass of catalog data.

(2) *System integration:* Currently, there is no standard query language and protocol for exchanging PLIB electronic catalog data among electronic catalog servers. The existing servers provide their own distinct ways of querying catalog contents. In order to realize open distribution of catalog contents, each server should be equipped with the query mechanism for any other catalog server if it retrieves and uploads catalog data over the Internet. However, such system integration is very complex and costly.

(3) *Various retrieval requests:* While the current PLIB standard does not include query ways, various query ways are required for utilizing elec-

Figure 2. Concept of Multi-Agent Framework Bee-Gent

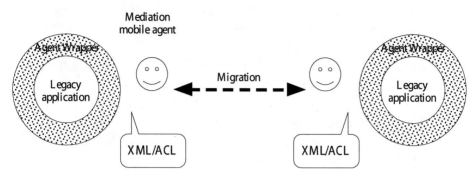

tronic catalog servers. For example, the way to retrieve catalog data in the specific class in a dictionary model and the way to retrieve any data, including specific manufacturers below a certain class, are required. Furthermore, the PLIB standard allows us to extend a dictionary model to add attributes such as a price for specific customers.

MULTI-AGENT FRAMEWORK BEE-GENT

Bee-gent (see Kawamura, 2000; Bee-gent, 1999) is a multi-agent framework for realizing a flexible open distributed system, which integrates existing heterogeneous software applications, such as WWW servers, databases, software packages, legacy systems, etc., through use of the network. Figure 2 illustrates the concept of Bee-gent.

Bee-gent is composed of two kinds of agents, an agent wrapper and a mediation mobile agent. The agent wrapper agentifies an existing application by encapsulating an implementation of the wrapping application. It manages the states of the application, invoking the application when necessary. The mediation mobile agent provides a coordination process between applications through communications. It also migrates among the sites of the applications when it interacts with agent wrappers. Furthermore, Bee-gent adopts XML/ACL as a representation format of the agent communication language FIPA Agent Communication Language (FIPA, 2000). By exchanging XML/ACL messages, agents can respond to the nature of received request messages and can determine the best action. Thus, inter-application coordination is realized through interactions between agent wrappers and mediation mobile agents.

DEVELOPMENT USING BEE-GENT

This section shows development of an electronic catalog retrieval system using the Bee-gent multi-agent framework to exchange catalog data among existing electronic catalog servers.

The architecture of the proposed system is shown in Figure 3. An operation user inputs both search conditions (parts types, parts vendors, create dates, etc.) and retrieval ways (the one to visit the designated servers, the one to visit the servers that store the catalog data of parts provided by the designated vendors, etc.). The operation user sends these data to a mediation agent on a web server and receives the retrieved results.

A mediation mobile agent realizes a coordination procedure which includes a migration plan and a query for each server among all electronic catalog servers. The mediation mobile agent migrates to the designated servers according to the search conditions and submits queries to an agent wrapper on the visited server. An agent wrapper agentifies an existing electronic catalog server and invokes it to retrieve catalog data when it receives a retrieval request from a mediation mobile agent.

As shown, the implementations of the electronic catalog servers are distinctly different. In order to encapsulate the implementations, we develop two conversion modules for each agent wrapper. One is from a retrieval request message in ACL to a search API of the wrapped server; the other is from an upload request message in ACL to an upload API of the wrapped server.

DISCUSSION OF ADVANTAGES

(1) *Reduction of retrieval time:* Generally, the submission of several queries is required to obtain the desired catalog data from millions of catalog data, since existing electronic catalog servers do not have interfaces that meet any retrieval request. Suppose that queries are realized by message exchanges. Then, for each query, a mass of catalog data is transmitted over the network, and the agents have to again retrieve the received catalog data to obtain the desired data. In the proposed system, mediation mobile agents migrate to each server and submit queries on the destination server. Since the agents filter retrieved data to obtain the desired results and bring them back to the departure server, only the desired catalog data are transmitted. Therefore, mobile agents are more effective than message exchanges for retrieving electronic catalog data. (Kawamura et al., 2001)

Figure 3. System Architecture of Agent-Based Electronic Catalog Retrieval System

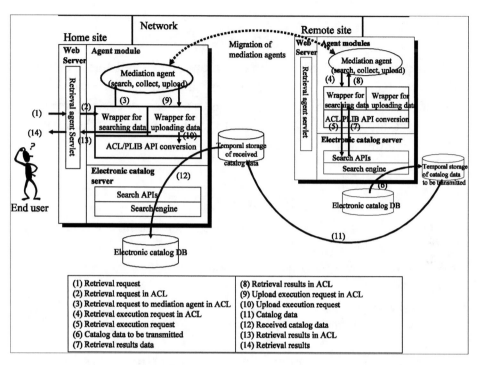

(1) Retrieval request	(8) Retrieval results in ACL
(2) Retrieval request in ACL	(9) Upload execution request in ACL
(3) Retrieval request to mediation agent in ACL	(10) Upload execution request
(4) Retrieval execution request in ACL	(11) Catalog data
(5) Retrieval execution request	(12) Received catalog data
(6) Catalog data to be transmitted	(13) Retrieval results in ACL
(7) Retrieval results data	(14) Retrieval results

show the quantitative comparison between message exchanges and mobile agents with respect to information retrieval.

(2) *Flexible integration:* Mediation mobile agents are unified and flexible processes, which realize integration procedures among existing electronic catalog servers. For example, agents can be designed to retrieve only classes of catalog data that specific servers require, or to select the next servers to be visited according to the data retrieved from the current visiting server. Agents can also be easily modified according to changes in integration procedures, which are due to the increase and decrease of electronic catalog servers and to changes in the retrieval orders of servers.

(3) *Prompt realization of various retrieval requests:* Agent wrappers provide common ACL conversation interfaces for accessing electronic catalog servers. By being wrapped, existing servers can exchange catalog data with each other, hiding their implementations. Even if the implementations of servers are partially changed, only processes in the agent wrappers corresponding to the implementation changes are modified.

Thus, various demands on retrieving catalog data can be promptly realized.

CONCLUSION

This chapter represents the development of an agent-based electronic catalog retrieval system by using Bee-gent, a multi-agent framework. It is expected to drastically reduce the running and maintenance costs of distributing electronic catalog data. We plan a quantitative evaluation of the developed system as a future work.

REFERENCES

Bradshaw, J. M. (ed.). (1997). *Software Agents*. Menlo Park, CA: AAAI Press/The MIT Press.

FIPA. (2002). *FIPA agent communication language specifications*. From http://www.fipa.org/

Kawamura, T. & Joseph, S. (2001). Designing multi-agent systems based on pairwise agent interactions. *IEICE Transactions, 84*(8), 968-980.

Kawamura, T., Hasegawa, T., Ohsuga, A., & Honiden, S. (2000). Bee-gent: Bonding and encapsulation enhancement agent framework for development of distributed systems. *Systems and Computers in Japan, 31*(13), 42-56.

Pierra, G. (1997). Intelligent electronic component catalogues for engineering and manufacturing. *Proceedings of the International Symposium on Global Engineering Networking*.

Pierra, G. et al. (1998). Exchange of component data: The PLIB model, standard and tools. *Proceedings of the CALS EUROPE'98*.

Toshiba Corporation. (1999). *Multi-agent framework Bee-gent*. From http://www.toshiba.co.jp/beegent/

Wooldridge, M. & Jennings, N. R. (1998). Pitfalls of agent-oriented development. *Proceedings of the 2nd International Conference on Autonomous Agents*.

Chapter XIII

Using Dynamically Acquired Background Knowledge for Information Extraction and Intelligent Search

Samhaa R. El-Beltagy,
Ministry of Agriculture and Land Reclamation, Egypt

Ahmed Rafea,
Ministry of Agriculture and Land Reclamation, Egypt

Yasser Abdelhamid,
Ministry of Agriculture and Land Reclamation, Egypt

ABSTRACT

This chapter presents a simple framework for extracting information found in publications or documents that are issued in large volumes and which cover similar concepts or issues within a given domain. The general aim of the work described is to present a model for automatically augmenting segments of these documents with metadata, using dynamically acquired background domain knowledge to help users easily locate information within these documents through a structured front end. To realize this goal, both document structure and dynamically acquired background knowledge are utilized. A real life example where these ideas have been applied is also presented.

INTRODUCTION

This work is motivated by the fact that enterprises and organizations often contain information rich texts, but they rarely have the means by which these resources can be intelligently searched. In many cases, the search interface that is adopted is based on keywords and, though the indexing/matching techniques employed by those search engines may be very sophisticated, this approach suffers from the same limitations associated with the existing web search model (see El-Beltagy, 2000; Han & Chang, 2002).

This chapter addresses the particular problem of trying to extract information from organizational publications that are issued in large volumes and which cover similar concepts or issues and from which information cannot be extracted through the use of the structure of a document alone. The end goal is to enable individual sections of those documents to be automatically augmented with metadata so that users can perform structured searches using a predefined set of categories or classifications and obtain, as a result, only segments or sections of documents that fit their search criteria. The class of documents targeted by this work is, thus, that of resources that contain a set of information entities, most of which fall under known categories, but which contain no special markup to differentiate them from other information entities. The approach adopted toward this problem is to attempt to make use of background knowledge about those categories and to employ that background knowledge for an intelligent search. Rather than forcing predefined static background knowledge, the work presented allows for the dynamic acquisition of this knowledge as the system evolves.

Our goal is, thus, twofold: first, to provide the tools that can assist in ontology building and to utilize the background ontology for document indexing; and second, to provide an intelligent interface to allow for the retrieval of the stored information.

BACKGROUND

Information is a vital resource to individuals and organizations; its timely location can influence key decisions that affect both. It is, thus, no wonder that massive research efforts have been undertaken in recent years with the aim of improving upon existing search facilitates, especially among unstructured and semi-structured resources, where the problem of information finding is most pronounced (Han & Chang, 2002). Looking into ways to extract information from semi-structured texts has been investigated in many system integration projects (El-Beltagy, 1998), such as TSIMMIS (Garcia-Molina et al., 1995) and Lore (McHugh et al., 1997). These systems have tried to provide an integrated view of related data scattered across various structured and semi-structured resources, and have, thus, developed templates and wrappers to extract structured information from semi-structured texts. The primary goal of such systems was to unlock the wealth of information stored within legacy applications and to integrate those with other related/similar data available in other resources. Toward this end, specific languages, representation models and ontologies were designed and adopted.

Also, much work has been carried out within the knowledge acquisition community with the aim of providing automatic support for the extraction of information from unstructured texts. This task is still proving to be a rather challenging one. Information Extraction (IE) systems have, thus, appeared with a more focused goal of supporting the task of extracting information from specific domains or for particular tasks (Vargas-vera et al., 2001).

IE systems often rely on templates, hand generated annotations, or domain dependant NLP knowledge. For example, the SoftMealy system (Hsu, 1998) and the system presented in Kushmerick et al. (1997) are both IE systems that attempt to extract information from web pages through examples of such pages, all of which exhibit similar structure. These systems work when structure templates of well-defined fields of content exist. For example, a page containing some country codes may have the name of a country formatted in bold and the code for that country formatted in italics (Kushmerick et al., 1997). It is possible, then, to use this formatting information to extract country-code pairs.

However, it is often the case that structure or formatting on its own cannot be used to extract information. One of the solutions intended to overcome this obstacle is to tag the information in a way that would enable its extraction. Indeed, XML (Bray et al., 1998) emerged as a way to achieve precisely that.

Taking this idea a step further is the approach that has been adopted by SHOE (see Heflin & Hendler, 2000a; Heflin & Hendler, 2000b). SHOE is a web-based knowledge representation language that can be embedded in web pages. By explicitly specifying the ontology being used within a web page and tagging information within that page, using that ontology, it is possible to appropriately extract information from that page and to infer relations and information not explicitly represented. This idea was the basis for the DARPA agent markup language (DAML) (DARPA, 2000). DAML, RDF (Lessila & Swick, 1999) and a number of other languages are all part of the Semantic Web, the goal of which is to enrich information resources with semantics that can be processed by computers (Fensel, 2000).

What can be said regarding this approach, in general, is that, for its successful application to existing documents, automatic metadata augmentation mechanisms have to be devised. Trying to manually re-author existing documents in order to comply with these emerging standards is simply not possible because of their sheer volume. The work presented here attempts to do just that, but only for documents that exhibit the characteristics outlined in the previous section and in the next.

PROBLEM SCOPE AND DEFINITION

It is often the case that a broad range of documents containing useful information exists, but with no way to access individual segments of these documents directly using a targeted or structured search.

A document is typically divided into a number of sections and subsections. For example, documents that cover common problems related to various electrical appliances and their solutions will usually have sections for each class of problems, each of which will have subsections that cover a specific problem belonging to that class. Without a targeted search, a user interested in finding a solution to a particular problem related to a specific electrical appliance must first try to locate the specific document that covers common problems and their solutions for that appliance, and then begin the tedious task of browsing that document in order to locate the problem he/she is interested in. A search engine that would allow the user to select the appliance for which he/she is attempting to find a solution, then allow the user to select the specific problem he/she is interested in, and finally return the exact section that covers that problem, would certainly save the user valuable time and effort. The same interface, may also allow a user to compare how a given problem is solved across a range of appliances.

Moving beyond this simple and hypothetical example, in this work, we've had to address a real problem related to agricultural extension documents issued primarily to assist farmers in cultivating and caring for certain crops. Each document is information-rich with respect to the crop which it covers. Depending on the importance of a given crop and how involved the issues related to it are, a crop may have more than one document to address it.

Because of the wealth of information contained within these documents, they're often used by researchers, as well as by farmers and extension workers.

A typical document will cover most aspects related to cultivating a crop, ranging from land preparation to harvest. Each section within a document targets a given problem or issue, and each subsection embodies a specialization of that issue. For example, a section called 'Diseases' will have as its subsections most diseases that are likely to affect a given crop. Similarly, a section covering operations will cover all agricultural operations that apply to that crop (irrigation, fertilization, etc.).

In this case and in similar cases, there are two elements that can work to the advantage of an intelligent search. The first is that the main elements of search can be identified beforehand over a broad class of documents. 'Diseases' and 'Operations' are two examples of search categories that can be readily identified. The second element is that individual mappings of instances related to the categories are more or less the same across all documents, and they are featured in either section or subsection headings. For instance, 'Fertilization,' 'Irrigation' and 'Land Preparation' all belong to the class of agricultural operations, while 'Powdery Mildew' belongs to the class of agricultural diseases. These classes and their instances will usually generalize across all crops. So, the individual instances of these general categories embody background knowledge that can be added to individual document segments as metadata.

There are some cases, however, when a general category can be identified, but the instances of which will rarely recur across a document set. Crop 'Varieties' is an example. In most extension documents, there is usually a section on varieties with various subsections on each variety and its different features. The name of a crop variety is specific to that crop and, as such, cannot be used as a general search term. To enable the location of information on any given variety for a given crop, the hierarchy of the document itself can be utilized to infer that each subsection of any section covering 'Varieties' is an instance of the general category 'variety.'

Generally speaking, augmenting various document sections with metadata involves a number of steps, which can be summarized as follows:

- Identifying the various categories onto which various document sections can be mapped.
- Acquiring and representing background knowledge in a way that can facilitate the mapping of various document sections into the identified categories.

- Segmenting various documents and employing background knowledge to map each document section to its corresponding category.
- Storing structured index information in a persistent data store, such as a database, or converting the document into an alternate representation (e.g., XML).
- Providing a user interface to enable searches across indexed documents.

MODELLING BLOCKS

In this work, it was important to adopt a flexible yet powerful way to represent both background information as well as a document. XML (Bray et al., 1998) was, thus, adopted to represent both. Background information is stored in an XML file, which is used to represent index terms. The file has the structure shown in Figure 1.

Figure 1. XML Representation of Background Knowledge

```
<indexTerms>
        <general_category indexChildNodes= "true" >
                <name> diseases </name>
                <sameAs> disorders </sameAs>
        </general_category>

        <general_category indexChildNodes= "true" >
                <name> Varieties </name>
        </general_category>

        <disease indexChildNodes= "false" >
                <name>Powdery Mildew</name>
                <sameAs> aSynonym </sameAs>
                <sameAs> ……….. </sameAs>
        </disease>
        …
        …
        <operation indexChildNodes= "false" >
                <name> aNameOfanOperation </name>
                <sameAs> aSynonym </sameAs>
        </operation>
        …
        …
        <pest indexChildNodes= "false" >
                <name> aNameOfaPest </name>
        …
        …
        </pest>
        …
        …
</indexTerms>
```

Figure 2. XML Representation of an Unindexed Document

```
<doc>
        <title> aTitle </title>
        <section>
                <id>102328933656>/id>
                <level>1</level> ←the level of a section within a document hierarchy →
                <heading> the text heading of the section </heading>
                <text> a pure text representation of the contents of the section </text>
                <html> <![CDATA[ the html text representation of this section ]] < /html>
        </section>
        <section>
                .....
                .....
        </section>
</doc>
```

This representation, despite its simplicity, allows for the mapping of various phrases to their corresponding categories, and provides a simple thesaurus using the <sameAs> tag. The *indexChildNodes* can be used to specify whether or not specializations of a given term should be indexed as belonging to that term, i.e. whether or not a document's hierarchy is to be utilized.

A document will have the XML representation illustrated in Figure 2.

SYSTEM OVERVIEW

The implemented system is a distributed one, in which a number of components communicate to achieve the required functionality. The main components of this system are: an indexing user interface; an indexing backend linked to a DBMS; and a search front end, also linked to a DBMS. Figure 3 shows the various components, each of which is described in the following subsections, and their interactions.

Indexing Backend

The indexing backend is the component responsible for augmenting input documents with metadata using background knowledge. The indexing backend is implemented in Java as a multithreaded HTTP server that is capable of receiving indexing requests embedded in HTTP requests. On start-up, the system loads the XML representation of background knowledge into a set of dictionaries and data structures that can facilitate the indexing process. A

Figure 3. System Components and Interactions

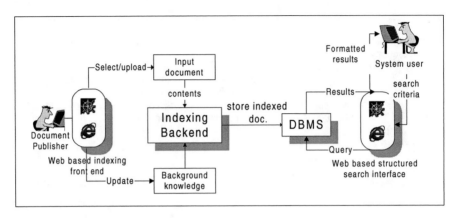

request to this component will contain the URL of the file that requires indexing, as along with the name of the crop for which this file belongs. Before carrying out any indexing, the component starts reading the specified document and breaks it down to the structure specified in Figure 2.

Following this segmentation phase, pattern matching techniques are applied to match section heading titles with index terms. An index record for each section is created, with each record containing fields for every pre-identified category (one for diseases, another for operations, etc.). Should a match be made between a heading and one of the input index terms, then the category of the section will be deduced. The field designated for that category will be filled with an ID pointing to the specific instance against which a match was made. A single section may match with more than one category.

After the analysis of a given section is completed and a record is created accordingly, the record, along with a pointer to the specific section for which it was derived, are sent to a remote storage component (a database) where they are kept. After analysis of the whole document is completed, an HTML page is returned to the user. Within that page, all section and subsection headings are displayed; beside each, it is indicated whether that section has been indexed. If the section has been indexed, it is indicated whether indexing was performed directly or indirectly (through the use of hierarchical information). Sections that have not been indexed are hyperlinked to an interface which allows the user to edit their text in order to update the background knowledge and re-index the input document.

Updating background knowledge can involve the creation of a new category instance or the creation of synonyms to associate with existing ones. The update request is encoded in a URL sent to indexing backend over HTTP. The indexing backend subsequently 'learns' this new information and updates its background knowledge file. Initially, some background knowledge could be acquired from a domain expert, or it could be completely learned through the indexing process (which also requires usage by someone familiar with the domain).

Indexing User Interface

Since it is anticipated that those users who will request document indexing will do so remotely, a web interface for facilitating the indexing and uploading of extension documents was implemented. This interface simply allows a user to select an extension document from their local machine, upload it to a web server, and then index this document through communication with the indexing backend.

Search Front End

A web search front end is provided to allow users to rapidly fetch their required information from the extension documents by selecting one or more values for index parameters, where the index parameters are those of the crop name as well as predefined indexing categories. The number of selected parameters defines whether the query will be a loose or a specific one. The more specific the query, the fewer records are returned.

After a query is entered, it is converted to SQL and dispatched to the database in which indexing information has been stored. The result is displayed in the form of an HTML page containing a list of index records that match the entered query. The output includes the following: the heading title of the matching section; a sample from the matching paragraph; and a hyperlink to the source section. On following the hyperlink, only the text of the selected section will be displayed. However, depending on the level of a section, extra information that defines the context of the section as part of the whole document might be displayed. In addition, a hyperlink to the source document will always be displayed.

RESULTS

Thus far in our real life example, 24 documents have been indexed using the system. The indexing resulted in the augmentation of 648 sections with metadata. Our testing of the system has revealed that, for any given query, none of the returned results were irrelevant.

Deploying this system into the real world, the search front end for this system was made available as one of the subsystems of a large information system devised to aid farmers in their farming activities. The system as a whole has six more subsystems, including two expert systems, a forum, a problem reporting facility, and a search front end for economic data, all of which are accessible from a web interface. Analyzing web log data for the first four months of the year 2003 has revealed that the page from which the search front end was made available was the second most-visited page (after the site's main web page). We believe that the reason for this page's popularity is the ease with which it allows users to locate specific items of interest, a task that would have otherwise been tedious even if a keyword search model was made available for these documents.

This system can also be a powerful research tool as researchers can, for example, easily study the manifestations of a single disease on different crops by specifying that disease and omitting any specific crop in the query, thus, loosening it.

FUTURE WORK

In building our prototype, the main categories under which extension document headings could be classified were hardwired into the code; for each of these categories, a table was created in the database. To enable our technique to work with any kind of document, we intend to remove any hardwired information and to allow for the definition of categories by the indexing user, i.e., by a user who knows enough about the domain and the documents. We will also extend our tool in order to enable it to automatically create any required DB tables and to dynamically generate the search interface. This will make our tool more generic and will enable its application in any domain.

Another area of future work that we intend to pursue is that of the agentification of the search component. By doing so, we will allow other agents within an agent-based framework to make use of it. For example, an expert system agent may use this service to link its conclusions with information available about these conclusions within the brochures.

CONCLUSION

This chapter has addressed the particular problem of attempting to locate, by using a user-friendly structured interface, information in organizational publications that are issued in large volumes and which cover similar concepts or issues. The general aim of the work described was to present a model for automatically augmenting segments of these documents with metadata, using dynamically acquired background domain knowledge, in order to assist users in easily locating information within these documents through a structured front end.

We have successfully applied the presented model for extension documents within the agricultural domain. The technique used to achieve this goal is a simple but powerful one, which could be generalized to apply to any collection of documents that cover similar concepts within a known domain.

ACKNOWLEDGMENTS

This work has been supported by FAO grant TCP/EGY/065

REFERENCES

Bray, T., Paoli, J. & Sperberg-McQueen, C. M. (1998). *Extensible markup language (XML) 1.0.* World Wide Web Consortium.

DARPA. (2000). *The DARPA agent markup language (DAML).* Available: http://www.daml.org/

El-Beltagy, S. (1998). *Approaches to System Integration for Distributed Information Management.* Southampton, UK: University of Southampton.

El-Beltagy, S. (2000). *Context, Queries, and the Web.* Southampton, UK: University of Southampton.

Fensel, D. E. (2000). The semantic web and its languages. *IEEE Intelligent Systems, 15*(6), 67-73.

Garcia-Molina, H., Hammer, J., Ireland, K., Papakonstantinou, Y., Ullman, J., & Widom, J. (1995). *Integrating and accessing heterogeneous information sources in TSIMMIS.* Paper presented at the AAAI Symposium on Information Gathering, Stanford, California.

Han, J. & Chang, K. C.-C. (2002). Data mining for web intelligence. *IEEE Computer, 35*(11), 64-70.

Heflin, J. & Hendler, J. (2000a). *Dynamic ontologies on the Web*. Paper presented at the 17th National Conference on Artificial Intelligence (AAAI-2000), Menlo Park, California.

Heflin, J. & Hendler, J. (2000b). *Searching the Web with SHOE*. Paper presented at the AAAI-2000 Workshop on AI for Web Search.

Hsu, C. (1998). *Initial results on wrapping semistructured web pages with finite-state transducers and contextual rules*. Paper presented at the AAAI-98 Workshop on AI and Information Integration, Madison, Wisconsin.

Kushmerick, N., Weld, D. S. & Doorenbos, R. B. (1997). *Wrapper induction for information extraction*. Paper presented at the International Joint Conference on Artificial Intelligence (IJCAI).

Lessila, O. & Swick, R. R. (1999). *Resource description framework (RDF) model and syntax specification*. World Wide Web Consortium.

McHugh, J., Abiteboul, S., Goldman, R., Quass, D. & Widom, J. (1997). Lore: A database management system for semistructured data. *SIGMOD Record, 26*(3), 54-66.

Vargas-vera, M., Domingue, J., Kalfoglou, Y., Motta, E. & Buckingham Shum, S. (2001). *Template-driven information extraction for populating ontologies*. Paper presented at the IJCAI 2001 Workshop on Ontologies Learning, Seattle, Washington.

Chapter XIV

A Study on Web Searching:
Overlap and Distance of the Search Engine Results

Shanfeng Zhu, City University of Hong Kong, Hong Kong

Xiaotie Deng, City University of Hong Kong, Hong Kong

Qizhi Fang, Qingdao Ocean University, China

Weimin Zheng, Tsinghua University, China

ABSTRACT

Web search engines are one of the most popular services to help users find useful information on the Web. Although many studies have been carried out to estimate the size and overlap of the general web search engines, it may not benefit the ordinary web searching users, since they care more about the overlap of the top N (N=10, 20 or 50) search results on concrete queries, but not the overlap of the total index database. In this study, we present experimental results on the comparison of the overlap of the top N (N=10, 20 or 50) search results from AlltheWeb, Google, AltaVista and WiseNut for the 58 most popular queries, as well as for the distance of the overlapped results.

These 58 queries are chosen from WordTracker service, which records the most popular queries submitted to some famous metasearch engines, such as MetaCrawler and Dogpile. We divide these 58 queries into three categories for further investigation. Through in-depth study, we observe a number of interesting results: the overlap of the top N results retrieved by different search engines is very small; the search results of the queries in different categories behave in dramatically different ways; Google, on average, has the highest overlap among these four search engines; each search engine tends to adopt a different rank algorithm independently.

INTRODUCTION

With the development of the World Wide Web, people can suffer from information overload. Since search engines help us locate what we need in the ocean of information, they have become one of the most popular services on the Web. Due to hard competition and financial pressure, some search engines were closed or stopped public searching service. One of those search engines is Northern Light (http://www.northernlight.com). By the end of July 2002, the most famous search engines included AltaVista (http://www.altavista.com), AlltheWeb (http://www.alltheweb.com), Google (http://www.google.com), HotBot (http://www.hotbot.com), Lycos (http://www.lycos.com), MSN Search (http://search.msn.com), Teoma (http://www.teoma.com) and WiseNut (http://www.wisenut.com).

Many web searching studies have been carried out to analyze the characteristics of searching on the Web. One type of study concentrates on the characteristics of search engines, such as coverage, overlap and dynamics, which could improve users' understanding of web searching and, thus, help users find desired information. The other type focuses on the characteristics of searching users, such as the most frequent searching queries, searching operators and modifiers, which are quite useful in designing more efficient search engines. Our study belongs to the first type.

As searching users, we are eager to know how to select a suitable search engine for search tasks. Since each search engine has its unique database, and distinct rank algorithm, it will retrieve and present its unique search results to the user. Naturally, we have many questions, such as: *With respect to same query, is there a significant difference among the searching hit lists of several different search engines? Do they rank the overlapped results in the same order?* In this study, we investigate the overlap and distance of search engine searching results for some popular queries. Four general search engines, AltaVista, AlltheWeb, Google and WiseNut, are examined.

According to several studies (see Hoelscher, 1998; Silverstein et al., 1999; Jansen et al., 2000), people seldom go beyond the top 10 hits of the result, which means that the list at the top is the most important to the users. Therefore, the top N (N=10, 20 or 50) results from each search engine are compared in this study. We measure not only how many hits are overlapped in the top N results of each search engine, but also the distance of overlapped results. The measurement of the overlap and distance will be given in the later sections. All 58 queries, which are chosen from a most popular query list provided by the WordTracker (http://www.wordtracker.com) service, are divided into three categories. In addition to helping users compare and choose suitable search engines, our findings could also shed light on proposing effective result-merging algorithms in metasearch engines and search engine evaluation algorithms.

BACKGROUND

Of the web searching studies on the characteristics of search engines, many of them try to estimate the coverage and overlap of the general web search engines. Using 575 queries obtained from the query log of NEC research laboratory, Lawrence and Giles (1998) estimated that, by the end of 1997, the indexable web contained 320 million pages. Bharat and Broder (1998) described a different technique for measuring the relative size and overlap of public web search engines. In contrast to Lawrence and Giles (1998), they adopted a different strategy of constructing more uniform random queries based on a lexicon of 400,000 words, which was built from the vocabulary of 300,000 pages present in the Yahoo! hierarchy. In a later study by Lawrence and Giles (1999), another method, random sampling of IP addresses, was introduced. They gave an estimate of 800 million pages as the size of the Web by February 1999. In all these studies, they found that the overlap among the general search engine's indexes database is surprising small. Some other researchers studied the dynamic characteristics of the Web, such as measuring search engine performance over time (see Bar-Ilan, 2001; Bar-Ilan, 2002) and the growth and update dynamics of search engines (Risvik & Michelsen, 2002).

Other studies emphasize the searching behaviors of web users by analyzing the query logs of practical web search engines (Silverstein et al., 1998) analyzed a six-week period (from August 2 to September 13, 1998) of AltaVista search engine query logs consisting of approximately 1 billion queries. Jansen et al., Spink et al. (2001) and Spink et al. (2002) analyzed Excite web search engine query logs three times, collected in September 1997, December 1999 and May 2001, respectively. All of them report similar findings. That is, users tend to submit short queries, they mostly view only a few top-ranked web pages, and they seldom modify the queries. Some of the most popular queries are identified in their studies. The latest study by Spink et al. (2002) shows that, although search topics have shifted, there is little change in user search behaviors. Other related studies also exist, such as the effect of advanced operators on simple queries (Jansen, 2000) and the term co-occurrence in Internet search engine queries (Wolfram, 1999).

However, from users' points of view, they care little about the size of the Web or about which search engine has the largest indexes database. The users are concerned more about the overlap of the top N (10, 20 or 50) hits of the general search engines on specific queries, which motivates this study of the overlap and distance of search engine results.

METHODOLOGY

Four general search engines (AltaVista, Google, WiseNut and AlltheWeb) are examined in the experiment. In order to perform the experiment, we first select suitable queries, and then we compare the overlap and distance of the searching results.

Sampling Queries

We select the 58 most popular queries from WordTracker's top 200 long-term keyword report on July 27, 2002. It provides access to the query logs of the metasearch engines MetaCrawler (http://www.metacrawler.com) and Dogpile (http://www.dogpile.com) stretching back for two months, which has a database of 301,687,926 search terms at the end of July 2002. The database is constantly updated, with new data added each week. The 58 queries are selected according to following criteria:

- We only select one from a group of similar queries. For instance, we select query *hotmail* from *hotmail* and *hotmail.com*.
- The sample queries are chosen according to the order of popularity. After reducing the redundancy of similar queries, the top 60 queries are selected as sample queries.

- Considering the popularity of adult-related queries, all eight adult-related queries out of the top 100 queries are selected.

These 58 queries account for approximately 55.22 percent of the total occurrence of all top 200 queries. Considering the characteristics of these 58 queries, we can divide them into three categories.

(a) **Very specific queries,** such as those for the name of a company, an organization or a product. Usually there exists a web site for these queries. This category includes 10 queries: *google, yahoo, hotmail, ebay, mapquest, ask jeeves, Kazaa, Winzip, southwest airlines,* and *warez.*

(b) **Very general queries.** This category includes 40 queries: *hotels, lyrics, jokes, pictures, maps, games, song lyrics, dictionary, weight loss, search engines, weather, music, april fools, snes roms, jobs, free people search, morpheus, clip art, mp3, wallpaper, recipes, computer deals, baby names, chat, poems, chat, travel, free games, quotes, used cars, airline tickets, movies, parent, lingerie, people search, spiderman, clipart, driving directions, dogs, greeting cards,* and *author.*

(c) **Adult-related queries.** This category includes eight queries: *sex, porn, free porn, literotica, lolita, xxx, erotic stories,* and *free sex stories.*

Comparing Search Results

Through the BookWorm metasearch service written by ourselves, each selected query is forwarded to four general search engines: Google, AltaVista, AlltheWeb and WiseNut. Then, the top 50 hits are fetched from each search engine and compared by a background program. The statistical data is recorded in a file for further processing. This mainly includes following steps.

Step 1. Normalizing the queries. All the queries are transformed into lowercase, and sent to search engines without any advanced operators like "AND", "OR" or "+".

Step 2. Retrieving the search results. To compare the search engines, we use the default settings of the search engines and site collapsing options if it is supported by search engine. When site collapsing options are enabled, the search engine tries to display many different sites in the result. The top 50 results from each search engine are saved for comparison.

Step 3. Calculating the overlap and distance of the searching results.
In this study, we only check the hostname of the URLs for matching. In other words, if two URLs with the same hostname are respectively retrieved by two search engines, we deem them as matching results when calculating the overlap. If several URLs with the same hostname are retrieved by the same search engine, the URL with the highest rank will be used to calculate the overlap and distance. Of course, we need a database to store the different hostnames of the same web site for the matching process. Three rounds of calculations are carried out on the top 10, top 20 and top 50 results. In some cases, the overlap of the top 1 result is also examined.

Step 4. Analyzing the results. The analysis of the results is carried out by utilizing the statistic tools of SPSS 10. We focus on following questions:

(a)   The difference of the overlap and distance of the searching results retrieved by four search engines (Google, AltaVista, AlltheWeb and WiseNut).
(b)   The difference of the overlap and distance over three categories.
(c)   The difference of the overlap and distance over three rounds (top 10, top 20, top 50).

In addition to these three questions, we also want to examine the search results in a general sense. For example, on average, what is the percentage of results retrieved respectively by only one search engine, two search engines, three search engines, or all four search engines? How many distinct results are retrieved by all four search engines?

Measurement on Overlap and Distance

Here we use an ordered list L to represent a search result returned by a search engine with respect to a specific query. Given a universe U, an ordered list L is a ranked subset S of U, i.e., $L = <x_1, x_2, ..., x_n>$ & $x_1 > x_2 > ... > x_n$, and $>$ is an ordering relation on S. Let $|L|$ denote the number of the elements in S, and $R(i)$ denotes the rank (position) of element i in L.

(a)   *Overlap measures*
Given two lists, L_1 and L_2, the overlap of L_1 and L_2 is given by $O(L_1, L_2) = |L_1 \cap L_2|$. That is to say, the overlap of L_1 and L_2 equals the number of elements occurring in both L_1 and L_2.

Given several ranked lists $J, L_1, L_2, ..., L_k$, the overlap of J to $L_1, L_2, ..., L_k$ is given by $O(J, L_1, L_2, ..., L_k) = (1/k)\sum_{i=1}^{k} O(J, L_i)$.

(b) *Distance measures*

Given two lists, L_1 and L_2 we first construct two new lists, N_1 and N_2, which only record the overlapped elements of L_1 and L_2 and which maintain the orders in the original lists. Then, we can calculate the distance between N_1 and N_2 by using the following method. We denote S as the set of elements in the newly constructed list.

Kendall tau distance. It counts the number of disagreements in the ordering between any two elements in the two lists (Kendall & Gibbons, 1990). Formally, the Kendall distance of L_1 and L_2 is given by:

$$K(L_1, L_2) = K(N_1, N_2) = |\{(i, j) \mid R_1(i) < R_1(j) \ \& \ R_2(i) > R_2(j) \ \& \ i, j \in S\}|,$$

where $R_1(i)$ and $R_2(i)$ are the rank positions of i in lists N_1 and N_2, respectively. Then, we can get the normalized distance by dividing the maximum possible distance $|S| * (|S|-1)/2$.

For $NK(L_1, L_2) = K(N_1, N_2)/(|S| * (|S|-1)/2)$, similarly, we can extend the distance measure for more than two lists. Given several lists $J, L_1, L_2, ..., L_k$, the distance of J to $L_1, L_2, ..., L_k$ is given by $NK(J, L_1, L_2, ..., L_k)$ $= (1/k)\sum_{i=1}^{k} NK(J, L_i)$.

From the definition of the distance, we see that the maximum possible value is 1, which means that the two list are totally reversed. The minimum possible value is 0, which means that the two lists are identical.

EXPERIMENT RESULTS

We carried out the experiment on August 2, 2002. All 58 queries were submitted to Google, AltaVista, AlltheWeb and WiseNut. The top 50 results from each search engine were retrieved for further analysis according to the principles described in last section. Here, we give our main results of the experiment.

Table 1. Number of Results Retrieved on Average Out of All 58 Queries in Three Cases: Top 10, Top 20 and Top 50

Case	Top 10	Top 20	Top 50
The number of results returned by only 1 search engine	22.36 (77.32%)	44.90 (77.29%)	107.91 (75.49%)
The number of results returned by 2 search engines	3.84 (13.28%)	7.24 (12.46%)	20.64 (14.44%)
The number of results returned by all 3 search engines	1.79 (6.19%)	4.14 (7.13%)	9.84 (6.88%)
The number of results returned by all 4 search engines	0.93 (3.21%)	1.81 (3.12%)	4.55 (3.19%)
The number of total distinct results	28.92	58.09	142.94

Overview

After analyzing the results returned by each search engine, we can get the basic situation of overlap between the results. Some results are retrieved by all four search engines, while most of the results are only returned by one search engine. In Table 1, we report the overview of the search results in three cases: top 10, top 20 and top 50. It gives the number of results retrieved, on average, out of 58 queries. From this table, we can see that over 75 percent of the total distinct results are retrieved by only one search engine, and only about 3 percent of the total distinct results are retrieved by all four search engines. Table 2 shows the case where the maximum and minimum distinct search results are retrieved. For instance, considering the top 50 results from each search engine, the maximum number of distinct returned results is 185 when submitting the query "xxx." At the same time, the queries which achieved maximum and minimum overlap in all four search engines are displayed in Table 3. For example, considering the top 20 results from each search engine, there are seven results retrieved by all four search engines when submitting the query "google."

Table 2. Maximum, Minimum, and Average Number of Distinct Results Retrieved Out of All 58 Queries in Three Cases: Top 10, Top 20 and Top 50

Case	Top 10	Top 20	Top 50
Maximum (The Query)	39 (free porn)	75 (porn)	185 (xxx)
Minimum (The Query)	17 (google)	38 (google)	106 (baby names)
Average	28.92	58.09	142.94

Difference Among Categories

As we noted in the last section, we divide all 58 queries into three categories. The queries in Category A are mainly composed of a specific name of a web site, a company or a product. Usually there exists a web site for this kind of query. In Category B, the queries are very general terms, such as *map*, *hotels*, *jokes*, etc. In Category C, the queries are mainly related to adult content.

In this experiment, we compared the search results for different categories. At first we compare the top1 hit from each search engine. As illustrated in Table 4, the search engines tend to agree with each other on Category A, but they behave totally differently on Category C. For each query in Category A, any two search engines will return same hit (web site) at the top1 position in 85 percent of the cases, while only a 6.25 percent overlap occurs for Category C.

Table 3. Maximum, Minimum, and Average Number of Distinct Results Retrieved by All Four Search Engines

Case	Top 10	Top 20	Top 50
Maximum (The Query)	4 (clip art)	7 (google)	15 (clip art)
Minimum	0	0	0
Average	0.93	1.81	4.55

Table 4. Number of Queries Having Same Top 1 (First) Result Between Search Engine Pairs Out of 58 Queries in Three Categories

Category	A(specific)	B(General)	C(adult)
Number of Queries	10	40	8
(Google-AltaVista)	9 (90%)	12 (30%)	0
(Google-AlltheWeb)	8 (80%)	13 (32.5%)	1 (12.5%)
(Google-WiseNut)	8 (80%)	15 (37.5%)	2 (25%)
(AltaVista-AlltheWeb)	9 (90%)	6 (15%)	0
(AltaVista-Wisenut)	9 (90%)	7 (17.5%)	0
(AlltheWeb-WiseNut)	8 (80%)	13 (32.5%)	0
Average	8.5 (85%)	11 (27.5%)	0.5 (6.25%)

In Table 5, we present the maximum, minimum, and average number of totally distinct search results for the queries in each category. In all three cases (top 10, top 20, top 50), we obtain the most results for the queries in Category C, and the fewest results for queries in Category A. But, the difference between the queries in Category A and Category B decreases when we fetch more results for merging from each search engine.

Overlap of the Search Results

In Tables 6, 7 and 8, we present the average overlap of the top N (N=10, 20 or 50, respectively) search results, between any two search engines, out of all 58 queries in three categories. We can see that AltaVista and WiseNut have the lowest overlap on the queries in Category A; Google and WiseNut have the highest overlap over the queries in Category B and Category C.

Table 9 shows the average overlap of the top N (N=10, 20 or 50) search results, between one search engine and any other search engine, out of all 58 queries in three categories. For instance: Overlap(Google)=1/3(Overlap(Google-AltaVista)+Overlap(Google-AlltheWeb)+ Overlap(Google-WiseNut)). The high value of average overlap means that the search engine is highly supported

Table 5. Number of Distinct Results Retrieved Out of 58 Queries in Three Categories for Three Cases: Top 10, 20 and 50

Case	Category	Maximum	Minimum	Average
Top 10	A (specific)	17	33	24.4
Top 10	B (general)	19	36	28.8
Top 10	C (adult)	31	39	35.25
Top 20	A (specific)	38	65	52.9
Top 20	B (general)	44	73	56.78
Top 20	C (adult)	64	75	71.13
Top 50	A (specific)	108	157	136.7
Top 50	B (general)	106	167	138.4
Top 50	C (adult)	160	185	173.5

by all other search engines. With respect to queries in Category B, the order of the search engines from high to low, according to average overlap, is Google, WiseNut, AlltheWeb and AltaVista, for all three cases (top10, top 20, top50). Different from Category B, the order for the queries in Category C for all three cases is Google, WiseNut, AltaVista and AlltheWeb.

Table 6. Average Overlap of Top10 Results Between Any Two Search Engines Out of 58 Queries in Three Categories

Category	A(specific)	B(General)	C(adult)
Overlap(Google-AltaVista)	3.6	2.13	1.13
Overlap(Google-AlltheWeb)	3.4	3.5	0.75
Overlap(Google-WiseNut)	3	3.9	2
Overlap(AltaVista-AlltheWeb)	3.3	1.43	0.5
Overlap(Altavista-WiseNut)	2.6	1.73	0.62
Overlap(AlltheWeb-WiseNut)	2.6	3.08	0.5
Average	3.08	2.63	0.917

Table 7. Average Overlap of Top 20 Results Between Any Two Search Engines Out of 58 Queries in Three Categories

Category	A(specific)	B(General)	C(adult)
Overlap(Google-AltaVista)	5.8	4.72	2.63
Overlap(Google-AlltheWeb)	6.6	7.55	1.25
Overlap(Google-WiseNut)	6.3	8.15	3.62
Overlap(AltaVista-AlltheWeb)	5.2	3.6	0.63
Overlap(AltaVista-WiseNut)	4.5	3.55	1.5
Overlap(AlltheWeb-WiseNut)	5.9	6.0	0.86
Average	5.72	5.60	1.75

Table 8. Average Overlap of Top 50 Results Between Any Two Search Engines Out of 58 Queries in Three Categories

Category	A(specific)	B(General)	C(adult)
Overlap(Google-AltaVista)	14.6	13.93	7.38
Overlap(Google-AlltheWeb)	15.2	18.8	3.5
Overlap(Google-WiseNut)	13.9	19.68	9.75
Overlap(AltaVista-AlltheWeb)	11.8	10.28	1.5
Overlap(AltaVista-WiseNut)	9.5	10.2	4.38
Overlap(AlltheWeb-WiseNut)	12.2	14.48	2
Average	12.87	14.56	4.75

Table 9. Average Overlap of the TopN (N=10,20 or 50) Results Between Each Search Engine and Any Other Search Engines Out of All 58 Queries in Three Categories

Case	Category	Google	AltaVista	AlltheWeb	WiseNut
Top10	A	3.33	3.17	3.1	2.73
Top10	B	3.18	1.76	2.67	2.9
Top10	C	1.29	0.75	0.58	1.04
Top20	A	6.23	5.17	5.9	5.57
Top20	B	6.81	3.96	5.72	5.9
Top20	C	2.5	1.58	0.92	2
Top50	A	14.57	11.97	13.07	11.87
Top50	B	17.47	11.47	14.52	14.78
Top50	C	6.88	4.42	2.33	5.38

However, in Category A, we don't have a consistent order for the queries for all three cases (top 10, top 20, top 50). In Category A, Google always obtains the highest overlap, and the difference among all four search engines is very small. As shown in Table 9, Google always achieves the highest overlap among all cases for the queries in all three categories.

Distance of the Search Results

In the previous section, we presented a method (*Kendall tau distance*) for computing the distance between two rank lists retrieved by different search engines. Since low overlap makes the distance less meaningful, we will eliminate some low overlap cases and consider the following cases for the experiment: Category A, top 20; Category A, top 50; Category B, top 20; Category B, top 50.

In this experiment, we calculated the Kendall tau *distance* between two search results retrieved by different search engines. Table 10 presents the results of the mean distance over any two search engines out of all queries in Categories A and B in two cases (top 20 and top 50). Since the overlap is very small for the queries in Category C, we don't calculate the distance for the queries in Category C. We can see that there are no obvious differences among all search engine pairs. Since all search engines tend to agree with the top 1 for queries in Category A, the distance for Category A is obviously smaller than the one in Category B.

Table 10. Average Kendall Distance of the Top N (N=20 or 50) Results Between Any Two Search Engines Out of All Queries in Category A and B

Category	A(Speicfic)	B(general)	A(specific)	B(general)
Top N	20	20	50	50
Google-AltaVista	0.215	0.404	0.282	0.43
Google-AlltheWeb	0.244	0.365	0.33	0.366
Google-WiseNut	0.242	0.326	0.294	0.348
AltaVista-AlltheWeb	0.176	0.424	0.333	0.402
AltaVista-WiseNut	0.152	0.369	0.284	0.432
AlltheWeb-WiseNut	0.243	0.385	0.334	0.381

In Table 11, we present the average Kendall *tau distance* between each search engine and any other search engines. We can see that AltaVista has the largest distance for the queries in Category B, while it has the smallest distance for the queries in Category A. In Category B, Google has the smallest distance.

DISCUSSION

In this experiment, the search results retrieved by the four search engines have little overlap. Over 75 percent of the total distinct results are returned by only one search engine, and less than 3 percent are retrieved by all four search

Table 11. Average Kendall Distance of the Top N (N=20 or 50) Results Between Each Search Engine and Any Other Search Engines Out of All 58 Queries in Category A and Category B

Category	Top N	Google	AltaVista	AlltheWeb	WiseNut
A	20	0.243	0.178	0.229	0.197
A	50	0.302	0.3	0.332	0.304
B	20	0.358	0.397	0.384	0.356
B	50	0.381	0.423	0.382	0.386

engines. We think this is due to the various ranking algorithms adopted and to different coverage of the index database. On the other hand, the distribution of the overlap is relatively steady in all three cases (top 10, top 20, top 50). It means that the overlapped results do not definitely occur in high ranks.

The search results for the queries in different categories behave very differently. For the queries in Category A (specific), all four search engines will retrieve same top 1 result in more than 80 percent of the time. However, they achieve little agreement on the queries in Category C (adult). In all three cases (top 10, top 20, top 50), the number of total distinct results retrieved for queries in Category C is, on average, 25 percent higher than that of the queries in Categories A or B. It also indicates that there are no obvious web site winners for adult-related content.

We present the overlap between any two search engines and the mean overlap of one search engine with any other search engine. There are, altogether, six search engine pairs for four search engines. Because the overlap is affected by several factors, such as the queries in different categories, and different cases (top 10, top 20 or top 50), no search engine pairs can obtain maximum overlap in all cases. However, when we calculate the average overlap for each search engine, Google always achieves the highest average overlap for all cases. It indicates that, in some degree, Google is highly recognized by other search engines.

Different from the overlap, the results for distance of search have a low variation over all search engine pairs. This may result from the fact that each search engine independently adopts different ranking algorithms. Since the distance is approximately 0.4 for most cases, it means that the ranking algorithms adopted by different search engines could, to some degree, achieve similarly ranked lists. The distance for the queries in Category A for the top 20 case is relatively lower than other situations, which is due to the highest overlap of the top 1 result for the queries in Category A.

FUTURE DIRECTIONS FOR RESEARCH

This study shows that, for some popular queries, each search engine will retrieve its distinct result. There also exist significant differences among queries in different categories. Since our study is on searching web pages, a natural extension of this research is to study searching news, FTPs, music and video, etc. On the other hand, the sampling queries in this study were some very popular and general queries. To study searching in a specific field, we could concentrate web searches on some of the most-used queries in that domain.

With the evolution of the search engine, keyword searching, linkage analysis and, now, paid for included (PFI) have been implemented in current web search engines. Due to PFI, business companies must pay a search engine company to be placed in the search results of some specific queries, such as travel and shopping. The most famous PFI search engine is Overture (http://www.overture.com). Although it increases the return on investment for a search engine, it may harm our efforts to search for objective information. The impact of PFI on web searching needs be investigated in detail.

CONCLUSION

In this chapter, we carry out a simple case study on the overlap and distance of search results, by multiple search engines, on some popular queries. We submitted 58 sample queries, provided by the WordTracker service, to four general search engines (Google, AltaVista, Alltheweb and WiseNut). These queries were divided into specific, general and adult-related queries. Three cases (top 10, top 20 and top 50) were considered in the experiment.

The highlights of our findings in this experiment are summarized as follows:

(1)   The search results by different search engines have little overlap.
(2)   The search results for the queries in different categories behave in dramatically different ways. Search engines usually return the same top 1 result for the query in Category A, while there is very little overlap on the query in Category C.
(3)   Different search engine pairs have different overlap of the search results. But, in all cases in this study, Google has the highest overlap with other search engines.
(4)   Compared with overlap, the distance of the search results retrieved by different search engines show only a slight variation. This indicates that each search engine independently adopts a different ranking algorithm.

Although only 58 popular queries and four major search engines were examined, this study illustrates that the distinct characterization of queries in different categories, and the independent ranking algorithm adopted by each search engine, result in distinguished search results. This will shed light on future research in the areas of proposing effective result-merging algorithms in metasearch engines and search engine evaluation algorithms.

ACKNOWLEDGMENTS

This work is supported by a joint research grant (N_CityU 102/01) of Hong Kong RGC and NNSFC of China.

REFERENCES

Bar-Ilan, J. (2001). Methods for measuring search engine performance over time. *Poster Proceedings of the 10th International WWW Conference,* Hong Kong.

Bar-Ilan, J. (2002). Methods for measuring search engine performance over time. *Journal of the American Society for Information Science, 53*(4), 308-319.

Bharat, K. & Broder, A. (1998). A technique for measuring the relative size of public web search engines. *Proceedings of the 7th International WWW Conference,* Brisbane Australia.

Hoelscher, C. (1998). How Internet experts search for information on the Web. In H. Maurer & R.G. Olson (Eds.), *Proceedings of WebNet98 - World Conference of the WWW, Internet & Intranet.* Charlottesville, VA: AACE.

Jansen, B. (2000). An investigation into the use of simple queries on web IR systems. *Information Research: An Electronic Journal, 6*(1).

Jansen, B., Spink, A., & Saracevic, T. (2000). Real life, real users, and real needs: A study and analysis of user queries on the Web. *Information Processing and Management, 36*(2), 207-227.

Kendall, M. & Gibbons, J. D. (1990). *Rank Correlation Methods.* London: Edward Arnold.

Lawrence, S. & Giles, C. L. (1998). Searching the World Wide Web. *Science, 5360*(28), 98-100.

Lawrence, S. & Giles, C. L. (1999). Accessibility of information on the Web. *Nature, 400*, 107-109.

Risvik, K. & Michelsen, R. (2002). Search engines and web dynamics. *Computer Networks*, 39(3), 289-302.

Silverstein, C., Henzinger, M., Marais, H., & Moricz, M. (1999). Analysis of a very large web search engine query log. *SIGIR Forum, 33*(1), 6-12.

Spink, A., Jansen, B., Wolfram, D., & Saracevic, T. (2002). From e-sex to e-commerce: Web search changes. *IEEE Computer, 35*(3), 107-109.

Spink, A., Wolfram, D., Janson, B., & Saracevic, T. (2001). Searching the Web: The public and their queries. *Journal of the American Society for Information Science, 52*(2), 226-234.

Wolfram, D. (1999). Term co-occurrence in Internet search engine queries: An analysis of the Excite data set. In *Proceedings of the 27th Annual Conference of the Canadian Association for Information Science* (pp. 438-451).

Chapter XV

Taxonomy Based Fuzzy Filtering of Search Results

S. Vrettos, National Technical University of Athens, Greece

A. Stafylopatis, National Technical University of Athens, Greece

ABSTRACT

Our work proposes the use of topic taxonomies as part of a filtering language. Given a taxonomy, we train classifiers for every topic of it. The user is able to formulate logical rules combining the available topics, e.g., (Topic1 AND Topic2) OR Topic3, in order to filter related documents in a stream of documents. Using the classifiers, every document in the stream is assigned a belief value of belonging to the topics of the filter. These belief values are then aggregated using logical operators to yield the belief to the filter. In that framework, we are concerned with the operators that provide the best filtering performance for the user.

In our study, Support Vector Machines (SVMs) and Naïve Bayes (NB) classifiers were used to provide topic probabilities. Fuzzy aggregation operators were tested on the Reuters text corpus and showed better results

than their Boolean counterparts. Moreover, the application of Ordered Weighted Averaging (OWA) operators considerably improved the performance of fuzzy aggregation, especially in the case of NB classifiers. Finally, we describe a filtering system to exemplify the use of fuzzy filtering.

INTRODUCTION

The primary way of interactively finding information on the Web is to make a query in a search engine and then browse a ranked list of possibly related web pages. Alternatively, we can browse a manually organized topic taxonomy to find pages related to the query that we have in mind. Although web taxonomies may be very large, they cover a small portion of the Web relative to search engines, primarily because they rely on human effort.

Text/Hypertext categorization (see Yang, 1999; Yang et al., 1999; Chen, 2000) promises to help maintain updated and large web taxonomies and also to improve query-based (Dumais, 2001) retrieval. The idea is to use topic classifiers, which have been trained using the portion of the well-structured web taxonomy, to organize the results of a query to the much larger, but unclassified, web portion indexed by a search engine. Basically, as regards the interface used to include topic information in the query results, it can be topic-oriented or list-oriented. In topic-oriented interfaces, results are organized in a flat or hierarchical taxonomy; in list-oriented interfaces, the original query list is enriched with topic meta-data.

Our work proposes the use of topic taxonomies as part of a filtering language. The user is able to formulate logical rules combining the available topics, e.g., (Topic1 AND Topic2) OR Topic3, in order to retrieve or filter related documents. In that framework, we are concerned with the operators that provide the best filtering performance for the user.

Typically, classification is a YES/NO assignment, so the Boolean model is a good candidate for the filtering task. Nevertheless, Boolean filtering provides no ordering, which is a drawback to both retrieval effectiveness and man-machine interaction. If perfect classifiers were available, Boolean filtering would be enough because all the true positive documents of the stream, and only them, would be retrieved. In that case, Boolean filtering would yield recall and precision equal to 1. Unfortunately, no perfect classifiers are available yet, and even the best performing classifiers in laboratory text corpora might have poor results in real, noisy environments such as the Web. In such cases, ranking according to some suitable measure of classification accuracy is able to improve retrieval performance. This improvement is gained either by improving recall through the retrieval of false negative documents that were not included in the answer set, or by improving precision through the ordering of true positive documents higher in the rank, above false positive ones.

To provide ordering of the filtering results, we used the Ordered Weighted Operators (OWA) to aggregate the topic probabilities of a document in a stream according to the logical rule defined. In our study, Support Vector Machines (SVMs) and Naïve Bayes (NB) classifiers were used to provide topic probabilities. OWA aggregation operators have been tested on the Reuters corpus, justifying their use over their Boolean counterparts.

TEXT CLASSIFICATION

Let D be a collection of m documents d_i, $i=1...m$, each one belonging to one or more of c categories (topics) c_j, $j=1...c$. The document feature vector space D^n is defined through the term–document matrix, TF, where tf_{ki} is the frequency of occurrence of the kth term, $k=1...n$, to the ith document of the collection.

A text classifier is a mapping f from the document feature vector space D^n to the category vector space C^c. The category vector space is defined through the category-document matrix CD, where $cd_{ji} \in \{0,1\}$ is the information of whether the ith document belongs to the jth category. To create such a mapping using machine learning, we need to split the document collection into a training set and a test set, and then use these sets to create and test the classifiers respectively.

Table 1. Term-Document Matrix TF

	d_1	...	d_i	...	d_m
t_1	tf_{11}	...	tf_{1i}	...	tf_{1m}
...	...	...	...	...	...
t_k	tf_{k1}	...	tf_{ki}	...	tf_{km}
...	...	...	...	...	...
t_n	tf_{ni}	...	tf_{ni}	...	tf_{nm}

Table 2. Category-Document Matrix CD

	Training Set				Test Set			
	d_1	...	...	d_i	d_{i+1}	...	...	d_m
c_1	cd_{11}	...	...	cd_{1i}	$cd_{1(i+1)}$	...	...	cd_{1m}
...	...	...	...	...	...	...	...	...
c_j	cd_{j1}	...	...	cd_{ji}	$cd_{j(i+1)}$	...	...	cd_{jm}
...	...	...	...	...	...	...	...	...
c_c	cd_{c1}	...	...	cd_{ci}	$cd_{c(i+1)}$	...	...	cd_{cm}

Support Vector Machines (SVMs)

In this work, we used Support Vector Machines (SVMs) as text classifiers (Dumais, 1998). The SVM model was proposed by Vapnik in 1979. In recent years, it has gained much popularity due to its strong theoretical and empirical justification. In the simplest linear form, a SVM is a hyperplane that separates a set of positive examples from a set of negative examples with maximum margin. A separating hyperplane (Cherkassky, 1998) is a linear function capable of separating the training data in the classification problem without error. Suppose that the training data consist of n samples $(x_1, y_1), ..., (x_n, y_n)$, $x_i \in R^d, y_i \in \{+1, -1\}$, which can be separated by a hyperplane decision function

$$D(x) = (w \cdot x) + w_0 \tag{1}$$

with appropriate coefficients w and w_0. A separating hyperplane satisfies the constraints that define the separation of data samples:

$$y_i[(w \cdot x_i) + w_0] \geq 1, \quad i = 1, ..., n \tag{2}$$

The minimal distance from the separating hyperplane to the closest data point is called the *margin*, denoted by ***T***. A separating hyperplane is called "optimal" if the margin is the maximum size. It is intuitively clear that a larger margin corresponds to better generalization.

The key to finding the optimal hyperplane is to find the coefficient vector w that maximizes the margin ***T***, or equivalently minimizing

$$\eta(w) = \|w\|^2 \tag{3}$$

with respect to both w and w_0.

In the case of training data that cannot be separated without error, positive slack variables ξ_i, $i=1,...,n$ can be introduced to quantify the nonseparable data in the defining condition of the hyperplane:

$$y_i[(w \cdot x_i) + w_0] \geq 1 - \xi_i \tag{4}$$

For a training sample x_i, the slack variable ξ_i is the deviation from the margin border corresponding to the class of y_i. Slack variables greater then 0 correspond to nonseparable points, while slack variables greater than 1 correspond to misclassified samples.

It is possible to pose the problem in terms of quadratic optimization by introducing the following equivalent formulation concept of the soft margin hyperplane. This hyperplane is defined by the coefficients w, w_0 that minimize the functional:

$$\frac{C}{n}\sum_{i=1}^{n}\xi_i + \frac{1}{2}\|w\|^2 \tag{5}$$

subject to the constraints and given sufficiently large (fixed) C. In this form, the coefficient C affects the trade-off between the complexity and proportion of nonseparable samples, and it must be selected by the user.

To relieve the problem of nonlinear separability, a nonlinear mapping of the training data into a high-dimensional feature space is usually performed according to Cover's theorem on the separability of patterns (Haykin, 1999). The separating hyperplane is now defined as a linear function of vectors drawn from the feature space rather than from the original input space. This expansion is usually realized based on a Radial-Basis inner product kernel:

$$k(x, \bar{x}) = \exp\left(-\frac{\|x - \bar{x}\|^2}{2\sigma^2}\right) \tag{6}$$

where the width σ^2 is specified a priory by the user and is common to all the kernels.

The constrained optimization problem is solved using the method of Lagrange multipliers. In this work, we used the OSU SVM Classifier Matlab Toolbox (OSU SVM) to train classifiers.

To obtain a good performance, the parameters C and σ (in the case of a Radial-Basis kernel) of the SVM model have to be chosen carefully (Duan, 2001). These "higher level" parameters are usually referred to as hyperparameters.

To provide an accurate measure of confidence, Platt (2000) proposed a parametric approach for SVM. This approach consists of finding the parameters A and B of a sigmoid function, and then mapping the scores $f_i = D(x_i) = (w \cdot x_i) + w_0$ into probability estimates

$$p_i = \frac{1}{1 + \exp(Af_i + B)} \tag{7}$$

such that the negative log-likelihood cross-entropy error function of the data

$$\min - \sum_i t_i \log(p_i) + (1 - t_i) \log(1 - p_i) \tag{8}$$

is minimized using maximum likelihood estimation.

Naïve Bayes

Bayes theorem can be used to estimate the probability $\Pr(c_j | d_i)$ that a document d_i is in class c_j.

$$\Pr(c_j | d_i) = \frac{\Pr(d_i | c_j) \cdot \Pr(c_j)}{\sum_{l=1}^{c} \Pr(d_i | c_l) \Pr(c_l)} \tag{9}$$

where $\Pr(c_j)$ is the prior probability that a document is in class c_j, and where $\Pr(d_i | c_j)$ is the likelihood of observing document d_i in class c_j.

$\hat{\Pr}(c_j)$, the estimate of $\Pr(c_j)$, can be calculated from the fraction of the training documents that is assigned to this class:

$$\hat{\Pr}(c_j) = \frac{|c_j|}{\sum_{l=1}^{c} c_l} \tag{10}$$

The probability of observing a document like d_i in class c_j is based on the naive assumption that a word's occurrence in class c_j is independent of the occurrences of the other words. Therefore, $\Pr(d_i|c_j)$ is:

$$\Pr(d_i \mid c_j) = \prod_{k=1}^{n} \Pr(t_k \mid c_j), t_k \in d_i \tag{11}$$

where t_k represents the kth term of the collection document. The estimation of $P(d_i|c_j)$ is now reduced to the estimation of $P(t_k|c_j)$ (Laplace estimator), which is the likelihood of observing t_k in class c_j:

$$\Pr(t_k \mid c_j) = \frac{1 + tf(t_k, c_j)}{n + \sum_{l=1}^{n} tf(t_l, c_j)} \tag{12}$$

where $tf(t_k, c_j)$ is the number of occurrences of the word t_k in category c_j, and where n is the number of the terms of the corpus.

In this work, we have used the NB algorithm for multi-topic categorization, so we define a threshold h_j related to each category j. If $\Pr(c_j|d_i) > h_j$, then document d_i is categorized under category c_j. Threshold selection is performed by measuring the F1-measure in a validation set (Sebastiani, 2002).

ORDERED WEIGHTED AVERAGING OPERATORS

In this work, we propose the use of topic classifiers as part of a filtering language. The user is able to formulate logical rules combining the available topics, e.g., (Topic1 AND Topic2) OR Topic3, in order to retrieve or filter related documents in an incoming document stream. Under this assumption, we are interested in finding the operators that provide the best filtering performance. We can either aggregate the final decisions or the estimated probabilities of the classifiers. In the first (Boolean) case, the final decision is influenced by the selection of the decision thresholds, and it provides no ordering. The second (fuzzy) case provides ordering and a means to optimize the selection of the operators.

Ordered weighted averaging operators (OWA) (Yager, 1994) is a family of mean like operators that can adjust the degree of "AND-ing" and "OR-ing" in an aggregation. OWA have been used in many applications, including machine leaning (see Yager, 1997; Cho, 1995).

More formally, an OWA operator of dimension n is a mapping $f: R^n \rightarrow R$ that has an associated vector $w = [w_1 \ w_2 \dots w_n]$, such that (1) $w_i \in [0,1]$ and

(2) $\sum_{i=1}^{n} w_i = 1$. Let α_i, i=1..n, be the membership values to be aggregated, then

$f(\alpha_1,\dots, \alpha_n) = \sum_{i=1}^{n} w_i \cdot b_i$ with b_i the ith largest of the α_i. Therefore, the weight

w_i is not associated with a value $\pm_i$ but with the ith ordered position, imposing nonlinearity in the aggregation.

The classical Min, Max, and Average aggregations are special cases of OWA operators:

(1) $F^*(\alpha_1,\dots, \alpha_n) = Max_i(\alpha_i)$, with associated vector $W^* = [1 \ 0 \dots 0]$

(2) $F_*(\alpha_1,\dots, \alpha_n) = Min_i(\alpha_i)$, with associated vector $W_* = [0 \ 0 \dots 1]$

(3) $F_A(\alpha_1,\dots, \alpha_n) = \frac{1}{n}\sum_{i=1}^{n} a_i$, with associated vector $W_A = \left[\frac{1}{n} \frac{1}{n} \cdots \frac{1}{n}\right]$

By appropriate choice of the weighting vector, we can move continuously from AND (Min) to OR (Max) type aggregation. A special family of OWA operators, called the S-OWA-OR (OR-like) and S-OWA-AND (AND-like) aggregations, are:

$$\tilde{v}_i \, \alpha_i = (1-\beta)\frac{1}{m}\sum_{i=1}^{m}\alpha_i + \beta \vee \alpha_i \qquad (13)$$

$$\tilde{\wedge}_i \, \alpha_i = (1-\alpha)\frac{1}{m}\sum_{i=1}^{m}\alpha_i + \alpha \wedge \alpha_i \qquad (14)$$

where α_i are the numbers in the unit interval to be aggregated. As we can see, for $b \in [0,1]$, the S-OWA-OR operator is between the mean and the maximum of numbers α_i, while for $\alpha \in [0,1]$, the S-OWA-AND operator is between the minimum and the mean of the numbers α_i.

EVALUATION AND RESULTS

To evaluate fuzzy filtering against Boolean filtering, we used the Reuters-21578 corpus. We consider the flat topic taxonomy that consists of the 10 most frequently assigned topic categories. A term-document matrix was created after removing the infrequent [Jochims] and the most commonly used English words. Using the labels of the topics, we are able to formulate filters of the form (Earn) AND (Trade), (Acq) OR (Money-Fx), and then use them to find relevant documents in a stream of data.

To specify the exact filters to use, and to measure their effectiveness as regards the logical operators, we considered the "ModApte" split, a standard commonly-used partitioning of the Reuters corpus into training and test sets. A search in the test set of the "ModApte" split yielded 213 documents that belong to two or more of the specified topics. These documents constitute the set F to be filtered and are mapped to 19 multi-category vectors in the table CM, where $cm_{ij} = 1$ implies that category c_j exists in multicategory vector m_i.

For every multicategory vector m_i, where $i=1...19$, of the filtering set, the logic operator AND is used to combine trained classifiers of all categories having $cm_{ji} = 1$, in order to find documents in F that belong to all of them. In the same way, the logic operator OR is used to combine trained classifiers of

Table 3. Category-Multicategory Matrix CM

	m_1	...	m_i	...	m_{19}
c_1	cm_{11}	...	cm_{1i}	...	$cm_{1,19}$
...	...	...	...	...	...
c_j	cm_{j1}	...	cm_{ji}	...	$cm_{j,19}$
...	...	...	...	...	...
c_{10}	$cm_{10,1}$	...	$cm_{10,i}$	...	$cm_{10,19}$

all categories having $cm_{ji} = 1$, in order to find documents in F that belong to at least one of them. Finally, the logic operator NOT is used in conjunction with OR to combine trained classifiers of all categories having $cm_{ji} = 1$, in order to find documents in F that do not belong to any of them. As a result, we form 19 filters and obtain their relevant documents in F for every logical operator.

SVM Training

To reduce dimensionality, we applied Principal Component Analysis (PCA) on the training set leaving the 300 most informative features. We trained and validated one two-class SVM classifier for every topic in the "ModApte" split. We took as positive examples all the samples that belong to the topic. As negative examples we took all the samples that do not belong to the topic.

To obtain the best possible classification accuracy, we optimized the hyperparameters of nonlinear SVM on the filtering set F. In Table 4, we give the classification accuracy of SVM on the test (filtering) set. The output of each SVM was transformed to probability using maximum likelihood, as described in Section 2, using the MATLAB optimization toolbox.

NB Training

We trained and validated one NB classifier for every topic in the "ModApte" split. For the 10 classifiers, we validated each combination of thresholds out of three different threshold values $(0.05, 0.1, 0.3)$ in the filtering set F. The best threshold set was selected based on the F1 measure and macroaveraging (Sebastiani, 2002). In Table 4, we give the classification accuracy of NB on the test (filtering) set.

Table 4. Classification Accuracy of SVM on the Test Set

Topic	SVM	NB
Earn	0.9812	0
Acq	0.9812	0.4
Money-fx	0.9531	0.5102
Crude	0.9624	0.4681
Grain	0.9484	0.7739
Trade	0.9635	0.0769
Interest	0.9108	0.5909
Ship	0.9531	0.5870
Wheat	0.9014	0.6197
Corn	0.9624	0.5179
Average	0.9518	0.4537

Table 5. Average Recall and Precision for All Filters and Operators

Operator	SVMs		NB	
	Precision	Recall	Precision	Recall
AND	0.36	0.39	0.21	0.15
OR	0.93	0.86	0.96	0.54
NOT	0.75	0.80	0.75	0.99

In the case of Boolean filtering, every document d in F was assigned the crisp value $\{0,1\}$, depending on whether it belongs to class c_j or not. For every filter, the related decisions were aggregated using Boolean logic. Because no ordering is available, Boolean filtering was evaluated by averaging recall and precision over all filters for both NB and SVM training of a logical operator (see Table 5).

In the case of fuzzy filtering, every document d in F was assigned a value indicating the estimated probability $Pr(c_j|d)$ that it belongs to class c_j. For every filter, the related probabilities $Pr(c_j|d)$ were aggregated using OWA operators to estimate whether d is relevant to the filter. Because fuzzy filtering provides ordering, a standard recall-precision diagram of a logical operator can be constructed (see Figure 1 and Figure 2). Different values of b, in the case of Fuzzy OR and NOT, did not show any difference in performance. On the contrary, the performance of the AND operator was improved for both $\alpha = 0.4$ for NB and $\alpha = 0.1$ for SVMs. It is worth noting that the improvement produced by OWA aggregation on the less accurate NB classifier was much greater than the improvement on the more accurate SVM classifier.

In all cases, fuzzy aggregation succeeded in improving retrieval performance. In the case of OR and NOT operators, the improvement was due to higher precision. This means that true positive documents are placed high in the ranked answer set. In the case of AND operators, fuzzy aggregation managed to improve both recall and precision.

AN EXAMPLE FILTERING SYSTEM

Generally, an information filtering system can be on the server side or on the client side. The proposed fuzzy filtering approach can be used both ways. In client-sided filtering, the taxonomy may be in the form of user's bookmarks, for example. The system creates the topic classifiers that the user uses to filter

Figure 1. Recall-Precision Diagram of the Logic Operators for NB Training

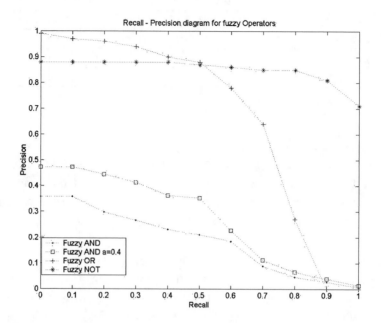

Figure 2. Recall-Precision Diagram of the Logic Operators for SVM Training

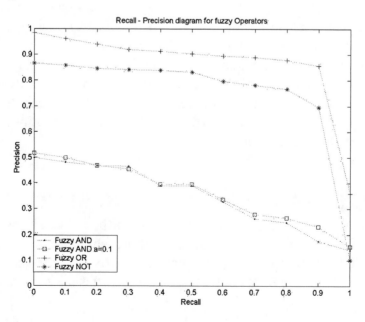

Figure 3. Client vs. Server-Sided Filtering Systems

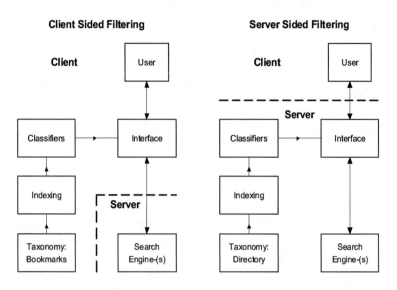

Figure 4. Fuzzy Filtering on the Web

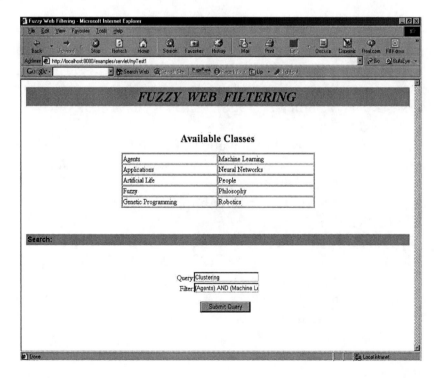

the results of a search engine, according to the method described. In server-sided filtering, the taxonomy may be in the form of a web directory.

In order to provide an example application, we have developed a server-sided filtering system on the Web using the Computers/Artificial Intelligence directory of the Open Directory Project (Dmoz). We created NB classifiers for 10 topics related to this directory, using about 40 web pages as training examples for each topic. The application is available from (ISLab). Through the interface, the user is able to create queries and rules in order to retrieve and filter web pages.

CONCLUSION

In this work, we present and evaluate a framework that can take advantage of a topic taxonomy as part of a filtering language. Fuzzy aggregation of the estimated topic probabilities proved to exhibit superior performance than Boolean aggregation. OWA aggregation operators improved fuzzy aggregation in an inversely proportional manner to classification accuracy. Future work includes the study of the proposed framework, including automatically learned OWA aggregation as well as further deployment of the framework on the Web.

REFERENCES

Chen, H. & Dumais, S. T. (2000). Bringing order to the Web: Automatically categorizing search results. In *Proceedings of the ACM SIGCHI Conference on Human Factors in Computing Systems* (pp. 145-152).

Cherkassky, V. & Mulier, F. (1998). *Learning from Data.* New York: John Wiley & Sons.

Cho, S.-B. (1995). Fuzzy aggregation of modular neural networks with ordered weighted averaging operators. *International Journal of Approximate Reasoning.*

Dmoz. *Open directory project.* From http://dmoz.org/

Duan, K., Keerthi, S. S., & Poo, A. N. (2001). *Evaluation of simple performance measures for tuning SVM hyperparameters.* ICONIP.

Dumais, S., Cutrell, E. & Chen, H. (2001, March). Optimizing search by showing results in context. *SIGCHI, 1*(2), 69-90.

Dumais, S., Platt, J. C., Heckerman, D. & Sahami, M. (1998). Inductive learning algorithms and representations for text categorization. In *Pro-*

ceedings of the ACM Conference on Information and Knowledge Management (pp. 148-155).

Haykin, S. (1999). *Neural Networks: A Comprehensive Foundation.* Englewood Cliffs, NJ: Prentice Hall. ISLab. http://www.islab.ntua.gr

Ohio State University. *OSU SVM classifier matlab toolbox (v. 3.00)* [Computer Software]. Retrieved from http://eewww.eng.ohio-state.edu/~maj/osu_svm/

Platt, J. C. (2000). Probabilities for SV machines. In A. J. Smola (Ed.), *Advances in Large Margin Classifiers.* Cambridge, MA: The MIT Press.

Sebastiani, F. (2002). Machine learning in automated text categorization. *ACM Computing Surveys, 34*(1), 1-47.

Yager, R. R. & Filev, P. D. (1994). *Essentials of Fuzzy Modeling and Control.* New York: John Wiley & Sons.

Yager, R. R. & Kacprzyk, J. (1997). Ordered weighted averaging operators. In *Theory and Applications.* London: Kluwer Academic.

Yang, Y. (1999). An evaluation of statistical approaches to text categorization. *Journal of Information Retrieval, 1-2*(1), 69-90.

Yang, Y. & Liu, X. (1999). A re-examination of text categorization methods. *SIGIR-99, 22nd ACM International Conference on Research and Development in Information Retrieval.*

Chapter XVI

Generating and Adjusting Web Sub-Graph Displays for Web Navigation

Wei Lai, Swinburne University of Technology, Australia

Maolin Huang, University of Technology, Australia

Kang Zhang, University of Texas at Dallas, USA

ABSTRACT

A graph can be used for web navigation. The whole of cyberspace can be regarded as one huge graph. To explore this huge graph, it is critical to find an effective method for tracking a sequence of the graph's subsets (web sub-graphs) based on the user's focus.

This chapter introduces our method for generating and adjusting web sub-graph displays in the process of web navigation. Any online web sub-graph should fit in the display window. To enhance the display, there should not be any overlap between node images in the web sub-graph. Our system ensures that any online web sub-graph has no overlapping node images by letting the user, or the system itself, define the visible and invisible parts of the web graph.

INTRODUCTION

Most web browsers, such as Netscape and Microsoft Explorer, cannot provide the contextual overview required for global orientation; instead, they can only give a set of URL lists.

A graph is more suitable for World Wide Web (WWW) navigation. Nodes in a graph can be used to represent URLs, and edges between nodes can represent links between URLs. We look at the whole cyberspace of the WWW as one graph — a huge and dynamic growing graph. However, it is impossible to display this huge graph on the computer screen.

Most current research interests involve "site mapping" methods (see Chen & Koutsofios, 1997; Maarek & Shaul, 1997; Pilgrim & Leung, 1996). That is, they try to find an effective way of constructing a structured geometrical map for one web site (a local map). This can only guide the user through a very limited region of cyberspace, and it does not help users in their overall journey through the cyberspace.

Huang et al. (1998) proposed an online exploratory visualization approach, which provides a major departure from traditional site-mapping methods. It does not pre-define the geometrical structure of a specific web site (a part of cyberspace); instead, it incrementally calculates and maintains a small visualization of a subset of cyberspace online, corresponding to the change of the user's focus. That is, it automatically displays a sequence of web sub-graphs with smooth animation following the user's orientation. This feature enables the user to logically explore cyberspace without requiring the whole structure of the cyberspace to be known.

However, the Huang et al. (1998) approach uses the FIFO (first in and first out) rule to animate web sub-graphs, which cannot help the user define a web sub-graph. Also, this approach cannot ensure that its web sub-graph layout has no overlapping node images. This chapter introduces an approach for web graph displays that can overcome these drawbacks.

To aid in web navigation using graphs, we should provide clear web graph displays so that the user can easily understand the relationships shown in a web graph. This requires that interaction facilities should be provided to the user for defining and adjusting a web sub-graph. Automatic web sub-graph displays, based on the user's current focus, should fit in the display window and should have no overlaps.

Two major features of our web graph displays are introduced in this chapter. One is that the user can interact with the web graph to let a node's sub-graph be visible or invisible. The other is that overlapping node images/sub-graphs are automatically detected and defined as visible or invisible, based on the user's selection.

EXAMPLES OF WEB GRAPH DISPLAYS

The best demonstration of our web graph display system is through some examples. Figure 1 shows an online web sub-graph. Our system can ensure that any online web sub-graph has no overlapping node images and fits in the window. We provide three kinds of modes for the user's intersection.

In the *LayoutAdjust* mode, the user can adjust a web sub-graph layout. For example, if the user clicks a node in the web sub-graph, the node's sub-graph is changed from invisible to visible, or from visible to invisible. Figure 2 shows the results after the user clicks the nodes — Phone, Fax and Teaching — in the web sub-graph shown in Figure 1. If the user clicks these nodes again, their sub-graphs would become invisible (i.e., they would disappear, as shown in Figure 1). In this way, the user can define a node's sub-graph as visible or invisible by direct manipulation.

When a node's sub-graph becomes visible, our system checks whether there will be overlaps between this sub-graph and any part of the current display. If so, those parts overlapping the sub-graph automatically become

Figure 1. A Web Sub-Graph Display

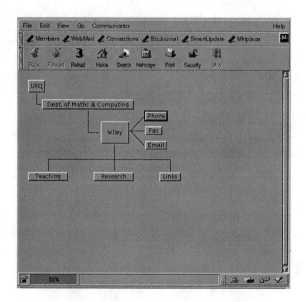

Figure 2. Some Sub-Graphs Become Visible After the User's Interaction

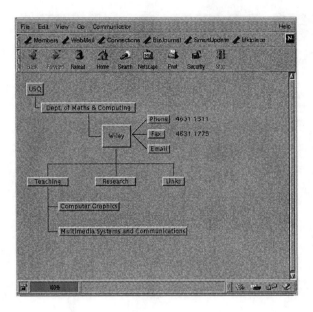

invisible. For instance, in Figure 3, after the user clicks the node with label Research, the sub-graph of this node appears and the sub-graph of the node Teaching automatically disappears.

A node in the web graph is linked to a URL. For example, the node with label Computer Graphics is linked to the web site of the unit 66333 —

Figure 3. A Sub-Graph Becoming Visible Makes Another One Invisible

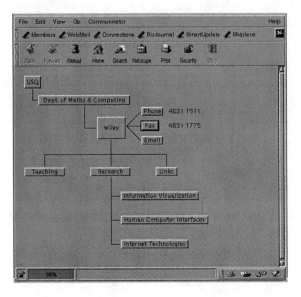

Figure 4. A Web Page Corresponding to a Node is Shown Up

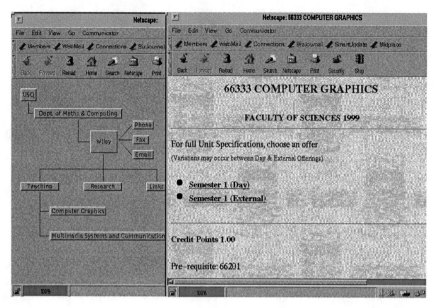

Computer Graphics. The user can switch into the *ShowPage* mode by clicking the middle mouse button. Our system can support the display of a detailed web page corresponding to a node in a web sub-graph (after the ShowPage model is set up). Figure 4 shows the result of the user selecting the node with label Computer Graphics in the *ShowPage* mode.

The third interaction mode is the *Navigation* mode, which can be selected by clicking the right mouse button. In this mode, the user can change the focused node to get another web sub-graph. Suppose that the user's current focused node is Wiley. After the user clicks the node Links, and then the node CNN under the node Link in the navigation model, we can get the web sub-graph corresponding to the user's new current focused node, CNN. This web sub-graph is shown in the window on the left in Figure 5. A web sub-graph keeps track of the user's navigation. That is, it includes two nodes — Wiley and Links — for indicating the previous two steps of navigation. The other nodes linking to the node with label CNN are formed in this way: our system analyzed the source HTML file of the CNN web site and extracted the URLs in this file to form those nodes. In this way, we could test whether the system can navigate from one web site to another.

Figure 5. Another Web Site and Its Web Graph

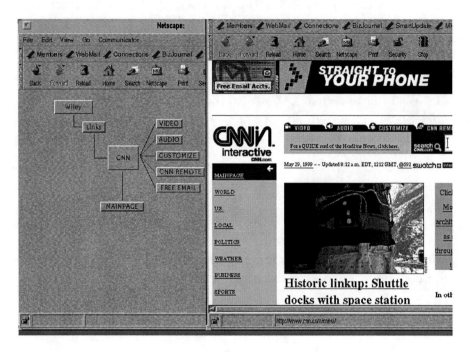

Figure 6. A Web Sub-Graph for the Focused Node "Dept"

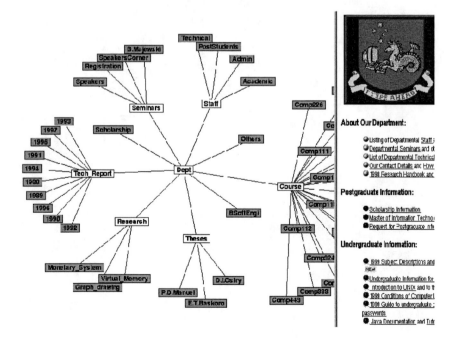

The user can switch among the three interaction modes. For example, after selecting the *ShowPage* mode, if the user clicks the node CNN, the web page of CNN appears (see Figure 5). The user can also use the *LayoutAdjust* mode by clicking the left mouse button. More complex web sub-graph displays are shown in Figure 6 and Figure 7.

Our online web sub-graph is formed dynamically, based on the user's focus. When the user changes the focus (i.e., he clicks a node in the *Navigation* mode), a new web sub-graph is formed by dropping old nodes and adding new ones. This is similar to driving a car: new views arrive in the front and old views vanish in the back.

SYSTEM ARCHITECTURE

Our system design integrates techniques for graphical user interfaces, automatic graph layouts, distributed computing, Internet and web programming, computer networks, and communications.

Figure 7. Navigating the Web Graph from the Node "Dept" to the Nodes "Staff", etc.

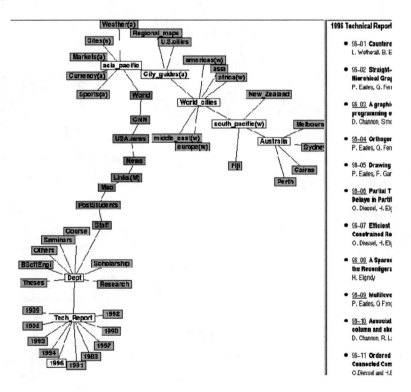

The architecture for our system includes two major components: a web graph user interface component for generating and adjusting web sub-graph displays, and a dialog component for communicating between the diagram user interface and the WWW.

The web graph user interface component displays web sub-graphs, allows layout adjustment, supports web navigation, etc. As mentioned in the previous section, it provides three kinds of modes for the user's interaction with the web sub-graph: *LayoutAdjust*, *ShowPage* and *Navigation*.

The dialog component supports the construction of web sub-graphs by communicating with web sites over the Internet. It can quickly search the entire neighborhood of the focused node to form a web sub-graph.

The dialog component has a web site parser and an information filter. The web site parser analyzes the HTML file of the web site corresponding to the focused node and extracts the hyperlinks embedded in the web site to form nodes and edges for the web sub-graph. To reduce the complexity of the web graph, the information filter removes unnecessary information (edges and nodes) generated by the parser; it only retains the essential part which the user requires. Then, the web graph user interface component maintains the user's orientation for web exploration, and it also reduces the cognitive effort required to recognize the change of views. This is done by connecting successive displays of the subset of the web graph and by smoothly swapping the displays via animation.

This chapter focuses on introducing layout techniques for the web graph user interface component.

AUTOMATIC GRAPH LAYOUT TECHNIQUES

This section introduces the automatic graph layout techniques used in our system to ensure that a web graph layout fits in the display window and has no overlaps.

The most difficult editing function for a web graph is layout — assigning a position for each node and a curve for each edge. The assignment must make the resulting picture easy to understand and easy to remember. A good layout can be like a picture — worth a thousand words; a poor layout can confuse or mislead the user. This problem is called the graph drawing problem — how to automatically create a nice layout. Automatic layout can free the user from the time-consuming and detail-intensive chore of generating a readable diagram. However, most existing systems that incorporate diagrams, such as CASE tools, do not support automatic layout; the layout decisions in these systems have to be made by the user, using the mouse and the screen to replace pen and paper.

Most classical graph drawing algorithms (Battista et al., 1998) produce aesthetically pleasing abstract graph layouts. These algorithms can be applied to draw practical graphs as long as the size of nodes take very little space. This is because such algorithms were often designed for abstract graphs where nodes take up little or no space.

However, in applications, the images of nodes are circles, boxes, diamonds and similar shapes; they may contain a considerable amount of text and graphics. In some systems (see Eades & Lai, 1991; Harel, 1988; Lai & Eades, 1995; Purchase, 1998), nodes are used to represent sub-graphs and may be quite unpredictable in size and shape. Applying such algorithms to practical graphs may result in overlapping nodes and/or edge-node intersections. Algorithms which exemplify this problem can be found in Eades (1984) and Kamada and Kawai (1989). They generate symmetric and well spread out diagrams which have great potential for use in the visualization of network structures. However, nodes of nontrivial size in a diagram produced by these algorithms tend to overlap.

We are interested in the problem of how to display diagrams, i.e., how to lay out practical graphs in applications. The term *abstract graph layout* refers to layout techniques for abstract graphs where nodes are negligible in size. The term *practical graph layout* refers to layout techniques for practical graphs where nodes vary in shape and size.

Our approach is to make use of existing classical graph drawing algorithms, i.e., to apply a classical graph drawing algorithm to a practical graph. Then, we need to develop some post-processes to avoid overlaps of node images and edge-node intersections by rearranging the graph layout (see Eades & Lai, 1991; Lai & Eades, 2002). The techniques for adjusting a graph layout should preserve the mental map of the original graph (see Eades et al., 1991; Misue et al., 1995).

The critical part of our approach is to remove overlapping nodes. We use the techniques for removing overlaps of node images and edge-node intersections (see Eades & Lai, 1991; Lai & Eades, 2002). We have experimented with these techniques using many sets of overlapping nodes and have found that it is quite effective. An example is shown. Figure 8 shows a graph layout generated by an abstract graph layout algorithm (the "spring" algorithm (Eades, 1984)). Figure 9 shows the result of replacing the nodes with rectangles, which gives us not only the overlapping nodes but also the edge-node intersections.

Figure 8. An Abstract Graph Layout

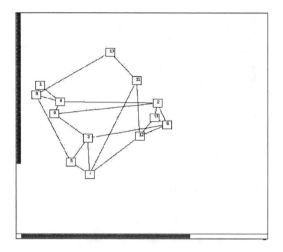

Figure 10 is the result of applying the "force-scan" algorithm (Lai & Eades, 2002) for removing overlaps of node images and edge-node intersections.

Although these techniques can make nodes in a diagram disjoint and as compact as possible, they cannot guarantee that the size of a diagram fits in the display window. So, we must also solve this problem. To this aim, our layout adjustment includes the following three parts:

Figure 9. A Practical Graph

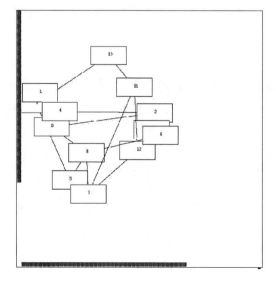

Figure 10. Layout Adjustment

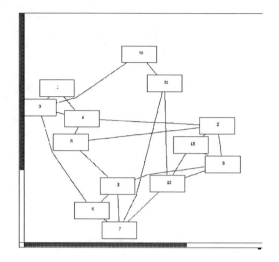

(1) Use the techniques (Lai & Eades, 2002) to remove overlapping nodes and edge-node intersections.
(2) If the size of the diagram exceeds the viewing area, find the minimum size diagram by changing the sub-graph layout.
(3) If the diagram still exceeds the viewing area, let some sub-graphs become invisible (in the order of those which overlap the user's currently selected sub-graph).

We used Java as the major software development tool for the implementation of our system. A prototype of the web graph user interface for WWW navigation has been developed.

CONCLUSION AND FUTURE WORK

This chapter introduces a new web graph display system. The major feature of the system is that it provides visible subsets of the web graph for WWW navigation. Our web sub-graph display technique creates an automatic layout that does not exceed the viewing area and which has no overlapping nodes.

Recent feedback from users is that they would like to combine our web graph interface with a current web browser (such as Netscape) for web navigation. It seems that they do not like to use the web graph interface alone for navigation.

We will continue to investigate layout techniques that will enhance the potential usability of the system. Purchase (1998) has presented a method for testing presentation and usability of graph layouts. We can adopt this method to evaluate the performance of our web graph layout.

We need to conduct usability studies of end-users to see whether they prefer this kind of interface for WWW navigation over more traditional styles.

REFERENCES

Battista, G. D., Eades, P., Tamassia, R., & Tollis, T. (1998). *Graph Drawing: Algorithms for the Visualization of Graphs*. Englewood Cliffs, NJ: Prentice Hall.

Chen, Y. & Koutsofios, E. (1997). WebCiao: A website visualisation and tracking system. *Proceedings of WebNet 97 Conference*.

Eades, P. (1984). A heuristic for graph drawing. *Congressus Numerantium*, *42*, 149-160.

Eades, P. & Lai, W. (1990). Visual interface design for relational systems. In *Proceedings of the 5th Australian Software Engineering Conference, Sydney,* Australia (pp. 259-263).

Eades, P. & Lai, W. (1991). Algorithms for disjoint node images. *Australian Computer Science Communications*, *14*(1), 253-265.

Eades, P., Lai, W., Misue, K., & Sugiyama, K. (1991). Preserving the mental map of a diagram. In *Proceedings of COMPUGRAPHICS 91*, (pp. 34-43).

Harel, D. (1988). On visual formalisms. *Communications of the ACM*, *31*(5), 514-530.

Huang, M. L., Eades, P., & Wang, J. H. (1998). Online animated visualization of huge graphs using a modified spring algorithm. *Journal of Visual Language and Computing*, *9*, 623-645.

Kamada, K. & Kawai, S. (1989). An algorithm for drawing general undirected graphs. *Information Processing Letters*, *31*(1), 7-15.

Lai, W. & Eades, P. (1995). CIGRAPHS: A new graph model. *Australian Computer Science Communications*, *17*(1), 262-270.

Lai, W. & Eades, P. (2002). Removing edge-node intersections in drawings of graphs. *Information Processing Letters*, *81*, 105-110.

Maarek, Y. S. & Shaul, I. Z. B. (1997). WebCutter: A system for dynamic and tailorable site mapping. In *Proceedings of the 6th International World Wide Web Conference* (pp. 713-722).

Misue, K., Eades, P., Lai, W., & Sugiyama, K. (1995). Layout adjustment and the mental map. *Journal of Visual Languages and Computing*, *6*, 183-210.

Pilgrim, C. & Leung, Y. (1996). Applying bifocal displays to enhance WWW navigation. *Proceedings of the 2nd Australian World Wide Web Conference*.

Purchase, H. (1998). Performance of layout algorithms: Comprehension, not computation. *Journal of Visual Languages and Computing*, *9*, 647-657.

Sugiyama, K. & Misue, K. (1991). Visualisation of structural information: Automatic drawing of compound digraphs. *IEEE Transactions on Systems, Man and Cybernetics*, *21*(4), 876-892.

Chapter XVII

An Algorithm of Pattern Match Being Fit for Mining Association Rules

Hong Shi, Taiyuan Heavy Machinery Institute, China

Ji-Fu Zhang, Beijing Institute of Technology, China

ABSTRACT

There are frequent occurrences of pattern match involved in the process of counting the support count of candidates, which is one of the main factors influencing the efficiency of mining for association rules. In this chapter, an efficient algorithm for pattern match being fit for mining association rules is presented by analyzing its characters, and it has been proved correctly and efficiently.

PRODUCTION

Association rules are one of the knowledge models in data mining. R. Agrawal developed the concept of association rules, which implies the relationships among a set of objects of transaction data set DB. Efficiency is the key to mining algorithms, owing to the frequent amounts of data included in DB. At present, the most effective algorithm of mining association rules is Apriori algorithm, presented by Agrawal and Srikant (1994).

Mining association rules may require iterative scanning of frequent transaction data sets and matching with candidates to count the support. Owing to the frequent data sets, the process of match is the main factor in efficiency. To resolve the question, we present a highly efficient pattern match algorithm being fit for mining association rules during exploiting, and we research the Market Basket Data Analysis System Based on Mining Associations Rules by analyzing some of the characteristics of pattern match included in mining association rules.

ASSOCIATION RULES DESCRIPTION

Given a transaction database DB, $I=\{I_1, I_2, \ldots, I_m\}$ is a set of itemsets with m different itemsets in DB. Each transaction T in DB is a set of items (i.e., itemsets), so $T \subseteq I$.

Definition 1: Itemset P is defined as $A_1 \cap A_2 \cap \ldots \cap A_k$, $A_i \in I$ (i=1,2,...,k), and P containing k items is called *k-itemset*.

Definition 2: The support of itemset P is defined as $\sigma(P/DB)$=the support account containing P in DB/the total transaction amount in DB=|A/DB|/|DB|.

Definition 3: If A and B are two itemsets, and $A \cap B = \Phi$, then the confidence of association rule $A \Rightarrow B$ in DB is defined as $\psi(A \Rightarrow B /DB)= \sigma(A \cap B /DB)/ \sigma(A /DB)$.

Definition 4: Let the minimum support be σ_{min}. Then the set of k frequent itemsets and the set of k non-frequent itemsets are defined separately as:

$$L_k = \{A_1 \cap A_2 \cap \ldots \cap A_k \mid A_i \in I (i=1,2,\ldots,k), \sigma(A_1 \cap A_2 \cap \ldots \cap A_k /DB) \geq \sigma_{min}\}$$
$$L_k' = \{A_1 \cap A_2 \cap \ldots \cap A_k \mid A_i \in I (i=1,2,\ldots,k), \sigma(A_1 \cap A_2 \cap \ldots \cap A_k /DB) < \sigma_{min}\}$$

To mine efficacious association rules in DB, minimum support σ_{min} and minimum confidence ψ_{min} must first be defined. Mining association rules find all of the association rules satisfying $\sigma(A \cap B /DB) \geq \sigma_{min}$ and $\psi(A \Rightarrow B /DB) \geq \psi_{min}$ in DB. Owing to the fact that the result of $\psi(A \Rightarrow B /DB)$ can be gotten from the value of $\sigma(A \cap B /DB)$ and $\sigma(A /DB)$, the key to mining association rule $A \Rightarrow B$ is to generate the set of k frequent itemsets. Therefore, the substantive study at present focuses on generating the set of k frequent itemsets (see Agrawal & Srikant, 1994; Feng et al., 1998; Zhang et al., 2000), which is the key to heightening the mining efficiency. We also focus on pattern match, which is the key to generating k frequent itemsets. The corresponding Apriori algorithm is as follows:

(1) C_1={candidate 1-itemsets}
(2) L_1={c∈C_1|c.count⩾σ_{min} }
(3) For (k=2; L_{k-1}≠ Φ; k++)
(4) C_k=apriori-gen(L_{k-1})
(5) Count_support(C_k)
(6) L_k={c∈ C1|c.counte⩾σ_{min}}
(7) Resultset=∪L_k
(8) Next

Here, C_k is candidate *k-itemsets*, L_k is *k-itemsets*, Count_support(C_k) is to count the support count of candidate *k-itemsets*, C_k, apriori-gen(L_{k-1}) is to generate C_k, which includes two steps. First, join L_{k-1} into *k-itemsets*. This is called the join step:

insert into C_k
select $P.A_1$, $P.A_2$,..., $P.A_{k-1}$,Q. A_{k-1}
from L_{k-1} P inner join L_{k-1} Q
where $P.A_1$= $Q.A_1$, $P.A_2$= $Q.A_2$,..., $P.A_{k-2}$= $Q.A_{k-2}$, $P.A_{k-1}$< $Q.A_{k-1}$

Then, delete any (k-1)-subitemsets of C_k which not be included in L_{k-1}. This is called the prune step:

For all itemsets c∈ C_k
    For all k-1_subitemsets s of c
        If (s∉L_{k-1}), then
            Delete c from C_k
and get the candidate *k-itemsets* C_k.

During the mining of association rules, pattern match mainly occurs in Count_support(C_k), which is the account of the support count of candidate *k-itemsets*. The resulting account is a match between the *k-itemsets* constructed by all the *k* items, compounded by each transaction in transaction data set and the set of candidate *k-itemsets* C_k(k=1,2,...). From the above, we know the pattern match of mining association rules is the match between any *k-itemsets* from each transaction of transaction data set whose item number is not less than *k* and any one itemset in the set of candidate *k-itemsets*.

PATTERN MATCH ANALYSIS

While exploiting and researching the Market Basket Data Analysis System Based on Mining Associations Rules, we analyzed the pattern match included in mining association rules. We discovered some characteristics of the transaction data set and the set of candidates:

(1) *Recording the item number and index can reduce the comparison time and enhance the efficiency of pattern match.* Sort all the items of each transaction in the transaction data set alphabetically. When preprocessing the transaction data set, do the sort, record the item number of each transaction and set it as an index. Then, choose a suitable algorithm to generate the *k-itemsets*. We get alphabetized *k-itemsets* which match.

(2) *The itemsets in the set of candidates can be alphabetized, not only in row, but also in a column.* The set of candidate *k-itemsets* generated by the join and prune steps, based on the set of candidate *(k-1)-itemsets* and C_1, is alphabetical. Then, through the SQL language as follows, we can get the alphabetic set of candidate *k-itemsets* in a row and in a column:

INSERT INTO C_k
SELECT TOP 100 PERCENT dbo.p.col$_1$, dbo.p.col$_2$,..., dbo.p.col$_{k-1}$, q. col$_{k-1}$ AS col$_k$
FROM dbo.l$_{k-1}$ p INNER JOIN dbo.l$_{k-1}$ q
ON dbo.p.col$_1$=q.col$_1$ AND dbo.p.col$_2$=q.col$_2$ AND ... AND dbo.p.col$_{k-1}$<q.col$_{k-1}$
ORDER BY P.col$_1$, P.col$_2$,..., P.col$_{k-1}$, Q.col$_{k-1}$

We can deal with the pattern match by the alphabetic characteristic. For two alphabetic linear objects, we can find the most efficient lookup algorithm to realize match easily. Then, we should look for a suitable algorithm to transform the alphabetic pre-match object into an alphabetic linear object. The simplest transformation method is to set the item number as weight and add up *k-itemsets* with weight as the object of match.

(3) *The item number of the longest itemset in a transaction data set is far less than the total item number |I|, and the transactions having longer itemsets take up only a small part of the total transactions.* When researching the market data set, which has 15,169 pieces of merchandise divided into 228 kinds of ware, we processed the mining based on 228 items, that is |I|=228. We discovered that the item number of the longest

transaction in the transaction data set is 33; 0.098 percent of the transactions have an item number larger than 20; 0.62 percent have an item number larger than 15; and 3.9 percent have an item number larger than 10.

(4) *The matching data object is larger, and the matching success ratio is lower.* When the *k-itemsets* number of each transaction in the transaction data set is larger, or when the transaction item number is larger, the itemset number of the set of candidates is larger. Then, the matching success ratio is lower. Owing to match being a process of lookup in nature, we can choose an algorithm which fits the match characteristic. In this chapter, that algorithm is bisearch, which has an average comparison time of $\log_2 n$ (n is the length of the object) and, therefore, can improve the efficiency.

(5) The match proceeded between two alphabetical obje found that the *k-itemsets* number of each transaction in the transaction data set, when k went from 1 to some scale, was always less than, or far less than, the itemsets number of the set of candidates. But above the scale, the *k-itemsets* number of each transaction in the transaction data set was more than the itemsets number of candidates. The results show determine data object should be applied to match the other one between the transaction data set and the set of candidates. But what's the determining principlecy.

Let the average transaction number of transaction itemsets in transaction data set DB be h. Then, the average *k-itemsets* number in each transaction is C_h^k. And, let there be m *k-itemsets* in candidate *k-itemsets* set C_k. Using the bisearch method, if we take each candidate in candidate k-itemsets set C_k to match the C_h^k-itemsets of each transaction in the transaction data set, then the total comparison time is $m\log_2 C_h^k$; conversely, if we take the C_h^k k-itemsets of each transaction in the transaction data set to match each candidate in candidate k-itemsets set C_k, the total compare time is $C_h^k \log_2 m$. Which one measure we should take is decided by the big and small of $m\log_2 C_h^k$ and $C_h^k \log_2 m$.

Then compare the big and small of $m\log_2 C_h^k$ and $C_h^k \log_2 m$.

$$\text{Let } x<y, h(x) = \frac{\log_2 x}{x}, \text{ then } h'(x) = \frac{1-\ln x}{x^2 \ln 2}.$$

When x>e(const), then ln>1, h'(x)<0, function h(x) is a monotone decrease function, and then $\dfrac{\log_2 x}{x} > \dfrac{\log_2 y}{y}$ is tenable. That is, when e<x<y, $x\log_2 y < y\log_2 x$.

To the pattern match of mining for association rules, there is $C_h^k > h > e$ and m is a positive integer.

When m>e, if $C_h^k < m$, then $C_h^k \log_2 m < m\log_2 C$, and we choose to take the C_h^k k-itemsets of each transaction in the transaction data set to match each candidate in candidate k-itemsets set C_k, which has a higher efficiency. On the contrary, if $C_h^k > m$, then $C_h^k \log_2 m > m\log_2 C_h^k$, and we choose to take each candidate in candidate k-itemsets set C_k to match the C_h^k k-itemsets of each transaction in the transaction data set, which has the higher efficiency.

When m=2, then $C_h^k > 2\log_2 C_h^k$; and when m=1, the question is changed into the match between one single data and an array of data. Therefore, when m<e, take each itemset in candidate k-itemsets set C_k to match the C_h^k k-itemsets of each transaction in the transaction data set.

From the above, when $C_h^k < m$, take k-itemsets of each transaction in the transaction data set to match the candidates set. Contrarily, when $C_h^k > m$, take the candidate k-itemsets set to match k-itemsets of each transaction in the transaction data set.

We can summarize the flow of the pattern match being fit for association rules as follows, through the preview analysis:

If k-itemsets of each transaction in the transaction data set match the candidate k-itemsets set, we should dispose of each k-itemsets of the candidate k-itemsets set by adding up their weights and putting them into a linear array to wait for match. Then, deal with current k-itemsets of the current transaction in the transaction data set by adding up the weight for each match, which is a match between a single data and an array, then choose, and then dispose and match the next k-itemsets of transaction. That method can be an effective use of the alphabetic characteristic of the transaction data set to make it more efficient. We can use a similar method when taking the candidate k-itemsets set to match k-itemsets of each transaction in the transaction data set.

DESCRIPTION OF PATTERN MATCH ALGORITHM

Following the analysis, we experimented and found that the function of realizing the pattern match MSPP is as follows. This MSPP is used to make the k-itemsets of transaction in the transaction data set match the candidate k-itemsets set.

Function MSPP:

(1) mspp(dqjy, ceng, maxceng, valu, star) //dqjy: an array conserving all the items of the current transaction in the transaction data set
(2)   For i = star To jygs - maxceng + ceng //jygs: the item number of the current transaction
(3)   If ceng = maxceng Then
(4)   eff dqjy, valu   // The transfer of function bisearch
(5)   Exit Sub
(6)   Else:
(7)   mspp dqjy, ceng + 1, maxceng, valu * maxsp + bb(i + 1), i + 1
(8)   End If
(9)   Next i
(10) End Sub

The transfer of function MSPP in main function:
(1) For i = 1 To jygs - k + 1
(2)   mspp?jyj, 1, k, jyj (i), 1?
(3) Next I

ALGORITHM ANALYSIS

Important point analysis The important point in the algorithm is how to take out the k items of each transaction itemset in an orderly fashion. Let the item number of the current transaction be n(n>k). Through combinatorics, we know that the formula for taking k items out of n is $C_h^k = \dfrac{n!}{(n-k)!k!}$. Owing to k not being certain, the method should be realized by recursion, which has been reflected in the above function MSPP. If the function is correct, the formula for taking k items out of n by the function should also be C_h^k. The proof is as follows:

Proof: Let g(n,k) be the number of k items taken from n by the function MSPP, then:

(1)   g(n,1): Owing to jygs=n, k=1, then g (n, 1) =n= C^1_n

(2)   g(n,2): Owing to jygs=n, k=2, then g (n, 2)= $\dfrac{n(n-1)}{2}$ = C^2_n

(3)   g(n,k): Use induction

Let i=k-1, g (n, k-1)=C^{k-1}_n is tenable, then prove that when i=k, g (n, k)= C^k_n is tenable also.

• The knowledge of combinatorics g (n, k) = g (n-1, k-1)+g (n-1, k) is tenable

• $C^k_n = C^{k-1}_{n-1} + C^k_{n-1}$ is tenable

That is, $\dfrac{n!}{(n-k)!k!} = \dfrac{(n-1)!}{(n-k)!(k-1)!} = \dfrac{(n-1)!}{(n-k-1)!k!}$ is tenable

And $\dfrac{(n-1)!}{(n-k)!(k-1)!} + \dfrac{(n-1)!}{(n-k-1)!k!} + \dfrac{k(n-1)!+(n-1)!(n-k)}{k!(n-k)} = \dfrac{n!}{k!(n-k)}$

= C^k_n

• The supposition is correct; the proposition is proved.

Efficiency Analysis

Let there be m rows in the candidate k-itemsets, and take the k-itemsets of transaction in the transaction data set to match the candidate k-itemsets set.

When using the ordinary pattern match method, we must also use the sequential lookup method owing to having not one times compare with the candidate k-itemsets set. The sequential lookup method's average comparison time is (m+1)/2, and the expense of the comparison between the k-itemsets of transaction in the transaction data set and the candidate k-itemsets set is k(m+1)/2.

When using this pattern match method, the match objects fall into an alphabetic linear array after being disposed because of their own alphabetization. The bisearch method is chosen because of the characteristics of alphabetization and linearity. Its expense is $\log_2 m$.

The expense can be known clearly from the above comparison.

CONCLUSION

One of the keys to data mining is efficiency, which is influenced mainly by the efficiency of pattern match. Toward that point, an efficient algorithm for pattern match being fit for mining association rules was presented in this chapter. It was approached through the alphabetization of the match objects, and used a fast lookup algorithm to advance the efficiency of match. Some key questions were analyzed and proved clearly in the chapter.

REFERENCE

Aggarwal, C. C., Procopiuc, C. & Yu, P. S. (2002). Finding localized associations in market basket data. Knowledge & Data Engineering, 14(1), 51-62.

Agrawal, R. & Srikant, R. (1994). Fast algorithms for mining association rules. In Proceedings of the 20th international conference on very frequent databases, Santiago, Chile, September 1994 (pp. 487-499).

Feng, Y. et al. (1998). Incremental updating algorithms for mining association rules. Journal of Software, 301-306.

Yan, W. (1997). The data structure. Beijing: Tsinghua University Press.

Zhang, J. et al. (2000). Updating association rule based on dynamic transaction item set. Computer Engineering, 26(7), 64-65.

Chapter XVIII

Networking E-Learning Hosts Using Mobile Agents

Jon T.S. Quah, Nanyang Technological University, Singapore

Y.M. Chen, Nanyang Technological University, Singapore

Winnie C.H. Leow, Singapore Polytechnic, Singapore

ABSTRACT

With the rapid evolution of the Internet, information overload is becoming a common phenomenon. It is necessary to have a tool to help users extract useful information. A similar problem is faced by e-learning applications. At present, commercialized e-learning systems lack the information search tools needed to help users search for course information, and few of them have explored the power of mobile agent. Mobile agent is a suitable tool, particularly for Internet information retrieval.

This chapter presents a mobile agent-based e-learning tool which can help the e-learning user search for course materials on the Web. A prototype system of cluster-nodes has been implemented, and experiment results are presented.

INTRODUCTION

Increasingly, our society is being reshaped by the Internet. In the past decades, the Internet evolved so rapidly that it made the information technology industry grow extremely fast. Internet-based applications, such as e-commerce, e-payment, e-billing, e-learning, etc., have had a tremendous influence on society. Among them, e-learning is one of the killer applications.

Currently, the traditional education system faces challenges arising from the development of a knowledge-based economy. As school enrollment increases with population growth, the level of education required for the new economy also increases, and the cost of higher education escalates. In the workforce training market, on the other hand, as the information economy develops, the demand for skilled workers increases; as the technology keeps changing, the workforce needs continuous training to maintain its productivity level. Hence, both formal school-based education and continuous workforce training have become a big business, and it will be even bigger in the future (Kerrey & Isakson, 2000). A more sophisticated education model is required to meet this challenge, and e-learning came into being.

Compared to traditional classroom teaching, e-learning provides one major advantage: it makes access to information much easier and more convenient. Hence, it makes learning — of all kinds, at all levels, any time, any place, any pace — a practical reality (Kolar, 2001). E-learning also provides a tremendous cost savings for both instructors and learners. The learning model is shifted from instructor-centered to learner-centered, which focuses primarily on the needs of learners. Updating online material is also much easier. Many e-learning systems can develop personalized and interactive applications that allow users to customize their individual e-learning models and to learn at their own pace. It can truly engage the user in a type of learning that involves simulation of real world events and sophisticated collaboration with other learners and instructors (Quah & Chen, 2002).

PARADIGMS FOR E-LEARNING SYSTEMS
Mobile Agent Paradigm

The server-client paradigm is popular in current e-learning applications. Mobile agent is an emerging technology. Because it makes the design, implementation, and maintenance of a distributed system much easier, it is attracting a great deal of interest from both industry and academia. In particular, the mobile agent paradigm has already been used to design applications ranging

Figure 1. Mobile Agent Paradigm

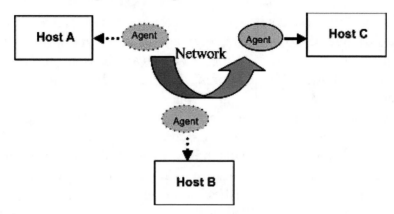

from distributed information retrieval to network management. Figure 1 shows a typical system based on a mobile agent paradigm.

A mobile agent is an autonomous, intelligent program that can migrate from machine to machine in heterogeneous networks, searching for and interacting with services on the user's behalf. Typically, agents are autonomous, adaptive, goal-oriented, collaborative, flexible, active, proactive, etc. (Smith & Paranjape, 2000). The mobile agent paradigm is used in distributed computing because improves the performance of the conventional client-server paradigm.

Under mobile agent paradigm, any host in the network is allowed a high degree of flexibility to possess any mixture of service code, resources and CPU time. Its processing capabilities can be combined with local resources. The service code is not tied to a single host, but rather is available throughout the network (Gray & Kotz, 2001).

Information Push and Pull Based on Mobile Agent

With the above features, the mobile agent paradigm is suitable for distributed information retrieval and e-commerce applications.

The rapid evolution of Internet-based services causes information overload on the Web. It has been estimated that the amount of information stored on the Internet doubles every 18 months, and the number of home pages doubles every six months or less (Yang et al., 1998). Therefore, it becomes difficult for the user to locate required information or services on the Internet from the huge amount of information.

Information Push and Pull technology makes easier the delivery of information from service providers to users. Push technology is the process of

Figure 2. Faded Information Field

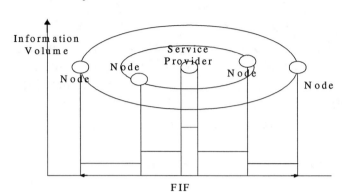

FIF

service provision by a provider in anticipation of its use; Pull technology is the process of searching information in the network.

Ahmad and Mori (2000), from the Tokyo Institute of Technology, proposed Faded Information Field (FIF) architecture. It is based on mobile agent technology to cope with fast-changing information sources and to reduce the information access time of the user.

In FIF, each component, such as user, provider, and node, is considered an autonomous entity. The information is distributed on these nodes, and the amount of information decreases away from the service provider, as shown in Figure 2. The nodes near the Service Center were allocated a larger volume of information, and those farther from central nodes were allocated a smaller volume of information.

In FIF, service providers generate push mobile agents to push information in the neighboring nodes in faded patterns. These agents negotiate with neighboring nodes and allocate information according to situation and importance level. Important information is stored on a higher number of nodes, and less important information is stored in a lower number of nodes. The user looks for information with pull agents. The pull agents navigate through the distributed nodes in FIF autonomously to locate appropriate information.

The algorithm for the design of autonomous information fading takes into consideration the popularity, size and lifetime of the information. A parameter access effort $E_g(i)$ is defined to assign a fading level to each information as:

$$E_g(i) = \frac{N_i \ln(d_i + 1)}{\ln(S_i + 1)} \tag{1}$$

where N_i, d_i, and S_i denote, respectively, the number of times accessed, the lifetime, and the size of the information unit. The information having high access effort is assigned high priority and is stored on all nodes.

Through the cooperation of Push agents and Pull agents in the FIF, the time it takes the user to access needed information is reduced. Since the user does not need to reach the service provider, he can get the required information at the nodes which are close to him. The service provider can avoid the congestion of the access, and the level of reliability is improved.

Keyword Search and Text Mining

The operation of a simple search engine is based on three main components: input of information, indexing information and storing it in a database, and retrieval of information.

Generally speaking, information retrieval from the Internet is done by using keyword matching, which requires user-entered keywords (or their synonyms) to be matched with the indexed keywords. In some cases, the information source may not match the keywords exactly. Even though the meaning matches, keyword matching will not retrieve the particular information file.

Takagi and Tajima (2001), from Meiji University, proposed a method to expand query context dependently using conceptual fuzzy sets. A fuzzy set is defined by enumerating its elements and the degree of membership of each element. It is used to retrieve information not only including the keyword, but also including elements which belong to the same fuzzy sets as the keywords. Keyword expansion should also consider context. The same word may have different meanings in various contexts.

A search engine using conceptual matching instead of keyword matching can effectively retrieve data relating to input keywords when there are no matches with such keywords. First, the search engine indexes the collected web pages, extracts nouns and adjectives, counts the frequency of each word, and stores them into the lexicon. When retrieving information, the user input keywords are collected and, using conceptual fuzzy sets, the meanings of the keywords are represented in other expanded words. The activation value of each word is stored into the lexicon, then matching is executed for each web page. The sum is used as a matching degree in the final evaluations of all words in each web page, and the matched web pages are sorted according to the matching degree. Those web pages with a matching degree exceeding a certain threshold are displayed to the user.

ADVANTAGES AND DISADVANTAGES OF USING MOBILE AGENT APPROACH

Comparing these three distributed paradigms — server-client, code on demand, and mobile agent — it can be seen that mobile agent exhibits greater flexibility. Furthermore, mobile agent possesses the following advantages:

(1) Mobile agent moves computation code to data, and the intermediate results passing are reduced. The network bandwidth consumption is reduced.
(2) The agents do not require a continuous connection between machines (Huhns & Singh, 1997). The client can dispatch an agent into the network when the network connection is healthy, then it can go offline. The network connection needs to be reestablished later only when the result was returned by agents from remote host. Hence, it provides a more reliable performance when the network connection is intermittent or unreliable (Pals et al., 2000).
(3) Agent operates asynchronously and autonomously, and the user doesn't need to monitor the agent as it roams in the Internet. This saves time for the user, reduces communication costs, and decentralizes network structure.
(4) With adaptive learning and automation added to agents, the agent can be tooled with AI for information retrieval and filtering.

The main problem with mobile agent is security (see Ghanea & Gifford, 2001), which is still an area of research on its own. In an agent system with a low level of security, the mobile agent may harm the host or the host may harm the mobile agent.

With the above properties, the software language to construct a mobile agent system should be object-oriented and platform independent, with communication capability and implement code security (James, 1996). At present, the languages being used for mobile agent include Java, Telescript, and Tcl. IBM Aglet with Java is a popular tool, and we selected it as the platform for this project.

E-LEARNING SYSTEMS

Existing Approaches

Some existing e-learning systems (some are university-based, others are not) have been studied and compared. Most of the systems were constructed based on server-client paradigms, and few provide search and user tracking functions. A few systems only provide course catalogs for the user to search. Currently, none of the systems uses mobile agent technology.

Mobile Agent Approaches

It is recommended to add a mobile agent-based search tool between the user and the e-learning system. This e-learning tool will help the user search for his preferred courses with some forms of AI and, at the same time, track the user's progress status continuously and report this information to the e-learning server. This information helps the online instructors know the progress of each learner and his status in the course, and then guide the learners differently. At the same time, the e-learning system administrator can also collect user status information for statistical purposes.

Through the e-learning tool, the learner and instructor are given an environment to interact with each other more easily and conveniently. A learner can decide whether to allow other learners to know his progress status information. When the learners' progress status is available among peers, competition and cooperation among learners are promoted. The more interactive the e-learning system, the more effective e-learning will be (Cupp & Danchak, 2001). In the following section, the method for implementing the e-learning tool will be discussed.

Construct E-Learning System Based on Mobile Agent Paradigm

We propose a new system architecture, based on mobile agent, to improve the performance of current systems. In our proposed system, a certain mobile agent-based software was pre-installed in the university centers and was connected, through Agent Transfer Protocol (ATP) in the Internet, to form a huge and powerful e-learning system. The client is a networked PC connected to the Internet, enabling it to connect to the Agent Server Center (ASC) to query the universities on behalf of the user. The ASC will then create a mobile agent, and it will roam to the university servers to hunt for required data. Each university center may offer some courses to users. Users may access the e-learning system through any web browser via the Internet.

All the university centers can be considered as different nodes in the network, and the courses are information distributed into these different nodes. We can construct a Faded Information Field (FIF) to implement the information push and pull technology, as discussed earlier, to improve users' access time to information, with a higher reliability.

The FIF system consists of logically connected nodes. Information providers and users correspond to these nodes, and information allocated to these nodes decreases in amounts away from the information center. That means the nodes adjacent to information center contain more information; farther nodes contain less.

The users' demand for the sub course materials changes dynamically over time. FIF provides an autonomous navigation mechanism by university centers through mobile agents to satisfy users' heterogeneous requirements. The university centers generate push mobile agents, and these agents carry out information fading by negotiating with the other neighboring nodes in the network. When the push agents perform the information fading, it needs to take into account the popularity, size and lifetime of the information, and then assign a priority level to each information. The information with higher priority is stored on more nodes, and low priority information is stored in fewer nodes.

All the nodes around the university centers are ranked according to distance. The nodes with lower traffic costs are ranked near to university center, and those with higher traffic costs ranked farther away from the university center. The information push agents perform their task at a certain network off-peak time to avoid network congestion.

Through the mobile agent-based architecture and Faded Information Field, the network structure is decentralized, and it can be easily extended to a larger scale by adding more university centers. The course materials are usually stored on more than one server so that the users can get the course materials from the nearest node, which saves information access time. When some nodes in the networks are down, users can still get course materials from other nodes; therefore, the reliability is increased. The system is robust and fault-tolerant.

Mobile Agent-Based Searching

Keyword searching/text mining, in which, the server collects the index of all the stored information, is commonly used by current search engines. When a user wants to retrieve information from the server, he is required to enter a keyword to query the server database. The server then searches all the indices that match the keyword entered by user and retrieves the information accordingly (Martin & Eklund, 2000) [e.g., Electronic Campus (Southern Regional Education Board, 2002)].

In this information retrieval mechanism, two problems may occur. Firstly, this mechanism is based on the assumption that user has a good understanding about the server-stored information and can express what he wants to retrieve in terms of correct and accurate keywords. If the query keyword is poorly structured, or if some typing error exists, the search will not work as the user expected; it may even return nothing. In order to overcome this problem, a thesaurus function is used to expand the search keys.

Secondly, if the query causes plenty of information to be returned to user at the client site, most likely not all the information is what the user wants. The user needs to browse through the retrieved information and discard that which is not important. This causes a waste of network bandwidth and user time. To assist the user, the system provides a weighted keywords function to gauge the importance of each piece of retrieved information.

Adding artificial intelligence to the keyword search will improve the search quality. One approach is to do a parsing on the user-entered keywords (Katz & Yuret, 1999). This process will generate several synonyms equivalent to the original keywords. When the query done with the original keywords is not satisfactory, the query based on its synonyms will be performed to return more information. Figure 3 illustrates the process of user query expansion.

One AI approach for e-learning course searches is to build web agents (Karjoth & Lange, 1997). The web agents will search for information on behalf of the user, according to his preferences. Such preferences are stored in a user profile database (Baek & Park, 1999). It has a learning function and can learn the user's likes and dislikes when the user searches the web with keyword searching.

Initially, the user enters the keywords and searches the Web. The monitor agent will save the keywords entered by the user, and then the search agent will start to roam the Web, searching for information (Cabri et al., 2000). As the search agent finds information, at remote sites, which matches the user's requirements, it will carry the information back to the user.

Figure 3. Thesaurus Module

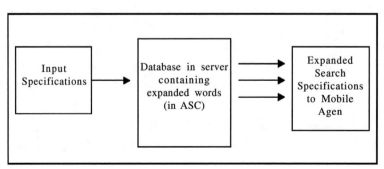

At the user site, the extraction agents will extract the keywords from the retrieved web documents. The keyword extraction includes two methods. One is based on the frequency of a word or phrase in a web document; the other is based on the frequency of a word or phrase in different web documents. The occurring frequency is then computed and weighted. If it exceeds a threshold value, the word can be treated as a keyword. It can then be saved into the user profile database together with the user-entered keywords. When the user reads through the retrieved web documents, some documents may not be what he wants. So, they are simply discarded by the user. The monitor agent will monitor this and add a negative preference with a weighting to the extracted keywords. For the correctly retrieved web documents, a positive preference weighting is added.

The next time the user does a keyword search, and enters similar keywords as the previous session, the user preference database will, first, find all the keywords stored with positive and negative weightings. Then, it will list those words and allow the user to pick the keyword he wants. The search priority is based on the weighting. Positive weighting indicates higher priority, and negative weighting indicates low priority. Since the negative weighting exceeds a certain threshold value, the web documents containing such key-words will not be retrieved in future sessions.

The monitor agent, search agent, and user preference database operate in close loop feedback, with learning ability. The user preference database will grow larger as the user does more keywords searches of the Web, and the search process will become more intelligent. Figure 4 shows the architecture of the search tool (Quah & Chen, 2002).

Mobile Agent-Based User Tracking

Among all the existing e-learning systems studied in this project, only "Corpedia" (Corpedia, 1998) and "Ninth House Network" (Ninth House, 1996) provide user progress tracking. Comprehensive and flexible user progress tracking provides useful information for both the e-learning instructor and the administration to improve the e-learning quality and make it more effective.

In our e-learning system, two kinds of agents are used for user tracking. One is a reporting agent, which is a mobile agent sitting at user machine; the other is the monitor agent, which resides at the e-learning center. After each e-learning session, the reporting agent will report the user's current status information to the monitor agent in a remote server via message passing. The

Figure 4. AI Search Engine Architecture

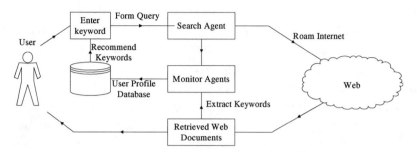

monitor agent will capture the information into the database. The instructor and administrator can check this information to analyze teaching effectiveness and to collect statistics.

By exploring mobile agent in user tracking, the user is freed from the burden of manually reporting his learning progress to server. All this is done automatically by the mobile agent, and the whole system is transparent to the user.

Overall Technical Architecture

In the proposed system, IBM Aglet workbench is used as the agent platform. Figure 5 shows the technical architecture.

Figure 5. Overall Architecture

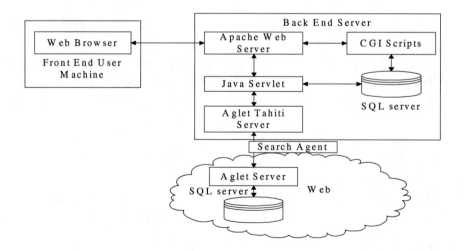

The whole system consists of three layers: the front end user machine, the back-end server, and the e-learning servers on the Web. The front end can be any PC connected to a back-end server. The back-end server has a SQL server database, which stores the user account information. It is used for user verification when logging into the system, and each new user needs to register his account with the back-end server. The handling of these data is through CGI scripts.

The addresses of all the e-learning servers which are to be visited by the searching mobile agent are also captured in the database, which forms a search directory for the searching Aglet. Each e-learning course center on the Web must pre-install the Aglet Tahiti server, and each must have a database server to store the course materials. These e-learning centers registered their addresses with the back-end server, thus providing a context in which the searching Aglet can operate.

Each time the user does a search, a Java Servlet will run at the back-end server, which, in turn, generates an Aglet carrying the searching criteria and sends it into the Web. The mobile agent will roam the Web, searching for the required information on the user's behalf. When information is found, the mobile agent sends it back and continues on to the next Aglet host in the predefined trajectory. The retrieved information will be filtered by the thesaurus module and then presented to user.

The filtering process is the reverse of the query expansion process. Text mining techniques are used to narrow down the search criteria; they also take into consideration the context in which the keyword is used.

CASE EXAMPLE

Nanyang Technological University (NTU) has adopted E-learning as a complementary tool for teaching and learning, combining it with the conventional classroom lecture and tutorial education. The system used at NTU is "*Edventure*" (NTU, 2002) supported by "Blackboard." In this environment, lecturers can post the course materials, exercises and project assignments to the forum. Students can download course materials from there, submit assignments and post questions regarding the course they are taking.

Although the "*Edventure*" system runs smoothly and plays an important role in conducting teaching and learning at the school, there are still some limitations. It is based on centralized client-server paradigms. So, the course materials are hosted at a single server (or dual servers), and the server's CPU has to service all the incoming requests from users. Some course materials in the school are only updated weekly by the lecturers. Within this short period of time, all students registered for the subjects need to download course materials from the *Edventure* server to prepare themselves for the lecture. The request hits to the server increase tremendously during this period, and not all the requests can be processed by the CPU in the *Edventure* server immediately. Some requests are queued until the CPU completes the current processing of client requests, which results in long response time for the user to bear with. The computation load at the server is also very heavy since the whole system depends on the centralized server. Under situations where the system administrator needs to perform system maintenance, or when the server is down accidentally, the whole system stops functioning until the server is recovered.

Course Information Distribution

Using the mobile agent-based E-learning system described, we reconstructed the Edventure system based on a highly decentralized network configuration — distributed mobile agent paradigm. Several proxy servers are needed in addition to the central server. Both the central server and the proxy servers are used to construct faded information field (FIF), in which both the CPU time and network bandwidth are distributed.

For the weekly updating of course materials — after the materials are posted to the central server by the lecturers, and when the user requests increase — the system calculates the access effort (Equation 1) of each information based on the number of hits, information lifetime, and size. The information with more hits will be assigned higher priority, and a push agent will push this higher priority information to the neighboring nodes. In this case, a user's request is directed to corresponding proxy nodes, which have a lower network traffic cost than other nodes. In a later period, after most students have downloaded the course materials, user requests will decrease, and the push agents will recalculate the access effort of the course information. This process will likely yield a smaller access effort, showing that users' demand for such course materials has decreased. Therefore, the push agent will erase the course materials from some proxy nodes. When a threshold access effort is reached, all the course materials will be removed from the neighboring hosts.

Customized Course Construction

The course structure in the previous Edventure system is fixed, and students have to take course modules in a fixed sequence. Thus, the reusability of course materials is low. For example, in the department where the authors of this article work, "Network Design and Simulation" and "Network Performance Analysis" are two typical courses. For both courses, the mathematics behind probability and statistics are the foundation for other theories and algorithms. Hence, if a student has taken "Network Design and Simulation," in which he has learned statistics and probability, he must still go through those lessons again when he takes "Network Performance Analysis." The fixed course structure decreases the reusability of course materials; students have to take redundant sub-courses and follow the fixed course structure at a pace not set by themselves.

Using a mobile agent system, the problem is solved by dividing an entire course into sub-courses, and categorizing them according to specific domain knowledge. Each sub-course material is related to a set of non-serialized reference materials, and these materials are available for students' ad-hoc retrieval. Customized course materials may be conducted by retrieving and linking sub-course materials together. In this case, the common parts, such as the probability and statistics in the above example, are separated; these common parts can be reused to construct other courses related to network technology. For each sub-course module, a student can optionally retrieve some reference material on the respective topics. With the structured course materials and unstructured reference materials, the course can be customized according to the student's pace and interest, and the sub-course reusability is improved. The construction of a course from sub-course materials and reference materials by students in order to study at their own pace also relieves the course authoring burden of lecturers.

Interactive User Tracking

It has been shown that the more interaction and cooperation between instructors and learners, the more effective learning will be. User tracking functions provide an interactive environment for lecturers and students to conduct teaching and learning. This environment can be realized through the cooperation of static agents at student machines and static agents that sit on an e-learning central server. These two groups of agents monitor the course status for a particular student, and communicate this information by message passing.

There are two types of tracking. At the lecturers' side, they receive feedback from students regarding the course materials effectiveness. For example, if the user tracking report shows a high access rate for a certain course material, it may mean the difficulty level of this course material is appropriate or that the course is taken by many students. On the contrary, if the access rates of certain courses are low, that may mean the courses are not very popular; either the difficulty levels are too high or the course formats are not user-friendly. With the feedback from students, the course materials can be customized to match students' learning pace and interest.

To test the effectiveness of student learning, after the course is taken, the system also provides some randomized questions for students in the form of quizzes. The quizzes will be graded by the e-learning server, and the server will feedback the grade information to each student. This is realized through the communication of two groups of static agents.

System Security

The Edventure system provides strict user authentication. Each student who has registered for some subjects has an independent account. Each user can only log in to his own account to search for course materials, and the system enforces regular password changes by users. At the server side, information on all transactions performed by an individual user is recorded into a log file. In the event that the system faces any security attack, it is easy to trace the source of attack from the log file.

A PROTOTYPE IMPLEMENTATION AND EXPERIMENT RESULTS

Load Balancing with Mobile Agent

An experiment was carried out to demonstrate how mobile agent realizes load balancing in a distributed e-learning environment. Figure 6 shows the network configuration used to simulate a typical Faded Information Field.

Response Time Evaluations

Figure 7 shows a model of a mobile agent network which depicts both the network architecture and the mobile agent behavior. In the network architecture, the processing part is represented as a set of nodes, such as "Server1," and they were capable of hosting and providing resources to the mobile agent

Figure 6. Network Configuration

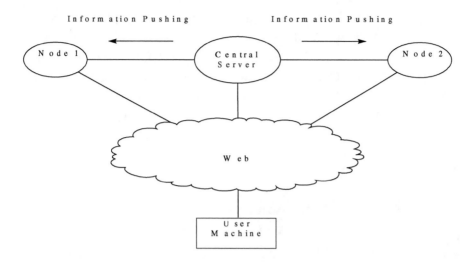

to make it execute its task. The network communication is represented by arrows that connect the nodes and support mobile agent migration and communication with the user by sending result messages.

The user interacts with the mobile agent network by initiating a mobile agent at the user machine. The agent then carries the user's search criteria to request required web documents at remote servers. The user's request and creation of the agent were random events; the agent migrates with a user-defined itinerary to the destination node to perform the data retrieval task, which is also a stochastic process. So, the mobile agent can be considered as

Figure 7. Mobile Agent Traversal

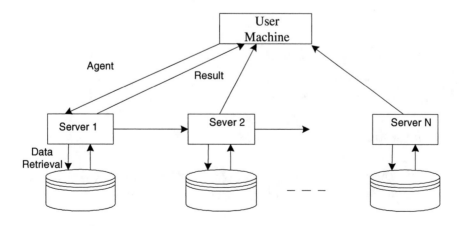

a network communication packet in the network queuing system that should be served at the server.

Response time is a typical parameter for measuring the performance of a queuing system. It is defined as the time interval between when a request is sent and when a response is returned. Response time is commonly used to evaluate parallel and distributed processing in telecommunications. We also adopted this method for our work with a mobile agent network.

With a higher level of abstraction, the response time for a mobile agent network is expressed as:

$$T = t_{process} + t_{migration} \tag{2}$$

T: mobile agent response time
$t_{process}$:   time taken to perform tasks at nodes
$t_{migration}$:   time taken to migrate within the network

Depending on the situation, $t_{process}$ will change. The factors that affect $t_{process}$ include the size of the mobile agent, the query size and complexity, and the size of the records inside the database. $T_{migration}$ is determined by the agent size and by the network bandwidth between agent hosts.

With these factors taken into consideration, Equation 2 is expanded as:

$$T = t_{agent} + \sum_{i=1}^{N} \left(t_{process}(i) + t_{agent}(i, i+1) \right) + t_{N+1} \tag{3}$$

With reference to the generic mobile agent network model in Figure 7 (the agent hosts were numbered from 1 to N), the parameters in Equation 3 are expressed below:

T: Mobile agent response time
t_{agent}:   Time taken to create a mobile agent and migrate it to the first host
$t_{process}(i)$:   Duration of the mobile agent execution at i_{th} server
$t_{agent}(i, i+1)$: Time taken by the mobile agent to travel from node i to node i+1
t_{N+1}:   Time taken by the mobile agent to travel back from the last host
           and destroy itself

The mobile agent-based searching was tested with a network configuration consisting of three agent hosts, as shown in Figure 6. The arrival and departure time at each host was recorded in the tables below to calculate the response time T.

Experiment results for the course metadata table with 10 records:

Table 1. Experiment Result (10 Metadata Records)

Runs	t_{agent}	t_1	t_2	t_3	t_4	T
1	0	1	2	4	5	5
2	0	1	2	2	3	3
3	0	1	2	2	3	3
4	0	1	2	2	3	3
Average	0	1	2	2.5	3.5	3.5

The parameters we used for Table 1 were:

Record Size: the number of records in database table to which the mobile search agent perform query

t_{agent}: the time at which search agent was created

t_1:   the time at which search agent arrived at host one

t_2:   the time at which search agent arrived at host two

t_3:   the time at which search agent arrived at host three

t_4:   the time at which search agent completed task and destroyed itself

With reference to t_{agent} and t_4 in Table 1, the response time T was calculated approximately with the following equation:

$$T = t_4 - t_{agent} \tag{4}$$

Table 1 shows that, for the first run of mobile agent searching, the response time is around five seconds. For subsequent runs, the response time drops to three seconds. The database query process takes a substantial percentage of the response time.

Querying the database for the first time differs from subsequent queries since the first query involves the additional overhead of loading the JDBC driver and establishing the communication channel. The subsequent queries already have some necessary program cached in computer memory from previous runs, so they take less time. For each query by mobile agent, a sufficient number of runs were carried out. The average response time for the specific data table was calculated according to Equation 5.

$$T = \frac{1}{n}\sum_{i=1}^{N} T_i \tag{5}$$

Another significant factor that we considered in our experiments was the size of the records in the database table and the size of query result. They directly affect the response time in two ways: in the time spent for the query to execute, and in the time required to transport the result to user machine.

The same experiment was performed to calculate the average response time for mobile agent-based search, with the database table records varying from 50 to 100 to 200.

Experiment results for the course metadata table with 50 records:

Table 2. Experiment Result (50 Metadata Records)

Runs	t_{agent}	t_1	t_2	t_3	t_4	T
1	0	1	3	5	6	6
2	0	1	2	3	3	3
3	0	1	2	3	3	3
4	0	1	2	3	3	3
Average	0	1	2.25	3.5	3.75	3.75

Experiment results for the course metadata table with 100 records:

Table 3. Experiment Result (100 Metadata Records)

Runs	t_{agent}	t_1	t_2	t_3	t_4	T
1	0	1	3	5	6	6
2	0	1	2	3	3	3
3	0	1	2	2	2	3
4	0	1	2	3	3	3
Average	0	1	2.25	3.5	3.75	3.75

Experiment results for the course metadata table with 200 records:

Table 4. Experiment Result (200 Metadata Records)

Runs	t_{agent}	t_1	t_2	t_3	t_4	T
1	0	1	3	5	6	6
2	0	1	2	2	3	3
3	0	1	2	2	3	3
4	0	1	2	2	3	3
Average	0	1	2.25	2.75	3.75	3.75

Experiment results for the course metadata table with 1000 records:

Table 5. Experiment Result (1000 Metadata Records)

Runs	t_{agent}	t_1	t_2	t_3	t_4	T
1	0	1	3	5	7	7
2	0	1	2	2	3	3
3	0	1	2	2	3	3
4	0	1	2	2	3	3
Average	0	1	2.25	2.75	4	4

The counterpart of mobile agent-based search is client-server search paradigm. Compared with our mobile agent system, the equivalent client-server system is shown in Figure 8.

Since the client-server paradigm is not synchronous, the user has to perform the search by himself, key in the search criteria, and wait for the request to be sent back from the server. If the user wants to search the three data servers one by one for required documents, he has to perform the same search operations three times. Those operations include opening the E-learning application, entering the search criteria, clicking the "start" button, etc.

The client-server network configuration is shown in Figure 8. Its response time is expressed as follows in Equation 6:

$$T = \sum_{i=1}^{N} \left(t_{query}(i) + t_{transmission}(i,0) \right) + \sum_{i=1}^{N} t_{user}(i) \qquad (6)$$

Figure 8. Client-Server Architecture

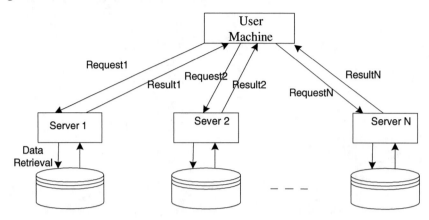

T:	Client-server response time
$t_{query}(i)$:	Time taken for the server i to perform the query on its database
$t_{transmission}(i, 0)$:	Time taken for server i to send query results to the user machine
$t_{user}(i)$:	Duration user performs operations during each search session

The client-server-based search was tested with the network configuration consisting of three servers (as shown in Figure 8), and the response time for each server was recorded in the table below. Since t_{user} is subject to the user's typing speed and reaction ability, we took t_{user} as 10 seconds for the average time a user takes to perform a search session. These values were summed up to get the response time to calculate the response time T.

The database used in testing was the same as the one used to test the mobile agent system. The query and query results were also the same. Thus, we performed a response time comparison between the two systems with the equivalent hardware and software components.

Experiment results for the course metadata table with 10 records:

Table 6. Experiment Result (10 Metadata Records) — Client-Server

Runs	t_1	t_2	t_3	t_{user}	T
1	1	1	3	10	35
2	1	1	3	10	35
3	1	1	3	10	35
4	1	1	3	10	35
Average	1	1	3	10	35

The parameters we have taken records in Table 6 were:

Record Size: the number of records in the database table to which the mobile
        search agent performed the query
t_1:   the time at which the search agent arrived at host one
t_2:   the time at which the search agent arrived at host two
t_3:   the time at which the search agent arrived at host three
t_{user}:   user's response
T: the response time for the client-server system

With reference to t_1, t_2, t_3 and t_{user} in Table 6, the response time T was calculated approximately using the following equation:

$$T = t_1 + t_2 + t_3 + 3*t_{user} \qquad (7)$$

To get a more accurate result for the response time, a sufficient number of runs were carried out to query the client-server system. Then, the average response time for the specific data table was calculated according to Equation 8.

$$T = \frac{1}{n}\sum_{i=1}^{N}T_i \qquad (8)$$

Experiment results for the course metadata table with 50 records:

Table 7. Experiment Result (50 Metadata Records) — Client-Server

Runs	t_1	t_2	t_3	t_{user}	T
1	1	1	4	10	36
2	1	1	3	10	35
3	1	1	3	10	35
4	1	1	3	10	35
Average	1	1	3.25	10	35.25

Experiment results for the course metadata table with 100 records:

Table 8. Experiment Result (100 Metadata Records) — Client-Server

Runs	t_1	t_2	t_3	t_{user}	T
1	2	2	5	10	39
2	1	1	5	10	37
3	1	1	4	10	36
4	1	1	4	10	36
Average	1.25	1.25	4.5	10	37

Experiment results for the course metadata table with 200 records:

Table 9. Experiment Result (200 Metadata Records) — Client-Server

Runs	t_1	t_2	t_3	t_{user}	T
1	2	2	6	10	40
2	2	2	5	10	39
3	1	1	5	10	37
4	1	1	4	10	36
Average	1.5	1.5	5	10	38

Experiment results for the course metadata table with 1000 records:

Table 10. Experiment Result (1000 Metadata Records) — Client-Server

Runs	t_1	t_2	t_3	t_{user}	T
1	3	3	9	10	45
2	2	2	9	10	43
3	2	2	9	10	43
4	2	2	8	10	42
Average	2.25	2.25	8.75	10	43.25

From the data collected, it was shown that, as the records in the database increase in size, the response time for both the mobile agent and the client-server systems increased. However, the response time of the client-server system was more sensitive to the database record size. Figure 9 shows the response time versus record size comparison for the two systems.

Figure 9. Response Time Comparison

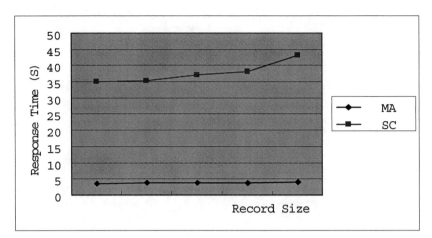

Figure 9 shows that the response time of the mobile agent-based search is much faster than that of the client-server search. This is mainly due to the asynchronous and autonomous nature of mobile agent. Mobile agent performs information searching tasks alone once a user creates it, and completes the task autonomously, without interaction or communication with the user. The user doesn't need to monitor the agent during its work, which brings the user tremendous time savings and reduces communication costs.

From our experiment data, mobile agent saved an average of 30 seconds compared to completing the same task with client-server system. The efficiency in performance can be attributed to the following reasons:

(1)   Mobile agent is not a stand-alone process. It is a thread that needs to work together with other programs in the agent host to complete the task. Hence, it is flexible and small in size. In our system, the search agent is only around 10K with small variation depending on user query size. Hence, the amount of time taken to transport mobile agent is small.
(2)   The mobile agent moves query computations to the data server, the repetitive request/response handshaking involved in the client-server system is eliminated. The mobile agent performs data selection at the remote server; only the selected documents are sent to user. In the client-server system, intermediate results and information need to be passed through the network between server and client. Hence, mobile agent reduces network traffic and improves performance in terms of response time.

Figure 10. Course Document Structure

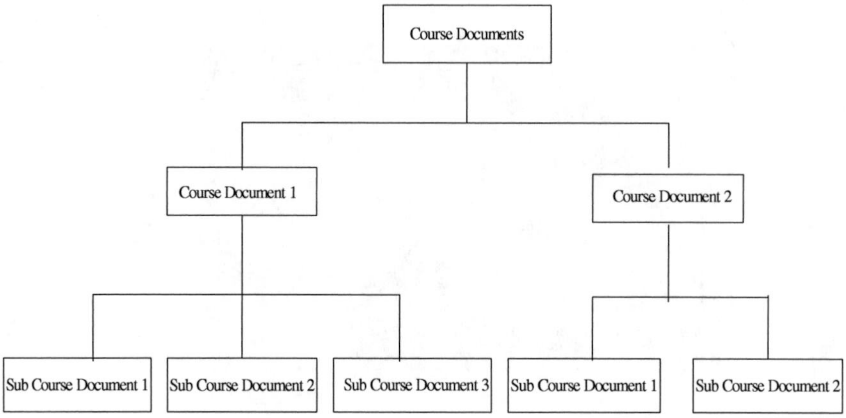

KEYWORD-BASED
INFORMATION SEARCHING

Domain Classification of Course Documents

In order to manage and search for course documents more accurately and efficiently, all course documents were analyzed and categorized according to the knowledge domain they belong to. Each course was further decomposed into sub-course documents to implement a new course scaffolding. In this way, the course documents' reusability was improved. The course documents were organized into tree hierarchy structures as shown in Figure 10.

In our experiment, the training documents include "Computer Architecture" and "Bio machine." Each has ten sub-course documents.

Keyword Selections and Document Indexing

Since the course documents can be very large in size, the system performance and speed can be degraded. To query and retrieve the course documents more efficiently, we selected a set of keywords from the sample documents and indexed them with the occurrence frequency and knowledge domain.

The index includes three parts: the selected keywords, its occurrences, and the knowledge domain it belongs to. The keywords are a set of vocabulary selected from the corresponding course document. Occurrences are the frequency with which the keywords appear in the document. The document

Table 11. Example of Index Table

Keyword	Knowledge Domain	Document	Occurrence
genetic	biology	BioMachine1	6
DNA	biology	BioMachine1	4
zoology	biology	BioMachine2	5
memory	computer	ComputerArchitecture1	7
Processor	computer	ComputerArchitecture2	5
disk	computer	ComputerArchitecture3	4
...	...	...	...

where the keywords appeared was also recorded in the index table to trace the location of the keywords. The index reflects the general concept of each document. An example of an index table is shown in Table 11.

The keywords in Table 11 were selected from each course document. In order to get the set of vocabularies that represents the general concept of the course document, text mining techniques were used on all the course documents. The algorithm involves three processes: word recognition, stop word elimination, and keyword selection.

Word recognition refers to the process of scanning the course document while ignoring the punctuation and word cases. In this process, the word prefixes and suffixes were removed to get the root word. Since words with common roots often have similar meanings, the root words were used for synonym generation and query expansion when the user searched for course documents.

In the process of stop words elimination, a list of stop words was deleted from the text. The stop words are non-semantic bearing words. They include a large number of pronouns, adjectives, and adverbs, including we, you, this, there, at, in, etc. Some high-frequency words that are too general to represent a document concept, such as say, listen, help, etc., were also deleted. Search engines usually do not index these stop words because doing so will result in the retrieval of a tremendous quantity and trivial records.

After word recognition and stop words elimination, the text was scanned to select the words with high occurrences and store them in the index table, as shown in Table 11.

Some words have high occurrences in many documents; they are too general to represent the content of the specific document. These words were ignored during our indexing process. What we were interested in were those words that have higher occurrences in only certain documents. These words were selected as the index keywords for particular documents, and they were used, with higher accuracy and speed, for data retrieval.

Using the above algorithm for selecting index keywords, Equation 9 takes into account the factors mentioned above. The word score was calculated to measure the weight of the word to each document.

$$ IS = tf_{xj} * \log \left(\frac{N}{df_j} + 1 \right) \qquad (9) $$

In Equation 9, *IS* stands for the index score. tf_{xj} is the term frequency, which is the number of occurrences of term *j* in document *x*. df_j is the document frequency, which is the number of documents in a fixed-size collection in which term *j* occurs. *N* is the number of document size. The calculated score *S* measures the weight of term *j* to document *x*.

With reference to Equation 9 and Table 11 by taking into account the document frequency, the index table was further evolved into Table 12.

Keyword-Based Searching

The search for e-learning course documents is based on keyword matching. A mobile agent carries user-entered keywords and roams in network to search for information on behalf of the user, according to the user's preference. As the search agent finds information that matches the user's requirements at remote sites, it sends the information back to the user via Aglet message. The monitor agent saves the keywords entered by the user to build the user's preference profile. Figure 11 shows the process of intelligent search with mobile agent.

Table 12. Index Table of Course Documents

Keyword	Knowledge Domain	Document	Term Frequency	Document Frequency	Collection Size	Index Score
genetic	biology	BioMachine1	6	2	10	10.75
DNA	biology	BioMachine1	4	4	10	4.39
zoology	biology	BioMachine2	5	1	10	11.99
memory	computer	ComputerArchitecture1	7	3	10	9.7
processor	computer	ComputerArchitecture2	5	4	10	5.49
disk	computer	ComputerArchitecture3	4	2	10	7.17
...	...	...	...	...	...	...

Figure 11. Document Search Process

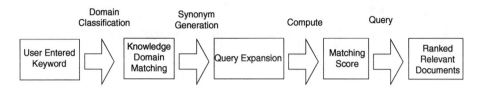

The user input keyword was first searched through the index table to find its suitable knowledge domain. In the next step, only the course documents under the relevant domain will be further queried. For example, if the user entered "hardware" as the search keyword, as the keyword reached the index table, it may be under domain of "computer" or "network," etc. Other domains, such as "biology" and "mathematics," will be eliminated from further query processing. By domain matching, the computing time was reduced and, as a result, the efficiency and accuracy of data retrieval was improved.

A thesaurus module was used to expand the user's query by generating synonyms corresponding to each user keyword. Its main purpose was to broaden the search criteria and to improve the document retrieval precision. The following figure illustrates the process of user query expansion.

At the agent host server, the query criterion carried by the mobile agent was used to retrieve course documents from document storage, based on the matching score of expanded user keywords and index words for each document. The matching score reflects the similarity between the user query and the course documents. It was calculated based on Equation 10.

Figure 12. Keyword Expansion

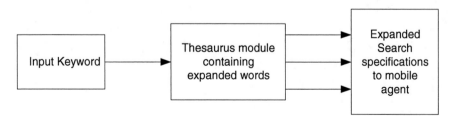

Word1 denotes the user-entered keyword for the search, and Q = {Word1, Word2, Word3 ... WordN} denotes the expanded query by thesaurus module that includes a list of synonyms to Word1. Then, the matching score between the expanded query and the course documents was calculated as follows:

$$MS = \sum_{i=1}^{N} Occur(Wordi) \qquad (10)$$

In Equation 10, MS stands for Matching Score; Word$i$ is the ith synonym in the expanded query; and Occur is the frequency Word$i$ appears in a particular document.

After the Matching Score for each document within the relevant knowledge domain was computed, the documents were sorted and ranked.

In our experiment, "Processor" was entered as the keyword for search. The mobile agent carried the keyword over to a remote agent host. The station agent at the remote host first classified the keyword "Processor" under the domain "Computer," and then the keyword was expanded by thesaurus module to widen the search criteria. The expanded query was {Processor, CPU, Controller, Microcontoller}. There were 10 course documents under the domain "Computer." The index table for the 10 course documents was scanned to retrieve the occurrences of each word in the expanded query. The occurrences of expanded keywords in each document were summed together to get the matching score, and the documents were ranked in descending order.

The ranked documents based on matching score are shown in Table 13.

Table 13. Ranking Retrieved Documents

User Keyword	Domain	Expanded Keywords	Document	Occurrences
Processor	Computer	Processor	ComputerArchitecture2	5
Processor	Computer	CPU	ComputerArchitecture2	3
Processor	Computer	Controller	ComputerArchitecture2	1
Processor	Computer	Microcontroller	ComputerArchitecture2	0
Processor	Computer	Processor	ComputerArchitecture5	3
Processor	Computer	CPU	ComputerArchitecture5	2
Processor	Computer	Controller	ComputerArchitecture5	1
Processor	Computer	Microcontroller	ComputerArchitecture5	0
...	...	...	...	...

Table 14. Ranked Documents

	Document	Matching Score
1	ComputerArchitecture2	9
2	ComputerArchitecture5	6
3	ComputerArchitecutre4	3
4	...	...

With reference to Equation 10, the matching score for the document "ComputerArchitecture2" was calculated as:

$$MS = \sum_{i=1}^{4} Occurr(Wordi)$$

= Occur (Processor) + Occur (CPU) + Occur (Controller) + Occur (MicroController)

= 5 + 3 + 1 + 0

= 9

In the same way, the matching score for the document "ComputerArchitecture5" was calculated to be 6. The ranked document list is shown in Table 14.

Which documents should be presented to the user from Table 14 was decided by applying the threshold. With a threshold matching score value of 5, the search agent sent the two documents "ComputerArchitecture2" and "ComputerArchitecture5" back to the user terminal.

CONCLUSION

E-learning and mobile agent are emerging technologies. In this chapter, we proposed and tested a method which combines both mobile agent and e-learning paradigms to support efficient and effective document retrieval, based on keywords entered by the user. This architecture can be use in furthering web-based distance learning.

ACKNOWLEDGMENTS

We would like to thank IBM for providing Aglet as a free source development tool for researchers to build mobile agents.

REFERENCES

Ahmad, H. F. & Mori, K. (2000). Push and pull of information in autonomous information service system. In *Proceedings of the International Workshop on Autonomous Decentralized Systems* (pp. 12-18).

Cabri, G., Leonardi, L., & Zambonelli, F. (2000). Mobile-agent coordination models for Internet applications. *Computer, 33*, 82-89.

Corpedia. (1998). *E-learning, web-based training, business management training and legal compliance.* Retrieved August 10, 2002, from: http://www.corpedia.com/

Cupp, E. L. & Danchak, M. M. (2001). The RSVP unibrowser: Bringing humanness and interactivity to e-learning. In *Proceedings of the IEEE International Conference on Advanced Learning Technologies* (pp. 67-69).

Ghanea, H. R. & Gifford, I. (2001). Solutions to security in mobile agent systems. In *Proceedings of the IEE Seminar on Mobile Agents* (vol. 5, pp. 1-4).

Gray, R. S. & Kotz, D. (2001). Mobile-agent versus client/server performance: Scalability in an information-retrieval task. In *Proceedings of the 5th IEEE International Conference on Mobile Agents* (vol. 2240, pp. 229-243).

Huhns, M. N. & Singh, M. P. (1997). Mobile agents. *IEEE Internet Computing, 1*, 80-82.

James, E. (1996). *White mobile agents.* Retrieved August 10, 2002, from: http://www.webtechniques.com/archives/1996/05/white/

Karjoth, G. & Lange D. B. (1997). A security model for Aglets. *IEEE Internet Computing, 1*, 68-77.

Katz, B. & Yuret, D. (1999). Integrating web resources and lexicons into a natural language query system. In *Proceedings of the IEEE International Conference on Multimedia Computing and Systems* (vol. 2, pp. 255-261).

Kerrey, S. B. & Isakson, J. (2000). *The power of the Internet for learning.* Retrieved July 25, 2002, from: http://www.ed.gov/offices/AC/WBEC/FinalReport/

Kolar, U. D. J. W. (2001). New web-based interactive e-learning in power electronics and electrical machines. In *Proceedings of the IEEE 36th IAS Annual Meeting Industry Application Conference* (vol. 3, pp. 1858 -1865).

Martin, P. & Eklund, P. W. (2000). Knowledge retrieval and the World Wide Web. *IEEE Intelligent Systems, 15*(3),18-25.

Nanyang Technological University. (2002). *Edventure*. Retrieved June 2, 2002, from: http://edventure.ntu.edu.sg

Ninth House. (1996). *Highly effective on-line training*. Retrieved May 23, 2002, from: http://www.ninthhouse.com/home.asp

Pals, H., Petri, S. & Grewe, C. (2000). FANTOMAS: Fault tolerance for mobile agents in clusters. *International parallel and distributed processing symposium online proceedings.* Retrieved June 25, 2002, from: http://ipdps.eece.unm.edu/2000/ftpds/18001241.pdf

Quah, T. S. & Chen, Y. M. (2002). Mobile agent assisted e-learning. *Proceedings of the IEEE International Conference on Information Technology and Applications.*

Smith, K. D. & Paranjape, R. B. (2000). An economic model for medical data retrieval using mobile software agents. In *Proceedings of the Canadian Electrical and Computer Engineering Conference* (vol. 1, pp. 230-234).

So, Y. J., Baek, H. J., & Park, Y. T. (1999). User profile-based personalized web agent. In *Proceedings of the 1st Asia-Pacific Conference on Intelligent Agent Technology Systems, Methodologies and Tools* (pp. 296-305).

Southern Regional Education Board. (2002). *Electronic campus*. Retrieved August 10, 2002, from: http://www.electroniccampus.org/

Takagi, T. & Tajima, M. (2001). Query expansion using conceptual fuzzy sets for search engine. In *Proceedings of the 10th IEEE International Conference on Fuzzy Systems* (vol. 3, pp. 1303-1308).

Yang, C. C., Yen, J., & Chen, H. (1998). Intelligent Internet searching engine based on hybrid simulated annealing. In *Proceedings of the 31st Hawaii International Conference on System Sciences* (vol. 4, pp. 415-422).

About the Authors

Masoud Mohammadian has completed his bachelor's, master's and PhD in Computer Science. His research interests lie in intelligent agents, adaptive self-learning systems, fuzzy logic genetic algorithms, neural networks and their applications in robotics, control, and industrial automation, and financial and business problems which involve real-time data processing, planning and decision making. He is a member of more than 30 international conferences, and he has chaired several international conferences on intelligent systems and computational intelligence. He is currently a senior lecturer at the School of Computing at the University of Canberra in Australia. He is a member of many professional (computing and engineering) organizations. He is also currently the vice chair of the Institute of Electrical and Electronic Engineering (IEEE) ACT section.

* * *

Yasser Abdelhamid is a lecturer at the Institute of Statistical Studies & Research (ISSR), Cairo University, as well as a researcher at the Central Laboratory for Agricultural Expert Systems (Egypt). Dr. Abdelhamid obtained his PhD from ISSR, with his research point being to build large-scale knowledge-based systems (KBS) from reusable knowledge components. His research interests include knowledge sharing and reuse, knowledge level modelling, library-driven KBS development, and software reuse.

R. Abi-Aad obtained his Bachelor of Computer Science from the Université du Québec à Trois-Rivières (1998). While completing his bachelor's degree, he twice won the Desjardins Foundation excellence award, chosen from among 260 candidates from nine universities. He got his master's degree in 2001 from Concordia University (Canada), under the supervision of Dr. Radhakrishnan. During his master's, he concentrated on user models, participated in many publications, won several awards, and became actively involved in the CITR project (Enabling Technologies for E-commerce) as the implementation team's main coordinator, collaborating with eight universities. In his secret nocturnal identity, Rony plays guitar, sings, and performs in bars. He also conducts a choir of 40 wonderful kids at St. John's primary school in Montreal.

Ignacio Aedo has a degree and a PhD in Computer Science from Polytechnic University of Madrid. Since 1991, he has been a lecturer at the University Carlos III in Madrid (Spain). His interests mainly focus on topics such as hypermedia, media integration systems, electronic books, electronic document systems, development methodology, and knowledge representation systems. In 1990, he started his research activity in the field of hypermedia systems, in which he is still involved.

Ricardo Aler is a lecturer in the Department of Computer Science at the University Carlos III, Spain. He has done research in several areas, including automatic control knowledge learning, genetic programming, and machine learning. He has also participated in international projects about automatic machine translation and optimizing industry processes. He holds a PhD in Computer Science from the Polytechnic University of Madrid (Spain) and an MSc in Decision Support Systems for Industry from Sunderland University (UK). He graduated in Computer Science from the Polytechnic University of Madrid.

A. Andreevskaia graduated from the Moscow State University, Russia, with a master's degree in Applied Linguistics. She continued her research at Moscow State University, looking into statistical methods in natural language analysis and processing. Three years later, she completed her PhD. In 2003, she obtained a master's degree in Computer Science at Concordia University, Canada, under the supervision of Dr. T. Radhakrishnan. She has won several major awards, including a NSERC scholarship in 2002. A. Andreevskaia is currently enrolled in the PhD program in the same University. Her interests include natural language processing, artificial intelligence, human-computer interactions, user modelling, and knowledge-based systems.

T. Beran has been at the Czech Technical University in Prague since 1992 (Czech Republic). He studied computer languages and translations in the Department of Computer Science and Engineering. During his studies, he worked for a company, where he developed banking applications. He finished his MSc in 1999. In his diploma thesis, he focused on the problem of optical recognition of scanned music sheets. After finishing his MSc, he began working toward a PhD at the same university and department. He has researched applications of binary neural networks for text processing tasks.

David Camacho is a lecturer in the Department of Computer Science at the University Carlos III of Madrid (UC3M) (Spain). He is member of the Complex and Adaptive Systems Group (SCALab) at this university. He holds a PhD in Computer Science from the University Carlos III of Madrid (Spain). He has a BSc in Physics from the Universidad Complutense de Madrid. He has done research in several areas, including multi-agent systems, planning, information gathering, and fuzzy logic. He has also participated in international projects about automatic machine translation and optimizing industry processes.

Rowena Chau obtained a Master of Business Systems from the School of Business Systems of Monash University (Australia) in 1996, followed by a PhD in 2002. She joined the School of Business Systems as an Assistant Lecturer in 1996. Her current appointment is a Post-doctoral Research Fellow. Her research interests include web content mining, multilingual information retrieval, soft computing, and computational intelligence.

Y.M. Chen is a research student at the Nanyang Technological University in Singapore. His research interests involve e-learning systems, mobile agent applications, intelligent systems, text mining, and Java technology. He was a master's student of Dr. Jon Quah.

Juan Cuadrado is a PhD student in the Department of Computer Science at the University Carlos III of Madrid (UC3M) (Spain). He is member of the Complex and Adaptive Systems Group (SCALab) at this university. He holds a BSc in Computer Science from the University Carlos III of Madrid. He is working in several research areas, including multi-agent systems, learning, and information gathering, webmapping and image processing.

Xiaotie Deng received the BS from Qinghua University, Beijing, China (1982), an MS from the Institute of Systems Sciences, Academic Sinica, Beijing (1984), and a PhD from Stanford University, Stanford, California in September 1989. He is currently a professor at City University of Hong Kong. His research interests include algorithms and complexity, and combinatorial optimization.

Paloma Díaz has a degree and a PhD in Computer Science from the Polytechnic University of Madrid (Spain). She is lecturer at the University Carlos III of Madrid, and she is the head of the ARCADE research group of the Computer Science Department, which is involved in areas concerning interactive systems, security issues, operating systems, and distributed systems. Within this group, her research work is done in the DEI Laboratory. Her interests mainly concern topics such as hypermedia, electronic document systems, CASE, software development methodology, and formal models for representing information. She is also interested in applying new technologies in education. She is a member of the executive committee of the IEEE Learning Technology Task Force.

Juan Manuel Dodero has worked as a lecturer in the Computer Science Department at the University Carlos III of Madrid (Spain) since 1999. He received his degree in Computer Science and MSc in Knowledge Engineering, both at the Polytechnic University of Madrid, and obtained his PhD in Computer Science at the University Carlos III. He had prior expertise as an object technology consultant and R&D engineer for Spanish companies. His research interests include technologies to support education and learning, knowledge management, computer-supported cooperative work, and multi-agent systems.

Julián Dorado is a professor in the Department of Information and Communications Technologies of the University of A Coruña, Spain. He finished his graduate in Computers in 1994 and began his PhD. In 1999, he became a Doctor, with a special mention of European Doctor. He has worked as a teacher at the university for more than six years. He has published many books and papers in several journals. He is currently working on evolutionary computing, artificial neural networks, computer graphics, and data mining.

Samhaa R. El-Baltagy is researcher at the Egyptian Central Laboratory for Agricultural Expert Systems. She also teaches at Cairo University. She received her PhD in Computer Science from the University of Southampton in the UK, with the focus of her research being on the development of a multi-agent framework for navigation assistance and information finding in context. Her research interests include agent and multi-agent systems and frameworks, adaptive hypermedia, distributed information management, and knowledge-based systems.

Qizhi Fang received her BS and MS degrees from Shandong University, China, in 1988 and 1991, and a PhD from the Institute of Systems Sciences, Academic Sinica, Beijing, China in 2000. She is currently an associate professor in the Department of Applied Mathematics, Qingdao Ocean University, Qingdao, China. Her research interests include algorithms and complexity, and combinatorial optimization.

Tetsuo Hasegawa received a BSc in Electrical Engineering from Waseda University in 1985 and completed an ME program in 1987. Subsequently, he joined Toshiba Corporation (Japan), and currently works in the Knowledge Media Laboratory, Corporate Research and Development Center. His research interests include distributed autonomous systems and software agent technology. He is a member of the Information Processing Society of Japan.

Maolin Huang is a senior lecturer at the Faculty of Information Technology, University of Technology, Sydney (Australia). His current research covers the ares of information visualization, software engineering and information retrieval. In the past seven years, Dr. Huang has published 50 referred journals and conference papers. His work has been well recognized by the international research community. His earlier research work has shown its large potential value and has been sold and build into the commercial software SimplyObjects, developed by Adaptive Arts Pty Limited. Dr. Huang also served as a PC member and session chair for many conferences and as a reviewer for some well-known journals.

Ric Jentzsch is a senior lecturer in Information Systems and Technology at the University of Canberra, Canberra, Australia. He has lectured in the USA, Canada, Australia, and several Asian countries. He has more than 25 years of industry experience in information technology, business management, and consulting. Dr.

Jentzsch has 34 publications in management and information technology. He has been an invited speaker at conferences, seminars, and universities. His current research interests include electronic business, intelligent agents, small to medium enterprises, and application of evolving and maturing technologies.

Kaïs Khrouf is currently a PhD student at IRIT Laboratory, Toulouse. He obtained his master's degree from Paul Sabatier University, Toulouse (2000) (France). His research interests include data and textual warehouses, information retrieval, advanced databases, query languages, ordered tree comparison, etc. He is the author of several articles in his subjects of interest.

Jin Sung Kim is an assistant professor of Management Information Systems at the School of Business Administration. His teaching and research interests are in the areas of intelligent decision support systems, especially in how information technologies support and enable effective decision making. In previous years, he has taught Systems Analysis and Design, Database Management, Internet Business, Management Information Systems, Data Analysis and Decision Support. Currently, he has responsibility for the Introduction to Management Information Systems, CGI programming, and Internet Business Modelling for business students for the BA program. Specific areas of research interest are the web-based decision support systems, negotiation support systems, the knowledge management practices of large organizations, data mining, and the development of intelligent systems to support multipurpose problem solving. He is specifically interested in exploring what "knowledge" is for large organizations, how it is created, how it is managed, and how it affects management action. Jin Sung Kim completed a PhD at the SungKyunKwan University, where he developed 'causal knowledge-based negotiation support systems' to mediate the suppliers and buyers simultaneously. He has a Master of Business Administration from the SungKyunKwan University. He has much experience in assessing how to develop the effectiveness of information systems, especially through the use of information technology. He has been involved in strategic planning, forecasting, web-based information systems development, management education, project management, research model analysis and development, and information systems design, policy and procedure development. He has had significant experience in technology assessment for artificial intelligence-based decision making. He also has experience sitting on the Boards of Directors of Korea Fuzzy Logic and Intelligent Systems Society.

Koichi Kurumatani received his PhD from the University of Tokyo in 1989. He worked for Electrotechnical Laboratory from 1989 to 2001. He has been conducting the CONSORTS project as multi-agent team leader, CARC, AIST (Japan) after 2001. The goal of the CONSORTS project is to provide multi-agent architecture for a ubiquitous computing environment and to provide a framework for mass user support that is socially coordinated among mass users or in society. His research interests are in software agents, multi-agent, ubiquitous computing, social coordination, and market and auction mechanism.

Wei Lai is a senior lecturer in the School of Information Technology at Swinburne University of Technology (Australia). He received his PhD from the University of Newcastle in 1993. His research interestes are software engineering, Internet and Web applications, user interfaces, and information visualization. He has published more than 60 papers in these areas.

C.H. Leow is currently a lecturer with the School of Business at Singapore Polytechnic. She has lectured in subjects including Retail Environment and Technology, Organizational Management, Management and Organizational Behavior, and Services Marketing. Ms. Leow has assisted in several key projects with retailers in Singapore in the area of successful business strategies. Her key area of research is business-related and technology applications for educational institutions and businesses. Prior to joining the Polytechnic, Ms. Leow worked for many years in the marketing and retailing practice with local and international companies, providing technical and professional advice to retailers and commercial companies. Ms. Leow is also a certified Casetrust auditor in Singapore.

T. Macek received his MSc from the Czech Technical University (Czech Republic), Faculty of Electrical Engineering in 1990. He received his PhD in 1998 at the same university. In his research work, he focused on pattern recognition, neural networks text processing, and parallel systems. He spent several years teaching, focusing particularly on distance learning and other modern teaching technologies. In the past, he worked both in academia and industry.

Shinichi Nagano received his ME and PhD in Computer Engineering from Osaka University, Japan (1996, 1999, respectively). In 1999, he joined Toshiba Corporation (Japan), and currently works at the company's Knowledge Media Laboratory, Corporate Research and Development Center. His research interests include software agent technology, XML web services, and formal verification. He is a member of the IEEE, the Institute of Electronics, Information and Communication Engineering (IEICE), and the Information Processing Society of Japan (IPSJ).

Akihiko Ohsuga received a BSc in Mathematics from Sophia University (1981) and a PhD in Electrical Engineering from Waseda University (1995). He joined Toshiba Corporation (Japan) in 1981. From 1985 to 1989, he worked with ICOT (Institute for New Generation Computer Technology), involved in the Fifth Generation Computer System project. He is currently a senior research scientist at Toshiba's Knowledge Media Laboratory, Corporate R&D Center. He is also a visiting Associate Professor in the Graduate School of Information Systems, the University of Electro-Communications. His research interests include agent technologies, formal specification and verification, and automated theorem proving. He is a member of the IEEE Computer Society, the Information Processing Society of Japan (IPSJ), the Institute of Electronics, Information and Communication Engineers, and the Japan Society for Software Science and Technology. He received the 1986 Paper Award from the IPSJ.

Alejandro Pazos Sierra is a professor in the Department of Information and Communications Technologies of the University of A Coruña, Spain. In 1987, he finished his graduate studies in Medicine and General Surgery at the University of Santiago. In 1989, he got the title of Master in Knowledge Engineering at the Polytechnic University of Madrid. In 1990, he became a Doctor of Computer Science and, in 1996, Doctor of Medicine. He has headed many research projects and published many papers and books, in areas such as medicine, knowledge engineering, artificial neural networks, expert systems, etc.

Nieves Pedreira is an assistant professor in the Department of Information and Communications Technologies of the University of A Coruña, Spain. She received a degree in Computer Science from the University of A Coruña in 1993. This was followed by a master's degree in Communications and Real Time Systems. After having worked in private enterprises, she returned to the University in 1997 as a PhD student and, currently, she is working on her thesis. She is also a tutor in the UNED (Distance Education National University) since 1998. Her research interests focus on distance learning and new technologies.

Jon T.S. Quah is currently an assistant professor with the School of Electrical and Electronic Engineering, Nanyang Technological University in Singapore. Dr. Quah lectures in both undergrad as well as graduate courses such as Software Development Methodology, Software Quality Assurance and Project Management, Object-oriented System Analysis and Design, and Software Engineering. His research interests include financial market modelling using neural network, software reliability, and Internet-related topics such as e-commerce and e-learning. Other than academic services, Dr. Quah has undertaken joint projects with major companies in the banking and airline industries, as well as with the statutory boards of the government body. Prior to his academic pursuit, Dr. Quah was a director of a local company dealing with industrial chemicals.

Juan R. Rabuñal is an assistant professor in the Department of Information and Communications Technologies of the University of A Coruña, Spain. He finished his studies of Computer Engineering in 1996 and, in 2002, he became a PhD in Computer Science with his thesis "Methodology for the Development of Knowledge Extraction Systems in ANNs." He has been a member of several Spanish and European projects, and he has published many books and papers in several international journals. He is working on evolutionary computing, artificial neural networks, and knowledge extraction systems.

T. Radhakrishnan graduated from the Indian Institute of Technology in Kanpur, India, with a PhD in Electrical Engineering. Since 1975, he has been working in the Computer Science Department at Concordia University, Canada. He is currently working as a professor and chair of the department. His interests are in human computer interactions, agent-based software systems, and multi-agent architectures. He has supervised well over 60 master's and doctoral theses in the past 28 years. He is a co-author of two computer science text books that are popular in India, and he holds two patents.

Ahmed Rafea is a professor of Computer Science at the American University in Cairo. He is also the supervisor of the Central Laboratory for Agricultural Expert Systems, Egypt. Dr. Rafea obtained his PhD in Computer Science from Universitee Paul Sabatier in France. Since his graduation, he has worked at Cairo University, where he chaired the Computer Science Department, San Diego State University, and the American University in Cairo. His main research interests are in knowledge engineering, knowledge discovery in database, intelligent information systems, and natural language processing.

Daniel Rivero was born in 1978 in A Coruña, Spain. In 1996, he began his studies of Computer Engineering, and he finished them in 2001. After that, he began his PhD in Computer Science and Artificial Intelligence. He has published several papers at international conferences and in journals on evolutionary computation, signal processing, image processing, artificial neural networks, and so on. He is working in the RNASA (Artificial Neural Networks and Adaptive Systems) Lab at the University of A Coruña.

Chantal Soulé-Dupuy is currently a professor at Toulouse I University and research manager at IRIT Laboratory (SIG team), Toulouse. She obtained her PhD from Paul Sabatier University, Toulouse (1990). She supervises a master's degree program at Toulouse I University, France. Her current research interests include information retrieval and filtering, neural networks, data mining, information systems, personalization, document warehouses, etc. She has published several research papers in her areas of interest. She is involved as a member of the program/organizing committees for a number of national and international conferences.

A. Stafylopatis was born in Athens, Greece, in 1956. He received the Diploma degree in Electrical and Electronics Engineering in 1979 from the National Technical University of Athens (Greece) and the Docteur Ingenieur degree in Computer Science in 1982 from the University of Paris-Sud, Orsay, France. Since 1984, he has been with the Department of Electrical and Computer Engineering at the National Technical University of Athens, where he is currently a professor. His research interests include neural networks, computational intelligence, parallel processing, and high-performance computing.

Yasuyuki Tahara received his BSc and MSc degrees in Mathematics from the University of Tokyo, Japan (1989 and 1991, respectively). He joined Toshiba Corporation (Japan) in 1991 and currently works at the company's Knowledge Media Laboratory, Research and Development Center. His research interests include software agent technology and software engineering, with particular reference to mobile agents and formal specification languages and methodologies. He is a member of the Information Processing Society of Japan and the Japan Society for Software Science and Technology.

S. Vrettos was born in Athens, Greece, in 1974. He received his Diploma degree in Electrical and Computer Engineering in 1999 from the National Technical University of Athens (N.T.U.A) in 1999. He is now a doctoral candidate in the Department of Electrical and Computer Engineering, National Technical University of Athens. His research interests include machine learning, fuzzy reasoning, and information retrieval.

Hui Yang is currently a PhD student at the University of Wollongong, Australia. She received her bachelor's degree in Electronics from Huazhong University of Science and Technology, China, in 1993, and a master's degree in Computer Science from Hubei University, China, in 1999. Her research topic is the methodologies and techniques of distributed informational retrieval on the Internet.

Chung-Hsing Yeh is currently an associate professor at the School of Business Systems at Monash University, Australia. He holds a BSc and an MMgmtSc from National Cheng Kung University, Taiwan, and a PhD in Information Systems from Monash University. His research interests include multilingual information processing, multicriteria decision analysis, fuzzy logic applications, operations scheduling and management, and transport systems planning.

Kang Zhang is an associate professor of Computer Science at the University of Texas at Dallas, USA. He received his BEng in Computer Engineering from the University of Electronic Science and Technology in China (1982), and a PhD from the University of Brighton in the UK (1990). He has held academin positions in China, the UK, Australia and the USA. Dr. Zhang's research interests are in the areas of software engineering, visual programming and Internet computing. He has published more than 120 papers in these areas. Dr. Zhang is a senior member of IEEE.

Minjie Zhang is an associate professor of Computer Science and Software Engineering at the University of Wollongong, Australia. She received her BSc from Fudan University, China, in 1982, and received her PhD from the University of New England, Australia, in 1996. She is a member of the IEEE, IEEE Computer Society, and ISCA. She is the author or co-author of more than 40 research papers. Her research interests include distributed artificial intelligence, distributed information retrieval, and agent-based software engineering.

Weimin Zheng received his BS and MS from Qinghua University, Beijing, China, in 1970 and 1982, respectively. He is currently a professor in the Department of Computer Science, Tsinghua Universtiy, China. His major research interests include parallel/distributed and cluster computing, compiler techniques and run-time system design for parallel processing systems.

Shanfeng Zhu is a research associate in the Department of System Engineering and Engineering Management, Chinese University of Hong Kong. He received his BS and MS degrees in Computer Science from Wuhan University, China, in 1996 and 1999, respectively, and a PhD in Computer Science from City University of Hong Kong in 2003. His research interests include information retrieval on the Web, recommender systems in e-commerce.

Index

NEW from Idea Group Publishing

- **The Enterprise Resource Planning Decade: Lessons Learned and Issues for the Future**, Frederic Adam and David Sammon/ ISBN:1-59140-188-7; eISBN 1-59140-189-5, © 2004
- **Electronic Commerce in Small to Medium-Sized Enterprises**, Nabeel A. Y. Al-Qirim/ ISBN: 1-59140-146-1; eISBN 1-59140-147-X, © 2004
- **e-Business, e-Government & Small and Medium-Size Enterprises: Opportunities & Challenges**, Brian J. Corbitt & Nabeel A. Y. Al-Qirim/ ISBN: 1-59140-202-6; eISBN 1-59140-203-4, © 2004
- **Multimedia Systems and Content-Based Image Retrieval**, Sagarmay Deb ISBN: 1-59140-156-9; eISBN 1-59140-157-7, © 2004
- **Computer Graphics and Multimedia: Applications, Problems and Solutions**, John DiMarco/ ISBN: 1-59140-196-86; eISBN 1-59140-197-6, © 2004
- **Social and Economic Transformation in the Digital Era**, Georgios Doukidis, Nikolaos Mylonopoulos & Nancy Pouloudi/ ISBN: 1-59140-158-5; eISBN 1-59140-159-3, © 2004
- **Information Security Policies and Actions in Modern Integrated Systems**, Mariagrazia Fugini & Carlo Bellettini/ ISBN: 1-59140-186-0; eISBN 1-59140-187-9, © 2004
- **Digital Government: Principles and Best Practices**, Alexei Pavlichev & G. David Garson/ISBN: 1-59140-122-4; eISBN 1-59140-123-2, © 2004
- **Virtual and Collaborative Teams: Process, Technologies and Practice**, Susan H. Godar & Sharmila Pixy Ferris/ ISBN: 1-59140-204-2; eISBN 1-59140-205-0, © 2004
- **Intelligent Enterprises of the 21st Century**, Jatinder Gupta & Sushil Sharma/ ISBN: 1-59140-160-7; eISBN 1-59140-161-5, © 2004
- **Creating Knowledge Based Organizations**, Jatinder Gupta & Sushil Sharma/ ISBN: 1-59140-162-3; eISBN 1-59140-163-1, © 2004
- **Knowledge Networks: Innovation through Communities of Practice,** Paul Hildreth & Chris Kimble/ISBN: 1-59140-200-X; eISBN 1-59140-201-8, © 2004
- **Going Virtual: Distributed Communities of Practice**, Paul Hildreth/ISBN: 1-59140-164-X; eISBN 1-59140-165-8, © 2004
- **Trust in Knowledge Management and Systems in Organizations**, Maija-Leena Huotari & Mirja Iivonen/ ISBN: 1-59140-126-7; eISBN 1-59140-127-5, © 2004
- **Strategies for Managing IS/IT Personnel,** Magid Igbaria & Conrad Shayo/ISBN: 1-59140-128-3; eISBN 1-59140-129-1, © 2004
- **Beyond Knowledge Management**, Brian Lehaney, Steve Clarke, Elayne Coakes & Gillian Jack/ ISBN: 1-59140-180-1; eISBN 1-59140-181-X, © 2004
- **eTransformation in Governance: New Directions in Government and Politics**, Matti Mälkiä, Ari Veikko Anttiroiko & Reijo Savolainen/ISBN: 1-59140-130-5; eISBN 1-59140-131-3, © 2004
- **Intelligent Agents for Data Mining and Information Retrieval**, Masoud Mohammadian/ISBN: 1-59140-194-1; eISBN 1-59140-195-X, © 2004
- **Using Community Informatics to Transform Regions**, Stewart Marshall, Wal Taylor & Xinghuo Yu/ISBN: 1-59140-132-1; eISBN 1-59140-133-X, © 2004
- **Wireless Communications and Mobile Commerce**, Nan Si Shi/ ISBN: 1-59140-184-4; eISBN 1-59140-185-2, © 2004
- **Organizational Data Mining: Leveraging Enterprise Data Resources for Optimal Performance**, Hamid R. Nemati & Christopher D. Barko/ ISBN: 1-59140-134-8; eISBN 1-59140-135-6, © 2004
- **Virtual Teams: Projects, Protocols and Processes**, David J. Pauleen/ISBN: 1-59140-166-6; eISBN 1-59140-167-4, © 2004
- **Business Intelligence in the Digital Economy: Opportunities, Limitations and Risks**, Mahesh Raisinghani/ ISBN: 1-59140-206-9; eISBN 1-59140-207-7, © 2004
- **E-Business Innovation and Change Management**, Mohini Singh & Di Waddell/ISBN: 1-59140-138-0; eISBN 1-59140-139-9, © 2004
- **Responsible Management of Information Systems**, Bernd Stahl/ISBN: 1-59140-172-0; eISBN 1-59140-173-9, © 2004
- **Web Information Systems,** David Taniar/ISBN: 1-59140-208-5; eISBN 1-59140-209-3, © 2004
- **Strategies for Information Technology Governance**, Wim van Grembergen/ISBN: 1-59140-140-2; eISBN 1-59140-141-0, © 2004
- **Information and Communication Technology for Competitive Intelligence**, Dirk Vriens/ISBN: 1-59140-142-9; eISBN 1-59140-143-7, © 2004
- **The Handbook of Information Systems Research**, Michael E. Whitman & Amy B. Woszczynski/ISBN: 1-59140-144-5; eISBN 1-59140-145-3, © 2004
- **Neural Networks in Business Forecasting,** G. Peter Zhang/ISBN: 1-59140-176-3; eISBN 1-59140-177-1, © 2004